D0713048

VIRGINIA WOOLF: DRAMATIC NOVELIST

Virginia Woolf: Dramatic Novelist

Jane Wheare

St. Martin's Press   New York

First published in the United States of America in 1989

Printed in Hong Kong

ISBN 0-312-02449-5

Library of Congress Cataloging-in-Publication Data
Wheare, Jane, 1961–
    Virginia Woolf: dramatic novelist / Jane Wheare.
        p.   cm.
    Originally presented as the author's thesis (doctoral—Oxford)
    Bibliography: p.
    Includes index.
    ISBN 0-312-02449-5: $35.00 (est.)
    1. Woolf, Virginia, 1882–1941—Criticism and interpretation
I. Title
PR6045.072Z899   1989
823'.912—dc19   88-18829
                                                          CIP

To my mother and father

though Turgenev could have said with Marianna ' . . . I suffer for all the oppressed, the poor, the wretched in Russia,' it was for the good of the cause, just as it was for the good of his art, not to expatiate, not to explain.

(Virginia Woolf, 'The Novels of Turgenev', *Collected Essays*, I, 252)

Contents

Acknowledgements

My first thanks are to Professor John Bayley, who supervised my doctoral thesis on Woolf. I should also like to thank Dr Vivien Jones and Dr Lyndall Gordon for criticising early drafts of this book, and Dr Nicola Bradbury and Professor Marilyn Butler for reading it in its final stages. Chapter Two, on *The Voyage Out*, is dedicated to Vivienne Harris and Mary Gibbs.

I am grateful to the Literary Estate of Virginia Woolf, to the Hogarth Press, and to Harcourt Brace Jovanovich, for permission to reproduce the extracts from *The Voyage Out* and *Night and Day*, by Virginia Woolf (copyright 1920 by George H. Doran Co., renewed 1948 by Leonard Woolf), and the extracts from *The Years* (copyright 1937 by Harcourt Brace Jovanovich, Inc., renewed 1965 by Leonard Woolf).

I am also grateful to the Bodleian Library for purchasing, at my suggestion, a microfiche of the *Virginia Woolf Manuscripts* (*Monks House Papers*). These form part of the Virginia Woolf holdings at the University of Sussex Library.

Above all, however, I thank Michael Banner for the friendship and love of the last six years.

J.W.

List of Abbreviations

A Room	*A Room of One's Own* (London: The Hogarth Press, 1929)
CE	*Collected Essays*, 4 vols (London: The Hogarth Press, 1966)
CSF	*The Complete Shorter Fiction of Virginia Woolf*, ed. Susan Dick (London: The Hogarth Press, 1985)
CW	*Contemporary Writers*, ed. Jean Guiget (London: The Hogarth Press, 1965)
Diary	*The Diary of Virginia Woolf*, ed. Anne Olivier Bell, 5 vols (London: The Hogarth Press, 1977–84)
Letters	*The Letters of Virginia Woolf*, ed. Nigel Nicolson, 6 vols (London: The Hogarth Press, 1975–80)
MHP	*The Virginia Woolf Manuscripts* (*Monks House Papers*) (Brighton: Harvester, 1985)

1

Introduction

(a) INTRODUCTORY: WOOLF – EXPERIMENTAL OR 'DRAMATIC' NOVELIST?

Existing criticism of Woolf tends to focus upon the experimental approach of her modernist novels, which finds its epitome in the esoteric, metaphorical style of *The Waves*. Her 'dramatic' novels – *The Voyage Out*, *Night and Day* and *The Years* – are often dismissed as unremarkable, the suggestion being that in writing them Woolf was conserving her imaginative energies for subsequent innovatory assaults upon traditional fiction.[1] Critics point to a pattern in Woolf's career as a novelist whereby a serious experimental novel would be succeeded by a frivolous or unimportant work in a more conventional mode. David Lodge, for example, argues that, 'The essential line of her literary development may be traced through the following novels: *The Voyage Out* (1915), *Jacob's Room* (1922), *Mrs Dalloway* (1925), *To the Lighthouse* (1927), and *The Waves* (1931) (her other books being, most critics agree, diversions, digressions or regressions from this line).'[2] In the following chapters I hope to modify this view, by emphasising the mastery of Woolf's 'dramatic' novels, and particularly *The Voyage Out* and *The Years*.[3]

That a novel can never lack artifice is an axiom which Woolf repeatedly emphasised. The method of her own experimental fiction – and especially *The Waves* – serves to draw attention to the element of illusion involved when a reader finds a novel 'natural' or 'realistic'. Like Proust, Woolf is extremely interested in the process whereby the reader accepts as 'true to life' those narrative conventions with which he or she is familiar. Her modernist novels pose questions about the nature of fiction, both through specific characters, such as Bernard in *The Waves* and Lily in *To the Lighthouse*, and also (implicitly) through their formal and stylistic experimentalism. In reading a novel as abstruse as *The Waves* one cannot

1

help but ask questions about narrative method, and particularly about the process whereby 'realist' novelists encourage us to 'believe in' their fictional world and characters. *The Waves* – with, for example, Joyce's *Ulysses*, Faulkner's *The Sound and the Fury* or Lessing's *The Golden Notebook* – is an essentially self-conscious work; it draws attention to its own artificiality and in so doing it makes statements about the novel. In its stylised 'discussion' of the problems facing the novelist or biographer and of the illusions implicit in their art *The Waves* complements Woolf's literary criticism. It constitutes both an attack on those writers who seem to adopt established narrative formulae unquestioningly, and a confession that the novelist can never be completely original; one can never wholly divorce oneself from linguistic conventions if one is to communicate with the public at all.[4]

In her 'dramatic' works, on the other hand, far from seeking to draw attention to the presence of artifice in a work of fiction, Woolf exploits the fact that the reader takes such artifice for granted. Whereas in her experimental novels she wishes to emphasise the trickery involved when one writes or reads a work of fiction, in *The Voyage Out*, *Night and Day* and *The Years*, she wishes simply to make use of such tricks.

If, broadly speaking, *The Waves* is a novel about the novel, a 'realist' work such as *The Years* is primarily about society. Whereas the experimental fiction belongs with Woolf's literary criticism, the 'dramatic' novels support her works of social comment. Another way of putting this would be to say that *The Waves* supplements 'Modern Fiction', whereas *The Years* illustrates *Three Guineas*. (This is not to deny, however, that in questioning the fictional narratives which we impose upon experience, *The Waves* makes a point not only about the novel but also about society.)

Much of Woolf's literary criticism, like that of her modernist contemporaries, emphasises the role of formal experimentation in fiction. Consequently many critics – amongst them left-wing poets of the 1930s and some feminists in more recent years – have condemned her as an amoral novelist who places technical inno-vation above social commitment in her writing. This is, however, not only to underrate Woolf's achievement as a modernist, but also to fail to recognise the significance of her 'dramatic' novels, works in which Woolf adopts the 'realist' approach as the most appropriate through which to express her ideas about society *obliquely*.[5] In the 'dramatic' works, Woolf employs a narrative method familiar to the educated reader, making use of technical devices with which we are so well acquainted that we accept them as 'natural'.[6] In reading the novel, therefore, one responds to the fictional characters as if they were real people, and in so doing becomes extremely receptive to the points of view which Woolf embodies in their narrative. One does not 'believe in' Jinny, Rhoda, Susan, Bernard, Louis and Neville in the way that one believes, for example, in Mary Datchet or William Rodney, our belief in these latter depending on the fact that in depicting them Woolf makes use of many conventional narrative devices.

In *The Waves*, largely through the novelty of her method, Woolf draws attention to the process of narration which one normally takes for granted in reading a 'realist' novel. In *The Voyage Out*, *Night and Day* and *The Years*, on the other hand, she induces the reader – through her use of familiar technical conventions – to 'believe in' her fictional characters, and in so doing, she encourages us at once to sympathise with, and to accept unconsciously, the ideological positions implicit in these novels.

Steve Neale analyses the way in which the 'realist' text may be a powerful vehicle of didacticism in an article in *Screen*.[7] Neale compares two types of anti-semitic film produced in Nazi Germany in the 1930s. The first – *Der ewige Jude* – is a documentary film involving overt propaganda, the second – *Jud Süss* – attacks the Jews more subtly through a 'realist' narrative. What makes the latter more persuasive is that the audience is likely to remain oblivious to the fact that the 'text' encourages specific responses on their part. Catherine Belsey makes a similar point about the novel when she remarks that 'the frequent overt authorial intrusions and generalizations of George Eliot are much easier to resist [than the implicit narrative viewpoint] since they draw attention to themselves as propositions'.[8] Within Woolf's *oeuvre*, *Three Guineas* corresponds approximately to the documentary film, whilst the 'dramatic' novels conform to the 'realist' model.

(b) THE EXPERIMENTAL NOVELS

Habit, Perception and the Novel

Being vain, I will broach the subject of beauty – just for a moment – and burst out in ecstasy at your defence of me as a very ugly writer – which is what I am – but an honest one, driven like a whale to the surface in a snort – such is the effort and anguish to me of finding a phrase (that is saying what I mean) – and then they say I write beautifully! How could I write beautifully when I am always trying to say something that has not been said, and should be said for the first time, exactly.[9]

The emphasis upon the writer's obligation to 'say something that has not been said', which we find in this letter from Woolf to the composer, Ethel Smyth, is typical of early twentieth-century modernist statements, which tend to focus upon the relationship between language, habit and experience.[10] Woolf's own experimental novels, like her criticism, examine the process whereby, in 'ordinary life', the individual's perceptiveness is dulled by habit. She identifies a comparable situation in the domain of art, when the artist's ability to portray experience vividly is limited by his or her acceptance of conventional formal devices and linguistic paradigms. Her concomitant belief that the novel should above all *be novel* is shared by many of her modernist contemporaries, among them Joyce, Dorothy Richardson, Marcel Proust and Gertrude Stein.[11] A commitment to formal and linguistic innovation also dominates the work of many of her contemporaries in related intellectual disciplines. One might single out, for example, the aesthetics of Roger Fry, the formalist criticism of Victor Shlovsky, or the philosophy of Henri Bergson.

Woolf has often been linked with Proust through the argument that the novels of each reflect Bergson's ideas on time and memory.[12] Although this approach has recently been discredited, there *is* a connection to be made between the three writers. What they have in common, and, indeed, share with a good many of their modernist contemporaries, is a belief in the limitations of conventional language as a medium for expressing the individual's unique experience.

Bergson's philosophy embraces Saussure's idea that languages 'do not simply name existing categories, they articulate their own'.[13] He argues that the scope of our language is determined by practical considerations. Since our use of language is governed by questions of economy, or ease of communication, our linguistic categories necessarily involve a simplification of sense-perception. It is Bergson's belief that the generalising tendency of language actually serves to mask experience, rather than to elucidate it. The obvious problem which he faces, as a philosopher, however, is that of communicating his own perceptions through the medium of that very language whose deficiencies he deplores. (Karin Stephen emphasises this point in her study of Bergson when she remarks that 'the intellectual activity by which we formulate general laws can only work among abstractions, and in order to explain a fact we are obliged to substitute for it either a class or word or other symbol'.[14] It is Bergson's view that the role of the philospher, unlike that of the scientist, should be to examine experience not from the practical, but from the speculative point of view.

> May not the task of philosophy [he asks] be to bring us back to a fuller perception of reality by a certain displacement of our attention? What would be required would be to turn our attention *away* from the practically interesting aspect of the universe in order to turn it *back* to what, from a practical point of view, is useless. And this conversion of attention would be philosophy itself.[15]

Bergson's notion of the philosopher can be linked with Roger Fry's idea of the artist. Fry suggests that the distinctive feature of a work of art is that it serves no practical purpose. Consequently, our perception of it is different in kind from our impressions of objects which have a purely functional status in our lives. In his 'Essay in Aesthetics' Fry argues that implicit in normal perception is a continuous process of unconscious selection. This theory can be illustrated, he maintains, by observing a street scene reflected in a mirror:

> It then, at once, takes on the visionary quality, and we become true spectators, not selecting what we will see, but seeing everything equally, and thereby we come to notice a number of appearances and relations of appearances, which would have escaped our vision before, owing to that perpetual economising by selection of what impressions we will assimilate, which in life we perform by unconscious processes.[16]

When a scene is reflected in this way we remain aloof from it, rather as we stand outside a striking work of art, and because we do not participate in it, our perception of it is less partial. Both

Roger Fry and Bergson argue that one's response to experience is sharpened when one lays aside practical considerations:

> In actual life the normal person really only reads the labels as it were on the objects around him and troubles no further. Almost all the things which are useful in any way put on more or less this cap of invisibility. It is only when an object exists in our lives for no other purpose than to be seen that we really look at it, as for instance at a China ornament or a precious stone, and towards such even the most normal person adopts to some extent the artistic attitude of pure vision abstracted from necessity.[17]

For Roger Fry, then, the mark of a work of art is not its resemblance to, but its distinction from 'real life'. Its value lies in its power not to stimulate, but to subvert, habitual modes of perceiving.[18]

At the time when Roger Fry was formulating his ideas on art in England, surprisingly similar arguments were being put forward by the Russian literary critic, Victor Shklovsky. In his essay on 'Art as Technique', the Formalist critic suggests that one should assess a work of art in terms of its power to make familiar experience strange, and thereby to intensify our response to it. Shklovsky, like Roger Fry, equates this process of defamiliarisation with formal innovation.[19] In the language of poetry, he argues, 'we find material obviously created to remove the automatism of perception. . . . A work is created "artistically" so that its perception is impeded and the greatest possible effect is produced through the slowness of the perception.'[20]

It was the desire to discredit the association between the novel and 'ordinary life', and hence to break down the equation between the habitual in art and the 'natural' (or 'real'), which led Woolf to emphasise the poetic quality of her own experimental fiction.[21] The argument of Woolf's modernist novels, and the formal devices which they employ, support Shklovsky's theory of defamiliarisation. In this respect they resemble Proust's *A la recherche du temps perdu* and Richardson's *Pilgrimage*. In all these novels formal innovation is accompanied by 'discussion' of conventional patterns in language and behaviour, and the tendency of such patterns to dull the individual's perceptiveness. All three writers associate mere imitation in art with the numbing effects of habit in life. In discussing, for example, his first train journey to Balbec, Proust's narrator emphasises the limitations of a life which, being habitual, is necessarily 'unconscious':[22]

> As a rule it is with our being reduced to a minimum that we live; most of our faculties lie dormant because they can rely upon Habit, which knows what there is to be done and has no need of their services. But on this morning of travel, the interruption of the routine of my existence, the unfamiliar place and time, had made their presence indispensable. My habits, which were sedentary and not matutinal, for once were missing, and all my faculties came hurrying to take their place, vying with one another in their zeal, rising, each of them, like waves, to the same unaccustomed level, from the basest to the most exalted, from breath, appetite, the circulation of my blood to receptivity and imagination.[22]

On the one hand, 'we are animals. We are not always aware by any means; we breathe, eat, sleep automatically'.[23] On the other hand, an event such as a journey may temporarily transform habitual living into conscious perception. Marcel's description of the effect of travel upon the individual's perceptiveness is echoed throughout Woolf's writing, notably in the diaries.[24] It is dramatised in *To the Lighthouse* at the moment in the third section when Lily Briscoe, coming out into the garden, remarks upon 'the unreality of the early morning hour. It was a way things had sometimes, she thought . . . they became unreal. So coming back from a journey, or after an illness, before habits had spun themselves across the surface, one felt that same unreality, which was so startling; felt something emerge. Life was most vivid then.'[25] Proust, Woolf and Richardson all argue that such a transformation may also be effected by a striking and original work of art. In Woolf's novel it is Lily Briscoe, in Proust's the artist Elstir, who acts upon the belief that art should serve to lift the veil of habitual perception and lay bare that which is strange, exciting, and indeed terrifying, in experience. At the opposite pole, in Proust's novel, the figures of M. and Mme Cottard represent a tendency in the 'consumer' to resist innovation in art. Like Bergson, Proust's Marcel suggests that it is in disregarding established categories of perception that the individual appreciates more fully the essence of his own experience. It is this 'honesty' of purpose which he identifies and admires in the work of the artist, Elstir:

> The effort made by Elstir to strip himself, when face to face with reality, of every intellectual notion, was all the more admirable in that this man who made himself deliberately ignorant before sitting down to paint, forgot everything that he knew in his honesty of purpose (for what one knows does not belong to oneself), had in fact an exceptionally cultivated mind.[26]

Lily Briscoe shares Elstir's determination to empty his mind of existing styles in art. She resists, for example, a temptation to imitate the popular artist Mr Paunceforte, with his particular combination of pastel shades. Since for Lily the 'jacmanna [is] bright violet; the wall staring white' these are the colours she attempts to capture in her picture.[27]

Both Proust's *A la recherche du temps perdu* and Woolf's experimental fiction make use of the visual arts to illustrate a theory of the novel. (The link between Post-Impressionist art and modernist fiction has often been made.) The artist who rejects familiar precedents in painting corresponds to the novelist who deliberately subverts existing narrative patterns.[28] Proust, like Shklovsky, equates value in life and art with the process of defamiliarisation. Where such a process is absent, life can have no meaning or worth.[29]

Experimental Novelists

The emphasis upon the importance of undermining habitual modes of perception, to be found in the critical writing of Bergson, Fry and Shklovsky, and of Proust, Richardson and Woolf, is put into practice in the novels of these latter through specific technical devices.

Proust, for example, experiments with various techniques which at once enable him to avoid a straightforward chronological sequence and to emphasise the arbitrary nature of accepted narrative forms. It is perhaps not surprising that *A la recherche du temps perdu* has affinities with Sterne's *Tristram Shandy*, a work described by Shklovsky and his fellow-critics as 'the most typical [that is, perfect] novel in world literature'.[30] Woolf connects Proust and Sterne through two separate remarks describing the technique of each writer as that of going backwards as well as forwards.[31] She herself employs the same device, notably in *Mrs Dalloway*, where the main characters' memories of Bourton are woven into the fabric of 'the present day'. This technique of displaced chronology draws attention to the fictional status of the novel and to the inadequacy of the 'realist' novelist's portrayal of life as a temporal sequence of public events. (Both Proust and Sterne reject such a sequence in favour of a portrait of the mind of their respective narrators – a mind which is not governed by the exigencies of clock-time.) Similarly, Proust's complex sentence-structure, like that of Henry James, draws attention to itself, and so impedes automatism of perception on the part of the reader. The demands of his syntax force the reader to focus upon the process of narration and to recognise the degree of artifice implicit in his fiction.

The narrative method of both Sterne and Proust is often described as 'feminine'. What is meant in this context is not that it is female, but rather that it is subversive or anti-conventional. The 'feminine' approach to narrative is typified in the early twentieth century in the work of Dorothy Richardson. In her unfinished novel, *Pilgrimage*, Richardson uses the fictional narrator, Miriam Henderson, to put forward her own criticisms of what she deems the traditional 'masculine' (or conventional) world-view, criticisms which correspond very closely to those contained in Woolf's experimental novels and essays.[32] (Both Richardson and Woolf have been attacked by some feminist critics because their references to a 'feminine' narrative method help, it is claimed, to perpetuate traditional sexual stereotypes. In fact, neither Woolf nor Richardson wishes to equate 'femininity' with the female.)[33] Like Woolf, Richardson defines her own narrative method in opposition to the 'Edwardian' tradition of Galsworthy, Bennett and, particularly, Wells. When she praises a narrative technique for its 'femininity', the implication is that it subverts this tradition. A 'masculine' style, on the other hand, is conventional and imitative.

Richardson's narrator shares Woolf's view that the 'masculine' framework traditionally imposed upon life and literature – epitomised for Miriam in the writing of Hypo Wilson – serves to misrepresent experience.[34] She argues that to adopt conventional narrative models, as Wilson does, is to refuse even to try to communicate the essence of individual experience. Such 'ready-made' phrases, she suggests – echoing Woolf – blind those who use them to the intensity of experience, 'the strangeness of the adventure of *being*, of the fact of the existence, anywhere, of anything at all'.[35] Miriam feels, like Woolf, that for most people the reality of the present is masked by an excessive interest in memories of the past or plans for the future. It is for the novelist to attempt to capture, through the unfamiliarity ('femininity') of his or her narrative approach, something of the vividness of 'ordinary' experience.

Like Woolf, Richardson's narrator believes that life does not exist 'more fully in what is commonly thought big than in what is commonly thought small',[36] 'what is commonly thought big' being the 'important events' which appeal to the 'masculine' (or conventional) writer and which draw attention away from the significance to be found in everyday life. Richardson's analysis of the traditional novel in 'Data for Spanish Publisher' echoes quite closely the argument of Woolf's 'Modern Fiction'. In the course of these notes she remarks, for example:

> The material that moved me to write would not fit the framework of any novel I had experienced. I believed myself to be, even when most enchanted, intolerant of the romantic and the realist novel alike. Each, so it seemed to me, left out certain essentials and dramatised life misleadingly. Horizontally. Assembling their characters, the novelists developed situations, devised events, climax and conclusion. I could not accept their finalities. Always, for charm or repulsion, for good or ill, one was aware of the author and applauding, or deploring, his manipulations. This, when the drama was a conducted tour with the author deliberately presenting his tale. Still more so when he imagined, as did Flaubert, that in confining himself to *'Constation'* he remained imperceptible. In either case, what one was assured were the essentials seemed to me secondary to something I could not then define, and the curtain-dropping finalities entirely false to experience.[37]

Both Richardson and Woolf deliberately suppress the traditional 'events' of fiction – the sentimental death-bed scenes or neat endings, for example – in their modernist works.[38] Death in Richardson's novel, as in *To the Lighthouse*, is depicted through the long-term effect which it has upon the characters who remain alive.

In the course of a discussion with Hypo Wilson about narrative techniques, which echoes very closely the views which Woolf puts forward through Bernard in *The Waves*, Miriam remarks:

> Oh, I *hate* all these written-up things: 'Jones always wore a battered cricket cap, a little askew.' They simply drive me *mad*. You know the whole thing is going to be lies from beginning to end.[39]

Like Bernard in *The Waves*, she rejects conventional narrative formulae, sharing his dislike of the attempts which most individuals make to 'tell life' as if it were a familiar story. Eleanor Dear's history has, for example, according to Miriam, the potential for being rewritten as a 'perfect recognisable story of a scheming unscrupulous woman', but to describe Eleanor's life in these terms is to outline 'the facts, leaving out all the inside things'. Miriam identifies such a tendency in novels: 'They showed only one side of people, the outside; if they showed them alone, it was only to explain what they felt about other people.'[40] In her own novel, Richardson endeavours to explore the consciousness of one person, rather than to portray her from an external point of view in terms of her interaction with other people. The development of so-called 'stream-of-consciousness' techniques in fiction can be explained in part in terms of an attempt by early twentieth-century novelists to expose the degree of caricature implicit in our external judgements of other people.

Through Miriam, Richardson draws attention to the fact that most novelists cater for a reading public which neither recognises nor accepts the importance or originality in fiction. As she reads *A Human Document*, for example, she remarks upon the fact that the whole concern of many readers is limited to 'the happy ending or the sad ending'. Thinking of her own very different method of reading she notes that most people 'thought it was silly, almost wrong to look at the end of a book. But if it spoilt a book there was something wrong about the book. If it was finished and the interest gone when you know who married who, what was the good of reading at all.'[41] Just as most people are incapable of appreciating the quality of the present moment because it is hidden beneath their memories of the past and their plans for the future, so too, in reading a book, they are concerned not with the quality of the prose, but with the superficial structure of the plot. According to Miriam, what remains absent from most novels is the richness and atmosphere of life itself quite apart from any 'momentous' happenings in life:

> There is something else; that's the worst of novels, something that has to be left out. Tragedy; curtain. But there never *is* a curtain, and even if there were, the astounding thing is that there is *anything* to let down a curtain on . . .[42]

Miriam admires Ibsen because his writing evokes the peculiar significance which permeates the whole of experience. A work like *Brand*, for example, although it reveals Ibsen as 'exactly like every one else, thinking and worrying about the same things', is remarkable because in it he puts these things down 'in a background that is more real than people or thoughts'.[43] In attempting to analyse Ibsen's technique Miriam can do no more than attribute to him the quality of 'genius'. Like Woolf, she uses the word to imply an ability to create a literary equivalent for the intensity of experience.

Both Woolf and Richardson, then, connect the traditional novelist's inability to capture the essence and multiplicity of experience with his or her willingness to accept established literary styles and forms. Miriam Henderson echoes Woolf's belief that it is only whilst language is continually remoulded that it remains alive and expressive. For example, as she entertains Michael Shatov with anecdotes drawn from her own life, she realises that '*that* was how talk was done . . . saying things over and over again to numbers of people, each time a little more brilliantly and the speaker a little more dead behind it. Nothing could be repeated'.[44] She argues that once an impression has been communicated in a particular way, the mode of expression becomes obsolete. Therefore, an author should neither develop a recognisable style nor imitate the method of other writers. The deadening effect of a borrowed narrative mode is illustrated, for Miriam – as she explains to Hypo Wilson – in her own conversation with Amabel:

> It may be that when I am trying to *describe* anything in return for all she has told me, she is bored by my *style* – because it becomes an imitation of hers – which I admire but which is a method of expression that does not belong to what I want to convey and so conveys nothing at all.[45]

Like Eleanor in *The Years* and Bernard in *The Waves*, Miriam laments the fact that language, being 'horizontal', cannot capture all the simultaneous aspects of experience which go to make up a 'moment of being'. 'If only', she thinks 'one could speak as quickly as one's thoughts flashed, and several thoughts together, all with a separate life of their own and yet belonging, everybody would be understood. As it was, even in the most favourable circumstances, people could hardly communicate with each other at all.'[46] Richardson's own 'feminine' (or innovatory) method can best be illustrated by a quotation from the text itself. A typical example is the following description from *The Tunnel* of a boy carrying a jug of milk:

> how shall I write it down, the *sound* the little boy made as he carefully carried the milk jug? . . . going along, trusted, *trusted*, you could see it, you could see his mother. His legs came along, little loose feet, looking after themselves, pottering, behind him. All his body was in the hand carrying the milk jug. When he had done carrying the milk jug he would run; running along the pavement amongst people, with cool round eyes, not looking at anything. Where the crowd prevented his running, he would jog up and down as he walked, until he could run again, bumping solemnly up and down amongst the people; boy.[47]

What is interesting about such a description is its poetic quality; the fact that it exists for its own sake, and not as a means of imparting information about the plot to the reader. The form the novel takes – as an account of experience within a single consciousness – gives Richardson the freedom to write in this way. The method is appropriate to Miriam's belief in the importance of *being* over *becoming*, of 'the moment' over past and future 'happenings'. Turning to Woolf's writing, the closest comparable method is, perhaps, to be found in her diaries. The diary form, like that of *Pilgrimage*, enables the writer to record significant thoughts and moments in experience apart from the constraints of a traditional plot structure. Both Richardson in her novel and Woolf in her diaries and experimental fiction are concerned to capture as closely as possible in language the precise atmosphere and peculiar significance of what are traditionally deemed unimportant moments in experience. The similarities between the technique of each author can be illustrated by comparing the account which each gives of an encounter with a group of 'mad' people.[48] Each writer's interest lies in re-creating, through language, something of the strangeness of the encounter, and in giving renewed substance to the condition behind the over-familiar and over-simplistic classification 'mad'.

Bernard, in Woolf's *The Waves*, like Miriam in *Pilgrimage*, represents those individuals who come to recognise the inadequacy of conventional language as a medium for communicating the multiplicity of experience. As in Richardson's *Pilgrimage*, this point of view is illustrated through the structure of Woolf's novel. Like Richardson, Woolf rejects stereotyped narrative models, but whereas Richardson employs in their place a 'stream-of-consciousness' technique, Woolf exploits the potential for poetic, metaphoric language in the novel.[49] In the closing section of *The Waves*, Bernard recalls the period of his youth when he still considered himself capable of mastering experience through ordinary language: 'The trees, scattered, put on order; the thick green of the leaves thinned itself to a dancing light. I netted them under with a sudden phrase. I retrieved them from formlessness with words.'[50] Bernard suffers a crisis as he begins to recognise the limitations of his own narrative style, and comes to reject his earlier tendency to impose patterns upon experience:[51]

> And sometimes I begin to doubt if there are stories. What is my story? What is Rhoda's?
> What is Neville's? There are facts, as, for example: 'The handsome young man in the grey suit, whose reserve contrasted so strangely with the loquacity of the others, now brushed the crumbs from his waistcoat and, with a characteristic gesture at once commanding and benign, made a sign to the waiter, who came instantly and returned a moment later with the bill discreetly folded upon a plate.' That is the truth; that is a fact, but beyond it all is darkness and conjecture.

Woolf suggests that in contrast with those who remain on the surface, the true artist must at least attempt to probe her way downwards into this 'darkness and conjecture'. What she deplores in the 'realist' novel is the writer's willingness to accept unquestioningly the narrative conventions which he or she inherits. Woolf, Proust and Richardson all suggest that in developing a new and unique narrative method, the novelist may overthrow accepted conceptions not only of the novel but of life itself. James's literary criticism reflects a similar belief that one should avoid conventional narrative modes in the novel. Indeed, Woolf links Proust with James in her essay, 'Phases of Fiction', when she describes both novelists as 'psychologists'. She praises each for his use of metaphor to illuminate psychological processes. In *What Maisie Knew*, for example:

> The visual sense which has hitherto been so active, perpetually sketching fields and farmhouses and faces, seems now to fail or to use its powers to illumine the mind within rather than the world without. . . . He says, she was 'a ready vessel for bitterness, a deep little porcelain cup in which biting acids could be mixed'. He is forever using this intellectual imagery. The usual supports, the props and struts of the conventions, expressed or observed by the writer, are removed.[52]

For James, the novel appears 'more true to its character in proportion as it strains, or tends to burst, with a latent extravagance, its mould'.[53] Woolf admires him for the audacity with which he employs metaphor to this effect in his novels:

> By cutting off the responses which are called out in the actual life, the novelist frees us to take delight, as we do when we are ill or travelling, in things in themselves. We can see the strangeness of them only when habit has ceased to immerse us in them, and we stand outside watching what has no power over us one way or the other. Then we see the mind at work; we are amused by its power to make patterns; by its power to bring out relations in things and disparities which are covered over when we are acting by habit or driven on by the ordinary impulses.[54]

The echoes of Bergson and Roger Fry, Shklovsky and Proust, are manifest. The reader, Woolf argues, remains outside the work of art – 'alienated' from it, in Brecht's terminology – in much the same way that Bernard, for example, after travelling to Rome, remains detached from the scene which he observes.[55]

The relationship between a new work of art and 'ordinary life' – or tradition – has affinities with that between tenor and vehicle in a particular metaphor. In each case it is the apparent incongruity of the comparison which brings into focus neglected aspects of both its constituent elements. Thus, an original novel encourages us to take a critical stance towards both art and life.[56]

Bernard is drawn to the pictures in the National Gallery, after Percival's death, because he feels that art, unlike language, need not specify.[57] The abstract quality of painting is one which seems to elude the novelist, who is bound to a verbal and linear medium. Conventional language, Bernard suggests, is too precise to capture what is essential, rather than general, in experience. Recalling, in his final soliloquy, his own complex mood of exaltation as a young man in love, he feels that 'there should be music. Not that wild hunting-song, Percival's music; but a painful, gutteral, visceral, also soaring, lark-like, pealing song to replace these flagging, foolish transcripts – how much too deliberate! how much too reasonable! – which attempt to describe the flying moments of first love. A purple slide is slipped over the day.'[58]

Woolf recognised that the novelist can never – as the term 'realist' erroneously implies – capture the complexity of experience in language.[59] Through formal innovation, however, and notably metaphor, the author can reveal hitherto neglected aspects of that experience. The writer, Woolf suggests, 'has the chance to live more than other people in the presence of . . . reality':

> It is his business to find it and collect it and communicate it to the rest of us. So at least I infer from reading *Lear* or *Emma* or *La Recherche du Temps Perdu* [sic]. For the reading of these books seems to perform a curious couching operation on the senses; one sees more intensely afterwards; the world seems bared of its covering and given an intenser life.[60]

The Waves has been criticised as a gratuitously esoteric novel devoid of social significance, but the novel's innovatory method in fact has not only aesthetic but also didactic importance. With early twentieth-century modernist works like *A la recherche du temps perdu* and *Pilgrimage*, Woolf's experimental fiction draws attention to the arbitrariness of the contemporary world-view; the fact that the way in which we 'see the world' depends upon how we describe it in our language. The modernist movement was not, then, simply an off-shoot of the late nineteenth-century interest in so-called 'art for art's sake'. Its experimentalism has social and political, as well as formal and aesthetic, implications. Indeed, the two are intimately bound together. (An obvious illustration of this point is Woolf's argument, in *Three Guineas*, that if women's experience is to be acknowledged by society it must first be recognised through the coinage of new terms – such as 'educated man's daughter' – in that society's language.)[61] In its 'feminine' tendency to undermine habitual modes of articulating experience, Woolf's experimental fiction has more in common, then, with her 'dramatic' novels than might at first sight be supposed.

(c) THE 'DRAMATIC' NOVELS

Critical discussion of Woolf tends, then, to focus upon her modernist works. Her name is traditionally associated with the idea of early twentieth-century experimentalism in fiction. To describe Woolf as a purely 'literary' novelist is, however, to ignore a substantial part of her achievement as a writer. Her novels in fact fall into two clearly defined groups. On the one hand she produced experimental works whose complex method provides a commentary upon the conventions of the 'realist' novel. These works could be said, then, to supplement her literary criticism. On the other hand we have the apparently more traditional novels – *The Voyage Out, Night and Day* and *The Years* – which could be described as 'dramatic' or 'external' works in the 'realist' mode. Whereas in her experimental novels Woolf is at pains to lay bare and undermine the illusions implicit in 'realist' fiction, in her 'dramatic' works she herself exploits many of these illusions. Whilst, then, her whole effort in a novel like *The Waves* is to draw the reader's attention to the presence of the author in her work of fiction, in *The Years*, for example, she wishes to disguise that presence. In very broad terms, then – and bearing in mind the provisos given above – one could say that if the subject of the experimental novels is literature, that of the 'dramatic' works is society.[62]

In the 'dramatic' novels Woolf remains true to her belief that fiction should never become a vehicle for overt didacticism. She avoids preaching directly, choosing instead to embody her private ideas about society in the lives of her fictional characters.[63] She encourages the reader to 'believe in' these characters and, in consequence, to respond sympathetically to the ideas which are dramatised through their narrative. Yet, although the 'dramatic' novels are not obviously didactic, they do illustrate, and therefore complement, many of the ideas put forward by Woolf in works of social criticism like *A Room* and *Three Guineas*. It is with Woolf's interest in the relationship between theoretical argument and fiction, and the implications of this interest for her 'dramatic' novels, that the rest of this study is concerned.

The question of the relationship between didacticism (or propaganda) and creative writing is one which dominates Woolf's criticism. Frequently, her assessment of a particular author or group of authors turns upon the degree to which they manage to avoid introducing undisguised theoretical argument into their work. On the one hand, she attacks certain writers because she finds their work 'personal' or 'autobiographical', they are too 'self-conscious'. On the other hand, she praises those who manage to efface personal experiences and private interests from their writing, remaining 'impersonal', 'aloof', 'anonymous' or 'unconscious'.

Woolf's most explicit exposition of her theory of 'unconsciousness' in creative writing is, perhaps, to be found in the essay 'The Leaning Tower' – a paper which she read to the Brighton Workers' Educational Association in May 1940. (The essay constitutes a reply to criticisms voiced by left-wing poets in the 1930s against the apparent lack of political commitment in Woolf's novels.) Woolf maintains that overt political partisanship cannot be reconciled with creativity in a work of art, sharing Eliot's view that, 'the more perfect the artist, the more completely separate in him will be the man who suffers and the mind which creates; the more perfectly will the mind digest and transmute the passions which are its material'.[64] Her argument is that

> Unconsciousness, which means presumably that the under-mind works at top speed while the upper-mind drowses, is a state we all know. We all have experience of the work done by unconsciousness in our own daily lives. You have had a crowded day, let us suppose, sightseeing in London. Could you say what you had seen and done when you came back? Was it not all a blur, a confusion? But after what seemed a rest, a chance to turn aside and look at something different, the sights and sounds and sayings that had been of most interest to you

swam to the surface, apparently of their own accord; and remained in memory; what was unimportant sank into forgetfulness. So it is with the writer. After a hard day's work, trudging round, seeing all he can, feeling all he can, taking in the book of his mind innumerable notes, the writer becomes – if he can – unconscious. In fact, his under-mind works at top speed while his upper-mind drowses. Then, after a pause the veil lifts; and there is the thing – the thing he wants to write about – simplified, composed. Do we strain Wordsworth's famous saying about emotion recollected in tranquillity when we infer that by tranquillity he meant that the writer needs to become unconscious before he can create?[65]

In this attempt to rationalise her own narrative method Woolf is, of course, more than a little disingenuous. It is difficult to see how any writer – *pace* W. B. Yeats and his fellow-enthusiasts for 'automatic writing' – could actually achieve such a state of unconsciousness. The most one could hope, or indeed want, to do, would be to create the impression of impartiality in a narrative, such that the reader – rather than the writer – would remain 'unconscious' of the author's private opinions and affiliations. Stephen Spender makes this distinction when he argues that, when Keats says that 'poetry should grow as naturally as the leaves of a tree. . . . he does not mean that poets should not work, but that the work itself should resemble the process of diligently growing rather than of being intellectualized'.[66]

Woolf's argument in 'The Leaning Tower' is that much of the writing produced in the 1930s is marred by self-consciousness. The poet of the thirties is acutely aware of the injustice of his own privileged position in society and cannot help but let this awareness affect the tone and content of his published writing. A remark in her diary shows that Woolf considers this a peculiarly modern problem:

I have been thinking about Censors. How visionary figures admonish us. Thats clear in an MS I'm reading. If I say this So & so will think me sentimental. If that . . . will think me Bourgeois. All books now seem to me surrounded by a circle of invisible censors. Hence their selfconsciousness, their restlessness. It wd. be worth while trying to discover what they are at the moment. Did Wordsworth have them? I doubt it. I read

Ruth before breakfast. Its stillness, its unconsciousness, its lack of distraction, its concentration and the resulting 'beauty' struck me. As if the mind must be allowed to settle undisturbed over the object in order to secrete the pearl.[67]

Woolf's criticism of Spender and his contemporaries is that the state of mind reflected in their poems and plays and novels is 'full of discord and bitterness, full of confusion and of compromise'.[68] The personal, egotistic tone of a poem like Louis MacNeice's *Autumn Journal* – which renders it 'feeble as poetry' albeit 'interesting as autobiography' – is, she feels, typical of much creative writing in the 1930s.[69]

Woolf's attack in 'The Narrow Bridge of Art' (1927) on the self-consciousness of modern writers anticipates the argument of 'The Leaning Tower'. In the earlier essay, she contrasts modern poets with Shakespeare, arguing that the strength of the Elizabethans stems from the fact that they remain 'unconscious' as they write.[70] Woolf deplored the lack of such 'unconsciousness' in Spender's poem *Vienna*, as she explains to him in a letter of 25 June 1935:

Here again my hatred of preaching pops out and barks. I dont think you can get your words to come till youre almost unconscious; and unconsciousness only comes when youve been beaten and broken and gone through every sort of grinding mill.[71]

Similarly, she finds Auden's *Letters from Iceland* 'mainly attitudinising, as if he were uneasy at heart, and must talk about himself in order to rid himself of some scabby itch'.[72] Woolf reiterates these criticisms of modern poetry in a letter to John Lehmann, where she suggests that the young poet's problem is that 'he doesnt reach the unconscious automated state – hence the spasmodic, jerky, self conscious effect of his realistic language'.[73] R. C. Trevelyan stands out, she feels, amongst contemporary poets because in his writing it is 'as though all superfluities had been consumed and whats left is very satisfying'.[74] In contrast, the work of the 'Leaning Tower School' is 'not unconscious, but stirred by surface irritation, to which the alien matter of politics, that cant be fused, contributes'.[75] Their writing, Woolf argues, remains weak when compared, for example, with that of Coleridge and Shelley, because it lacks suggestive power. As far as Woolf is

concerned, the best poetry is probably 'that which is most suggestive', which is 'made of the fusion of many different ideas, so
that it says more than is explicable'. The 'Leaning Tower' poets
compromise their writing because they 'must teach; they must
preach. Everything is a duty – even love'.[76]

It was not only Spender and his fellow poets who criticised
Woolf's novels for being apolitical. Katharine Mansfield –
according to Woolf – objected on moral grounds to the 'aloofness'
of *Night and Day*, and Woolf's literary disputes with Margaret
LLewelyn Davies and Janet Case often turned, to her annoyance,
upon the question whether a work of art should be overtly moral-
istic.[77] Throughout her career Woolf remained firmly convinced
that there is no place for overt propaganda or didacticism in a
work of fiction, that 'If we use art to propagate political opinions,
we must force the artist to clip and cabin his gift to do us a cheap
and passing service'.[78]

Woolf always took pains to disguise the element of autobiography in her own fiction.[79] Whilst at work on *To the Lighthouse*
she was worried that she would be, 'held up for personal
reasons[.] It will be too like father, or mother', and in consequence
she felt that the choice of subject was probably 'a little unwise'.[80]
Although she used this work to put her childhood, and particularly her feelings about her parents, into perspective, the autobiographical influences in the novel are carefully integrated into the
fictional mode.[81] In writing *Mrs Dalloway* Woolf was equally
concerned to avoid the autobiographical approach, asking herself
in her diary, 'Have I the power of conveying the true reality? Or do
I write essays about myself?'[82] Similarly, in planning the opening
section of *The Waves* she noted, 'this shall be Childhood; but it
must not be *my* childhood'.[83] On the publication of *Three Guineas*,
too, she found herself, 'uneasy at taking this role in the public
eye – afraid of autobiography in public'.[84]

Woolf's opposition to preaching in literature can be linked with
a more general dislike of violent partisanship.[85] She explains her
position in a letter to Ethel Smyth of 18 May 1931:

> what I can't abide is the man who wishes to convert other men's
> minds; that tampering with beliefs seems to me impertinent,
> insolent, corrupt beyond measure. . . . some cousins in
> particular, the daughters of Fitzjames, rasped and agonised us
> as children by perpetual attempts at conversion.[86]

Hence Woolf's indignation when her friend Jean Thomas sent her
a copy of Tolstoy's *What I believe*, accompanied by a 'long serious
letter' exhorting her to Christianity.[87] Her feeling is that to adopt
a militant approach over political and moral issues is at once to
insult and to alienate the sensitive 'potential convert'. Thus it is
on diplomatic as well as artistic grounds that she is careful to avoid
preaching in her own novels.[88]

Woolf's hostility to the work of D. H. Lawrence – a hostility
which, towards the end of her life, she considered to have been
excessive[89] – rests upon her dislike of the preaching in his writing:

> To me Lawrence is airless, confined: I dont want this, I go on
> saying. And the repetition of one idea. I dont want that either.
> I dont want 'a philosophy' in the least; I dont believe in other
> people's reading of riddles. What I enjoy (in the Letters) is
> the sudden visualisation . . . but I get no satisfaction from his
> explanations of what he sees.[90]

It is Lawrence's ability to dramatise experience which Woolf
admires, his attempts to analyse and interpret that experience she
finds merely abhorrent. Her argument is that a fictional 'scene'
should seem to speak for itself, an idea implicit in her advice to
aspiring novelists at the end of *A Room* to think of 'things in
themselves'.[91] Lawrence's fault, according to Woolf, is that, like
Wells, he insists on preaching in his fiction, on 'delivering judgment when only half the facts are there'. It is this determination
to give 'advice on a system' which alienates Woolf. Her own view
is that 'if you want to help' you should 'never systematise – not
till you're 70: and have been supple & sympathetic & creative &
tried out all your nerves & scopes'. She cannot concur with
Huxley's description of Lawrence as an 'artist' because she believes
that art 'is being rid of all preaching: things in themselves: the
sentence in itself beautiful'.[92] Lawrence, she feels, spoils his
writing by his 'mix up of inspiration, and prophecy', 'the whole
doctrine of preaching, of causes; of converting; teaching etc'.[93] She
distrusts 'the platform' in his writing, 'the "I'm right" pose in
art'.[94]

Henry James takes a similar line in his essay on 'Dumas the
Younger', criticising Dumas for his tendency to paraphrase the
argument of his fiction 'in an occasional and polemical pamphlet'.[95]
James, like Woolf, believes that:

In a story written in the interest of a theory two excellent things are almost certain to be spoiled. . . . when once an author has his dogma at heart, unless he is very much of an artist, it is sure to become obtrusive at the capital moment, and to remind the reader that he is, after all, learning a moral lesson.[96]

He deplores the fact that for many novelists 'the scales and the judicial wig . . . have taken the place, as the symbols of office, of the kindly, disinterested palette and brush', considering that the novel should be a vehicle not of overt didacticism, but of moral imagination.[97] 'The essence of moral energy is', he contends, 'to survey the whole field', 'the "moral" sense of a work of art' depending upon 'the amount of felt life concerned in producing it'.[98] Like Woolf, James came to define his own approach to art against that of H. G. Wells. Wells felt that the difference between their respective approaches was that James regarded literature as an end in itself, whereas he himself considered it to be a means to an end, like architecture.[99] In making such a distinction, however, Wells failed to take account of the fact that where he disagreed with James – and, indeed, with Woolf – was not as to whether the novel should be a vehicle of morality, but as to whether it should be manifestly such.

Woolf's chief criticism of Wells is that in his fiction he lets his theoretical ideas interfere with his characterisation; he is, she says, 'a mere scribbler', 'taking upon his shoulders the work that ought to have been discharged by Government officials'.[100] His fiction has, she feels, battened upon a 'swarm of ideas', and it is these ideas, rather than the characters, which dominate a novel like *Joan and Peter*.[101]

Woolf posed the question of the relationship between didacticism and fiction when she was at work on *The Waves*. Her interest at that time in the possibility of writing a polemical essay on feminism and fascism distracted her from the 'unconscious', trance-like mood in which, she claimed, she needed to sink herself in order to write her novel:

Too much excited, alas, to get on with The Waves. One goes on making up The Open Door [*Three Guineas*], or whatever it is to be called. The didactive [sic] demonstrative style conflicts with the dramatic: I find it hard to get back inside Bernard again.[102]

Woolf maintains that to introduce didactic passages into a novel is to draw the reader's attention away from the fictional characters to the person of the author.[103] The true novelist, as opposed to the pamphleteer, should, she feels, avoid commenting overtly on her characters' behaviour, or interpreting it explicitly. This is not to argue, of course, that novelists should not tell us about their characters, but that they should not obviously direct our response to them. Woolf would argue that whenever the author's ideas are allowed to intrude into the novel, without being assimilated into the characterisation, the effect can only be distracting. She feels, for example, that Huxley's *Point Counter Point* fails because of its author's 'interest in ideas', he 'makes people into ideas' and is a little 'theoretical, about religion & sex'.[104] Whilst at work on a draft of her penultimate novel, *The Years*, Woolf noted in her diary, 'the burden of something that I wont call propaganda. I have a horror of the Aldous novel: that must be avoided. But ideas are sticky things: wont coalesce; hold up the creative, subconscious faculty: thats it I suppose'.[105] She objects to Forster's early novels because his fictional characters are clearly the mouthpieces for specific theoretical ideas and attitudes. In *Howards End*, for example:

> The poet is twitched away by the satirist; the comedian is tapped on the shoulder by the moralist; he never loses himself or forgets himself for long in sheer delight in the beauty or the interest of things as they are. . . . just as we are yielding ourselves to the pleasures of the imagination, a little jerk rouses us. We are tapped on the shoulder. We are to notice this, to take heed of that. Margaret or Helen, we are made to understand, is not speaking simply as herself; her words have another and a larger intention. So, exerting ourselves to find out the meaning, we step from the enchanted world of the imagination, where our faculties work freely, to the twilight world of theory, where only our intellect functions dutifully.[106]

It is the minor characters in *Howards End*, such as Tibby and Mrs Munt, who remain most interesting to Woolf, because they seem to 'go where they like, say what they like, do what they like'. Margaret, Helen and Leonard Bast, on the other hand, 'are closely tethered and vigilantly overlooked lest they may take matters into their own hands and upset the theory'. *A Passage to India* is, she argues, more persuasive than the earlier novels because we cannot say of its characters that they 'will be allowed to go only so far and no further lest they may upset some theory of the author's'.[107] Woolf criticises Meredith on the same grounds as the early Forster, namely that he fails to remain 'anonymous' in his fiction and to portray characters who appear to be free, autonomous individuals. She maintains that his teaching is, like that of D. H. Lawrence, 'too strident', 'too insistent' and obtrudes into his fiction, 'and when philosophy is not consumed in a novel, when we can under-line this phrase with a pencil, and cut out that exhortation with a pair of scissors and paste the whole into a system, it is safe to say that there is something wrong with the philosophy or with the novel or with both'. Meredith's characters resemble Lawrence's in being too obviously the vehicle for their author's polemic. We feel that they 'have been called into existence merely to express Mr Meredith's views upon the universe'.[108]

In an essay on George Moore, Woolf criticises that novelist for his lack of 'dramatic power', contrasting his fiction with that of Tolstoy:

> The great novelist feels, sees, believes with such intensity of conviction that he hurls his belief outside himself and it flies off and lives an independent life of its own, becomes Natasha, Pierre, Levin, and is no longer Tolstoy. When, however, Mr Moore creates a Natasha she may be charming, foolish, lovely, but her beauty, her folly, her charm are not hers, but Mr Moore's. All her qualities refer to him.[109]

She recognises that no writer can be 'wholly impersonal', that even Flaubert – as Richardson notes in her 'Data for Spanish Publisher' – can never disappear completely from his fiction.[110] None the less, she sympathises with the French novelist's narra-tive approach.[111] Flaubert's belief that the novelist 'doit, dans sa création, imiter Dieu dans la sienne, c'est à dire, faire et se taire' is implicit in those novels in which the author makes a conscious attempt to disguise his or her presence from the reader.[112] What distinguishes such novels from, for example, those of George Eliot is not, of course, the absence of authorial point of view and direc-tives, but the illusion of such an absence. The distinction has often been expressed in terms of the difference between *telling* and *showing*. Another way of describing it would be to say that whilst Eliot's novels are 'didactic' those of Henry James, for example, are 'dramatic'. Whereas Eliot's narrator obviously intervenes in her text, directing our reading of it, James attempts to conceal the fact that his narrative is designed to elicit a certain response from the reader. It is not enough, however, simply to avoid overt authorial intrusion into a text. Woolf rightly remarks, in her essay on 'Phases of Fiction', that 'Style may carry with it, especially in prose, so much personality that it keeps us within the range of that personality'.[113] A novelist may undermine the reader's 'belief in' the world of the novel through excessive technical difficulty or ingeniousness. This is the case, she suggests, with James's *The Wings of the Dove:*

> His manipulations become so elaborate towards the end that instead of feeling the artist you merely feel the man who is posing the subject. . . . Finally, after all this juggling & arranging of silk pocket handkerchiefs, one ceases to have any feeling for the figure behind. Milly thus manipulated, disappears.[114]

Surprising parallels can be drawn between Woolf's objections to the complexity of James's fiction and early criticisms of her own experimental novels, parallels which serve to highlight a contradiction inherent in Woolf's criticism as a whole. Woolf's theoretical justification for the method of her modernist fiction rests on the presupposition that originality, or ingenuity, is a fundamental criterion of the good novelist's art. The writer should, above all, avoid adopting a familiar, or imitative, narrative method. In this context, complexity becomes a virtue since it serves to draw her readers' attention to the novel's fictionality, thereby preventing automatism of perception on their part. In rationalising the 'realist' approach of the 'dramatic' novels, on the other hand, Woolf takes the opposite line. Here she argues that the novelist should at all costs refrain from drawing attention to him or herself in a work of fiction, and for this reason the technical difficulty attendant upon originality and formal innovation should be avoided. It is neither possible nor necessary to reconcile these two strands in Woolf's criticism, which should, rather, be regarded as disparate attempts, at specific moments in Woolf's career as novelist and critic, to provide a theoretical basis or 'apology' for the method of particular novels.

Woolf considered women, by virtue of their peculiar treatment by history and society, to be particularly susceptible to the temptations of self-consciousness in their writing. She found her friend Ethel Smyth's obsession with her own personality, for example, incomprehensible, arguing that Smyth's egotism seriously mars the opening chapters of *Female Pipings in Eden*.[115] Instead of talking in general terms about the status of women in the music profession in this section of the book, Smyth insisted on recounting her personal experience of sex-discrimination. Woolf considered the later chapters of *Female Pipings* far superior to Chapter Two, for example, because, as she put it, 'they dont preach; they expound'.[116] For her own part, Woolf was careful in an essay like *A Room of One's Own* to avoid all such personal complaint and bitterness, as she explained to Ethel Smyth:

> I didnt write 'A room' without considerable feeling even you will admit; I'm not cool on the subject. And I forced myself to keep my own figure fictitious; legendary. If I had said, Look here am I uneducated, because my brothers used all the family funds which is the fact – Well theyd have said; she has an axe to grind; and no one would have taken me seriously . . .[117]

Similarly, as Woolf points out to Ethel Smyth, when, in response to a particularly hostile review, she was prompted against her better nature to draft a bitter and angry reply, she decided against publishing it.[118] One has only to trace – as Katharine Rogers has done[119] – the consistently vindictive and vitriolic campaign waged against feminists during the nineteenth century in the supposedly liberal *Saturday Review*, to appreciate the supreme degree of self-control manifested in Woolf's own feminist writings.

In *A Room*, Woolf divides women novelists into two groups; those whose work remains undamaged in spite of their subservient social position, and those whose writing is adversely affected by it.[120] *A Room* is based on two papers which Woolf read to the women students at Newnham and Girton in 1928, and was published in the autumn of the following year.[121] The proposed subject of the papers was that of 'women and fiction' and Woolf approaches it through a series of fictional sketches which illustrate (or dramatise) some of the absurd prejudices with which women have had to contend over the centuries and against which they were still struggling in the 1920s. As a polemical essay, *A Room* is differentiated in Woolf's mind from pure works of fiction, which (she argues in the course of the essay) ought always to remain free of theoretical argument. She considered it essential that the woman writer, like all professional women, should not become the victim of her own anger. She remarked, for example, in a speech to the London/National Society for Women's Service of 21 January 1931:

> You are bound I am afraid to meet with a great deal of derision and opposition. You will want all your strength and courage. And for this reason it is of the highest importance that you should not add to your burdens a very heavy and unnecessary burden, the burden of bitterness.[122]

Even in the 'non-fictional' *A Room*, Woolf is careful to maintain a certain lightness of touch, not wishing her argument to be 'pitched in too high a voice', to have 'a shrill feminine tone'.[123] To this end, she makes use of the fictional persona ('call me Mary Beton, Mary Seton, Mary Carmichael or by any name you please') which enables her to disguise, distance and generalise her private interests and experiences in her narrative.[124] She experienced a similar anxiety over the tone of *Three Guineas* – her response in the 1930s to the threat of war in Europe – rejecting the idea of calling the essay 'Men are like that?' on the grounds that this title was 'too patently feminist'.[125]

The persuasiveness of such works as Ray Strachey's *The Cause* and Olive Schreiner's *Woman and Labour* can be related to the dispassionate manner in which each author approaches her subject. Both adopt a broadly historical, rather than a fiercely polemical, line of argument. Schreiner, for example, seeks to account in sociological terms for the subservient position of women in modern society, implicitly criticising those who would, as she puts it, 'represent the suffering and evil of woman's condition, as wrongs intentionally inflicted upon her, where they are merely the inevitable results of ages of social movement'. Schreiner argues that,

> It is a gracious fact, to which every woman who has achieved

success or accomplished good work in any of the fields generally apportioned to men will bear witness, whether that work be in the field of literature, of science, or the organised professions, that the hands which have been most eagerly stretched out to welcome her have been those of men; that the voices which have most generously acclaimed her success have been those of male fellow-workers in the fields into which she has entered.[126]

In contrast with the work of Schreiner and Strachey, the insistent, personal tone of Florence Nightingale's unpublished autobiographical writings, for example, has the effect of alienating the unsympathetic reader.

In both *A Room* and *Three Guineas* Woolf puts into practice her belief that theoretical ideas make the deepest impression when they are dramatised through fictional scenes or episodes.[127] The narrator in *A Room*, for example, imagines herself in a number of different situations: visiting Oxbridge and being ordered off the grass by a Beadle; being refused entry to a library; lunching in a men's college and dining in a women's; talking with her friend Mary Seton and discussing the life of her mother; visiting the British Museum; reading a paper in a restaurant; looking at different books in her house by the river. She considers what it would be like to be a particular woman: Shakespeare's younger sister, Judith; Lady Winchelsea; Margaret, Duchess of Newcastle; Dorothy Osborne; Aphra Behn; George Eliot; the Brontës; Mary Carmichael. All the ideas in the essay are visualised through such fictional scenes culminating in the image of a couple getting into a taxi which, it could be argued, represents in both *A Room* and *The Years* the ideal of 'androgyny' or co-operation between the sexes. In her essays, then, Woolf is careful to avoid that aggressive sex-consciousness which she believed to be as great a hindrance to women's writing as she considered Marxism to be to the poets of the 1930s.[128] Women are often, she feels, too much aware of the need to assert their own identity to be able to achieve that state of 'unconsciousness' which she considers an essential preliminary to creative writing:

Women writers have to meet many of the same problems that

beset Americans. They too are conscious of their own peculiarities as a sex; apt to suspect insolence, quick to avenge grievances, eager to shape an art of their own. In both cases all kinds
of consciousness – consciousness of self, of race, of sex, of
civilisation – which have nothing to do with art, have got
between them and the paper, with results that are, on the
surface at least, unfortunate.[129]

In the essay 'Professions for Women', based on her aforemen-
tioned speech to the London/National Society for Women's
Service, Woolf outlines the ways in which sex-consciousness
affected, or threatened to affect, her own career as a writer. She
describes the degree of resolution which she needed as a young
reviewer if she were to avoid adopting the traditional 'feminine'
role of sympathiser to men, or 'Angel in the House', in her writing.
(The phrase is borrowed from Coventry Patmore's poem-
sequence.) As a novelist she faced a similar challenge. Wishing to
remain as 'unconscious' as possible, she was yet stung into self-
consciousness by the conflict between her own approach to her
art and the approach which male critics expected her to take. She
was tempted to 'adopt a view in deference to authority', and
thwarted in her attempts to write by the conventionality of men's
beliefs as to what a woman could appropriately say in print.[130] As
Woolf points out in *Three Guineas*, the 'educated man's daughter'
may have gained nominal entry into the professions, but she has
still to fight against *atmosphere*, a nebulous concept which can be
as powerful as, and considerably more insidious than, the law.[131]
In a letter to Violet Dickinson describing her experience in helping
her sister Vanessa over a miscarriage, she remarks: 'I know most
of the parts of the female inside by now, but that is useless knowledge in my trade, the british public being what it is.'[132] Her
point is that there are certain subjects upon which it is considered
unladylike for a woman to express herself in public. The knowledge that this is the case makes it impossible for Woolf to forget
her sex and write freely and 'unconsciously'. 'The problem of art
is', she feels, 'sufficiently difficult in itself without having to
respect the ignorance of young women's minds or to consider
whether the public will think that the standard of moral purity
displayed in your work is such as they have a right to expect from
your sex.'[133] Elaine Showalter supports Woolf's argument when
she points out that although nineteenth-century women novelists

were, in theory, able to write about 'female physical experience, including childbirth and maternal psychology, they faced many obstacles to self-expression in their own sphere'. There were strong taboos against women writers sharing their experiences with men.[134] Woolf enlarges upon her theory of the sex-consciousness in women's writing in the essay 'Women and Fiction' which, in effect, summarises the argument of *A Room*. Here, she suggests that in the past, and particularly during the nineteenth century, women writers have tended to use the novel as a vehicle for expressing anger and resentment over their treatment by society, and their writing has suffered in consequence:

> The desire to plead some personal cause or to make a character the mouthpiece of some personal discontent or grievance always has a distressing effect, as if the spot at which the reader's attention is directed were suddenly twofold instead of single.[135]

The reader has both to sustain a 'belief in' the fictional characters and to respond to the author's private grievances; two demands which prove to be incompatible. Woolf looks forward, then, to a time when the novel 'will cease to be the dumping-ground for the personal emotions' and women writers will express their private opinions in 'essays and criticism', 'history and biography' rather than in fiction.[136]

In both *A Room* and 'Women and Fiction' Woolf singles out George Eliot and Charlotte Brontë as examples of women writers whose work is marred by sex-consciousness.[137] She maintains that in *Jane Eyre*, as in *Middlemarch*, 'we are conscious not merely of the writer's character, as we are conscious of the character of Charles Dickens, but we are conscious of a woman's presence – of someone resenting the treatment of her sex and pleading for its rights'.[138] Eliot's inability to remain 'anonymous' in her fiction leads Woolf to conclude that her talents are primarily those of the historian or biographer rather than the novelist.[139] She suggests that both Eliot and Charlotte Brontë probably adopted male pseudonyms, 'not only with a view to obtaining impartial criticism', but also 'in order to free their own consciousness as they wrote from the tyranny of what was expected from their sex'.[140]

At the opposite pole from Eliot and Charlotte Brontë stand Emily Brontë and Austen, women novelists whom Woolf praises in

'Women and Fiction' for their ability to avoid partisanship and to remain 'anonymous' in their writing:

> The genius of Jane Austen and Emily Brontë is never more convincing than in their power to . . . hold on their way unperturbed by scorn or censure. But it needed a very serene or a very powerful mind to resist the temptation to anger. The ridicule, the censure, the assurance of inferiority in one form or another which were lavished upon women who practised an art, provoked such reactions naturally enough.[141]

As Woolf points out in *A Room*, it is understandable that a woman should react with anger to the attitudes epitomised in Professor von X's monumental work on *The Mental, Moral and Physical Inferiority of the Female Sex*.[142] It is the more remarkable, then, that both Austen and Emily Brontë should have resisted the temptation to do so.

Woolf argues that Emily Brontë is a more consummate artist than her sister because the 'impulse which urged her to create was not her own suffering or her own injuries'.[143] In *Wuthering Heights*:

> the characters of Heathcliff and Catherine are perfectly natural; they contain all the poetry that Emily Brontë herself feels without effort. We never feel that this is a poetic moment, apart from the rest, or that here Emily Brontë is speaking to us through her characters. Her emotion has not overflowed and risen up independently, in some comment or attitude of her own. She is using her characters to express her conception, so that her people are active agents in the book's life, adding to its impetus and not impeding it . . .[144]

She finds Austen remarkable, too, as an example of 'a woman about the year 1800 writing without hate, without bitterness, without fear, without protest, without preaching'.[145] Even in the early work, *Love and Friendship*, for example, Austen manages to portray the aristocratic figure, Lady Greville, without revealing any 'trace of anger at the snub which Jane Austen, the clergyman's daughter, no doubt once received'.[146] Indeed, all her novels are remarkable, Woolf suggests, for their 'dramatic' presentation of character. She remains aloof from her fictional scenes, being compelled by her genius 'to absent herself':[147]

> She wishes neither to reform nor to annihilate; she is silent; and that is terrific indeed. One after another she creates her fools, her prigs, her worldlings, her Mr Collinses, her Sir Walter Elliotts, her Mrs Bennets. She encircles them with the lash of a whip-like phrase which, as it runs round them, cuts out their silhouettes for ever. But there they remain; no excuse is found for them and no mercy shown them.[148]

Austen's narrative method is, Woolf suggests, 'Shakespearian' in its freedom from overt partisanship. Shakespeare is the archetypal artist for Woolf because his mind appears to have 'consumed all impediments', his 'grudges and spites and antipathies are hidden from us'.[149] Both writers manage, she contends, 'to infuse the whole of themselves into their works, yet contrive to universalize their identity so that, though we feel Shakespeare everywhere about, we cannot catch him at the moment in any particular spot'.[150]

What, in Woolf's view, Austen has in common with Shakespeare, and indeed with Sir Walter Scott, is her 'dramatic' approach to characterisation. Reviewing a production of *Twelfth Night* at the Old Vic, Woolf commented that: 'When Sir Andrew says "I was adored once", we feel that we hold him in the hollow of our hands; a novelist would have taken three volumes to bring us to that pitch of intimacy.'[151] Scott's approach to characterisation in a novel like *The Antiquary* is, she suggests, essentially the same.[152] It is possible, she argues, to read Scott's novels 'over and over again, and never know for certain what Scott himself was or what Scott himself thought'. We know his characters intimately, however, by 'their talk and by their acts'; his is 'the Shakespearean art, of making people reveal themselves in speech'. Nor would it be valid to argue, she maintains, that this 'dramatic' approach to characterisation is more superficial than the analytic, psychological approach. For Scott 'has the power of the artist who can create a scene and leave us to analyse it for ourselves':

> When we read the scene in the cottage where Steenie Mucklebackit lies dead, the different emotions – the father's grief, the mother's irritability, the minister's consolations – all rise spon-

taneously, as if Scott had merely to record, and we have merely to observe.[153]

Herein lies the attraction, for Woolf, of the 'realist' tradition. Through the 'dramatic' approach to character portrayal, she can create the illusion of absence from her own text.[154] This was, indeed, James's justification for his choice of the 'dramatic' approach in *The Awkward Age*, if the remarks in his Preface to the 1908 edition are to be believed:

> The divine distinction of the act of a play – and a greater than any other it easily succeeds in arriving at – was, I reasoned, in its special, its guarded objectivity. This objectivity, in turn, when achieving its ideal, came from the imposed absence of that 'going behind,' to compass explanations and amplifications, to drag out odds and ends from the 'mere' storyteller's great property-shop of aids to illusion: a resource under denial of which it was equally perplexing and delightful, for a change, to proceed.[155]

To describe either *The Awkward Age* or Austen's novels as 'dramatic' is not, of course, to deny that in each we are presented with something quite distinct from the typescript of a play. In her fiction, Austen tells us a great deal about her characters – their history, for example, and their thoughts – which could not easily be conveyed to an audience from the stage. James, likewise, notwithstanding his claim that the portrayal of Nanda Brooken-ham's situation 'abides without a moment's deflexion by the principle of the stage-play',[156] supplies the reader with a certain amount of such additional information, notably facts about his characters' states of mind.[157] Yet he creates the illusion that he is merely deducing these facts from the characters' speech, gestures and facial expressions. The careful addition of a qualifying word or phrase enables him to disguise the fact of his own omniscience from the reader.[158] The illusion of objectivity so achieved offered a peculiar attraction not only to James but also to Woolf at certain points in her career as a novelist. The 'dramatic' approach provided her with a method for those novels in which she wanted – for the sake of her art as well as her cause – to disguise her presence from the reader.

It is, perhaps, surprising to find a novelist renowned for her repudiation of 'Edwardian realism' objecting so frequently to particular nineteenth- and twentieth-century novels on the grounds that they are 'unrealistic'. It is, however, worth repeating that the account of Woolf's *oeuvre* which describes her as a purely modernist writer limits her scope as an author. Alongside her experimental works, Woolf produced novels in the 'realist' mode whose narrative method enabled her to express her ideas about society obliquely. If 'Modern Fiction', then, is a blueprint for the narrative approach of *The Waves*, 'Sir Walter Scott' is one amongst numerous essays which illuminate the rationale behind the method of Woolf's 'dramatic' novels.

2

The Voyage Out

(a) INTRODUCTORY

Woolf's criticism of a great many novelists – and particularly women – centres upon the fact that they use their writing as a vehicle for confessional autobiography. A writer is, perhaps, particularly likely to use the first novel to unburden personal obsessions and experiences. Given that this is the case, the 'objective' tone of Woolf's own first novel is the more remarkable. In writing *The Voyage Out* Woolf did, of course, draw upon the details of her own life. One thinks, for example, of her mental instability, her sister Vanessa's illness and brother Thoby's death from typhoid, her voyage to Spain and Portugal with her younger brother Adrian in the spring of 1905, and, particularly, her interest in feminism.[1] In the novel, though, these personal experiences are transformed from autobiography into fiction.[2] The emphasis in *The Voyage Out* falls not upon Woolf the private individual, but upon her fictional characters. It is primarily the lives of these latter, rather than that of the author, which sustain our interest.[3]

Notwithstanding her own interest in 'the woman question', Woolf is careful to avoid introducing didactic discussion of feminist issues – of the kind to be found, for example, in *Three Guineas* – into her fictional text.[4] Instead, she embodies various aspects of the feminist debate in the lives and opinions of her characters. This is not to deny that Woolf directs her reader's response to these characters and therefore to the ideas which they represent or hold, but she does so obliquely. Indeed, she makes use of two particular techniques to draw the reader's attention to specific ideas and points of view in the novel, whilst avoiding overt authorial intrusion into her narrative. First, she exploits specific characters – notably Helen Ambrose and Terence Hewet – through whom she encourages the reader to react in a particular way to the other figures in the novel. Since Woolf's portrayal of Helen and Terence is essentially sympathetic, we are inclined to accept their point of view as, to a large degree, authoritative. In what is essentially a *Bildungsroman*, Woolf traces her heroine's development under the guidance of Helen and Terence, and the reader, being encouraged to identify with Rachel, is caught up in this educational process. When, for example, Helen tells Rachel how to respond to the Dalloways, or when Terence persuades her to think more deeply about women, they also influence the reader's response to the novel.

The second technique whereby Woolf directs our reading of her narrative, without appearing to do so, is through her use of repetition. Repetition enables her to draw attention obliquely to important ideas in the novel. It also serves to suggest an underlying pattern to experience, an idea which – as we shall see – is extremely important to Woolf.

(b) FEMINISM

Woolf believed that 'it was for the good of the cause, just as it was for the good of [her] art' not to introduce theoretical argument in her own voice into a work of fiction.[5] In *The Voyage Out*, therefore, she dramatises her ideas so that they become an aspect of her characterisation and are integrated into the novel as a whole. She assigns the various attitudes to feminism which she was later to examine theoretically in, for example, *A Room* and *Three Guineas* to the novel's main characters. On the one hand Willoughby Vinrace, Richard Dalloway, St John Hirst and Ridley Ambrose betray varying degrees of prejudice against women. Set against them are Helen Ambrose and Terence Hewet, both of whom share (though in differing degrees) their author's feminist outlook. Rachel's development consists of a movement away from the world-view epitomised by the Dalloways, towards that represented by Terence. Woolf uses Terence in *The Voyage Out*, much as James exploits Ralph Touchett in *The Portrait of a Lady*, as the spokesman for her own point of view.[6] Terence not only recognises and explains to Rachel – and, by extension, to the reader – the immense value of the 'feminine' sensibility manifested by other characters in the novel, but also possesses, and therefore illustrates, this sensibility himself. Since Terence is a credible and interesting individual, however, we do not regard him as a mere tool in his creator's hands.

Through characters like Miss Allan and Mrs Thornbury, Woolf dramatises Terence's argument that the apparently obscure lives of certain women are in fact uniquely valuable.[7] In her account of the rise of the feminist movement, Ray Strachey points to the difficulties encountered by feminists in the 1890s in putting across arguments which 'were, of necessity, the same as they always had been'.[8] Mary Datchet, the feminist in *Night and Day*, similarly, faces the problem of delivering the old arguments 'with unexampled originality'.[9] In *The Voyage Out*, Woolf's feminist ideas are embodied in a narrative whose characters are interesting in their own right, and through them she is able to reawaken the reader's interest in a cause whose arguments may well be all too familiar.

The distinction between the 'masculine' and the 'feminine' is one which recurs implicitly or explicitly throughout Woolf's writing, and is therefore worth examining in some detail. For, as Simone de Beauvoir remarks, 'as soon as the "sexual" is distinguished from the "genital", the idea of sexuality becomes none too clear'.[10] In her *Vindication of the Rights of Woman*, Wollstonecraft attacks Rousseau on the grounds that he perpetuates the belief that 'femininity' and 'masculinity' are innate sexual characteristics.[11] 'According to the conventional view', argues Carolyn Heilbrun, ' "masculine" equals forceful, competent, competitive, controlling, vigorous, unsentimental, and occasionally violent; "feminine" equals tender, genteel, intuitive rather than rational, passive, unaggressive, readily given to submission.'[12] Mary Poovey suggests that by the end of the eighteenth century, ' "female" and "feminine" were understood by virtually all men and women to be synonymous'.[13] Barbara Taylor notes that the

> notion that women had a unique moral mission to perform was popular among all kinds of people in the early nineteenth century, anti-feminist as well as feminist. Its ideological function was highly ambiguous. In the hands of anti-feminists, it usually served merely to buttress sentimental dogmas of domestic womanhood ('the Angel in the House'), but even among feminists it led to a celebration of female specialness and moral superi-

ority which jostled uneasily with arguments against the concept of an innate femininity.[14]

Both Taylor and Poovey suggest that women had a vested interest in accepting such sexual stereotypes, since in doing so they gained recognition and grateful approval from men. In consequence, however, 'they found it increasingly difficult to recognize that the stereotype was prescription, not description'.[15]

Opposed to the concept of innate psycho-sexual characteristics are those who see 'masculine' and 'feminine' traits as the product of conditioning. Taylor contends that 'The idea that women's apparent inferiority was a produce of "vicious circumstances" rather than innate deficiencies had been a key theme in feminist writings from the early eighteenth century on, but it was in Owenite feminism that the argument was most fully developed'.[16] In her reading of Lessing's *The Golden Notebook*, Showalter suggests that Lessing 'does not . . . wish us to understand women's ability to manipulate the subconscious in terms of a stereotyped "feminine intuition". She presents women as being more practiced than men in interpreting inner space, but she chooses a male protagonist in *Briefing for a Descent into Hell* to emphasize the nonexclusivity of the gift.'[17] In the same way Woolf, in both *The Voyage Out* and *Night and Day*, goes out of her way to portray 'feminine' men. Whilst it is true that for Woolf the adjectives 'masculine' and 'feminine' carry their traditional associations, they are definitely not synonymous with 'male' and 'female'. Indeed, as the chapter on *Night and Day* which follows will suggest, Woolf's ideal individual is 'androgynous', combining in his or her personality both 'masculine' and 'feminine' characteristics. In all her novels, moreover, Woolf presents male and female characters who can be seen as the victims of traditional sexual stereotyping.

In *The Voyage Out* Woolf makes use of her central character, Rachel Vinrace, to illustrate her own interpretation of the life-style afforded to many middle-class women in the late nineteenth century. Rachel's relationship with her father, for example, reflects Woolf's belief – one which she was later to put forward explicitly in *Three Guineas* – that the conventional father educates his daughter not for her own sake but in order to make her useful to

men, and particularly to himself.[18] In this respect, Willoughby
Vinrace's attitude to Rachel echoes Gilbert Osmond's treatment of
his daughter Pansy in *The Portrait of a Lady*. Rachel's upbringing
and education also resemble those experienced by the pupils at a
German finishing school in Richardson's *Pilgrimage*, or at Madame
Beck's school in Brontë's *Villette*, or by the Baines girls in Bennett's
The Old Wives' Tale, to name but a few examples. Discussing her
own childhood with Terence Hewet, Rachel remarks that 'A girl
is more lonely than a boy. No one cares in the least what she
does' (*The Voyage Out*, p. 261). Her comment is borne out by
Bennett's description of the girlhood of Sophia Baines in *The Old
Wives' Tale*, a novel which merits further consideration in this
context.[19]

The episode in Bennett's novel in which Sophia Baines elopes with
Gerald Scales can be seen as the direct result of Sophia's parents'
complete indifference to her education and career.[20] The Baines
parents exert the type of emotional pressure upon their daughter
which Woolf condemns in *Three Guineas*. Like the Brangwens in
Lawrence's *Rainbow*[21] they remain deeply hostile to their daughter's desire for a career, considering that to earn a living must be
a second-best for a woman when compared with staying at home
or securing a husband:

> Orphans, widows, and spinsters of a certain age suddenly
> thrown on the world – these were the women who, naturally,
> became teachers, because they had to become something. But
> that the daughter of comfortable parents, surrounded by love
> and the pleasures of an excellent home, should wish to teach in
> a school was beyond the horizons of Mrs. Baines's common
> sense. (Bennett, *The Old Wives' Tale*, p. 38)[22]

Sophia's education is, like that of Rachel Vinrace, pitifully narrow
and useless, consisting of: ' "a sound and religious course of
training," "study embracing the usual branches of English, with
music by a talented master, drawing, dancing, and calisthenics."
Also "needlework plain and ornamental"; also "moral
influence" . . .' (p. 59). That the Baines's attitude to Sophia's

education is typical is illustrated by a passage from the report of the Schools Enquiry Commission published in 1868:

> We have had much evidence showing the general indifference of parents to girls' education, both in itself and as compared to that of boys. It leads to a less immediate and tangible precuniary result; there is a long-established and inveterate prejudice . . . that girls are less capable of mental cultivation, and less in need of it than boys; that accomplishments and what is showy and superficially attractive are what is really essential for them; and in particular that, as regards their relations to the other sex and the probabilities of marriage, more solid attainments are actually disadvantageous . . . It must be fully admitted that such ideas have a very strong root in human nature.[23]

The contrast between Sophia's upbringing and that of her nephew, Cyril Povey, serves as a far more persuasive commentary upon the inequality of the sexes than would any overt authorial interpolations in Bennett's text. Cyril is as much the focus of the Poveys' interest and ambition as Sophia is the object of the Baines's indifference. Like Galsworthy's Forsytes, the inhabitants of Bursley take it for granted that a son is absolutely more important than a daughter:

> His mother's thoughts were on Cyril as long as she was awake. His father, when not planning Cyril's welfare, was earning money whose unique object would be nothing but Cyril's welfare.   (p. 179)

The scenes between Cyril and the servant, Amy (pp. 189–90, 204), suggest the degree to which, unlike Sophia, he is able to assert his own will in his parents' household. The importance, moreover, which the Poveys attach to Cyril's first day at school – '(real school, not a girls' school, as once)' (p. 192) – is in marked contrast with the Baines parents' hostility to Sophia's education. Whereas Sophia, during her brief period as apprentice-teacher, is actively discouraged by her family, Cyril's schooling becomes the focus of the Povey family life, and is treated with deep seriousness: 'The parlour table was consecrated to his lessons. It became generally known that "Cyril was doing his lessons" ' (p. 194).[24] Unlike Sophia, Cyril is able, by dint of his sex and education, to gain a

moral ascendancy over his parents. This point is illustrated early
in the novel through that scene in which he orders his mother not
to come into his bedroom to look at him when he is asleep (p. 194).
Cyril's behaviour illustrates J. S. Mill's remark that

> people are little aware . . . how early the notion of his [the
> boy's] inherent superiority to a girl arises in his mind; how it
> grows with his growth and strengthens with his strength; how
> it is inoculated by one schoolboy upon another; how early the
> youth thinks himself superior to his mother, owing her perhaps
> forbearance, but no real respect.[25]

From his early childhood the Poveys are obsessed with Cyril's
future, as the Baineses are indifferent to Sophia's, so that by the
time he reaches the age of nine, each is 'dying to discuss his
ultimate career' . . . Constance was relieved to find that Mr Povey
had no thought whatever of putting Cyril in the shop. No; Mr
Povey did not desire to chop wood with a razor. Their son must
and would ascend. Doctor! Solicitor! Barrister! Not barrister –
barrister was fantastic' (p. 195). The passage brings to mind the
Dalloways' desire, in *The Voyage Out*, for a son who would succeed
in public life. The irony in Bennett's novel is that, despite the
restrictions imposed upon Sophia by provincial prejudice, it is she,
and not Cyril, who pursues what would be considered in Bursley
a successful career.

Rachel Vinrace's education resembles Sophia Baines's in that it is
marked by an absolute indifference on the part of her relatives to
her mental development. Rachel, that is,

> had been educated as the majority of well-to-do girls in the last
> part of the nineteenth century were educated. Kindly doctors
> and gentle old professors had taught her the rudiments of about
> ten branches of knowledge, but they would as soon have forced
> her to go through one piece of drudgery thoroughly as they
> would have told her that her hands were dirty. (*The Voyage
> Out*, p. 31)[26]

Rachel's upbringing recalls that of Austen's Emma, whose sole critic is her would-be lover, Knightley. Both women suffer because their intellectual education is of no importance to their relatives. Rachel's development has been governed by questions of health and of 'manners and morals' (p. 232; see also p. 32), the theory being that through the ministrations of her aunts her mental and physical virginity can be preserved, leaving her a marketable object to be sold in the 'masculine' world. Woolf remarks of Rachel's father that 'he loved his own possessions' (p. 77), and not the least of these is, of course, his daughter Rachel. As a result of his wife Theresa's early death, Willoughby Vinrace thinks of Rachel as 'the only thing that's left to me' (p. 96).

In her treatment of Rachel and her father Woolf draws in part, of course, upon her own relationship with Leslie Stephen. But, with a skill which is remarkable in a first novel, she disguises the fact that she herself has been the victim of male autocracy and tyranny. *The Voyage Out* remains as free as Austen's novels from private bitterness on the part of the narrator on the subject of the relations of the sexes. In order to avoid any such personal animosity and yet to cast an ironic and critical light on certain characters in the novel, Woolf puts forward many of her own opinions through Helen Ambrose. None the less Helen remains a convincing character in her own right.

It is part of Woolf's method in *The Voyage Out* to create a series of entertaining scenes in the manner of Austen which illustrate feminist ideas, and whose persuasiveness stems largely from the fact that they are amusing and light-hearted.[27] One such episode is that in which Helen suggests to Willoughby that she should undertake the social education of his daughter. Willoughby responds with enthusiasm to the idea, because he recognises the personal benefits which accrue to such a scheme. In describing to Helen the way in which a more confident Rachel could aid him were he to follow Richard Dalloway into Parliament, Willoughby reveals the fact that his daughter is primarily of importance to him only in so far as she can help to further his own career:

I should want Rachel to be able to take more part in things. A certain amount of entertaining would be necessary – dinners, an occasional evening party. One's constituents like to be fed, I believe. In all these ways Rachel could be of great help to me. (p. 97)

The outrageousness of Willoughby's attitude speaks for itself. Should the reader miss her satirical purpose, however, Woolf exploits Helen to underline just how ridiculous is Willoughby's idea of his daughter as 'a Tory Hostess' (p. 98). Helen recognises that Willoughby's superficial air of concern for Rachel masks a good deal of selfishness (p. 98), and in noting this fact she draws the reader's attention to it. Willoughby has much in common with Mr Hilbery in *Night and Day*, whose jealousy over his daughter leads him to oppose her marriage to Ralph Denham. Whereas in the later novel, however, it is chiefly through caricature that Woolf emphasises the absurdity of Mr Hilbery's position, in *The Voyage Out* she makes Helen the spokeswoman for her own dislike of the self-centred and over-possessive father. Helen considers Willoughby's neglect of his daughter's education little short of criminal. The state of ignorance in which Rachel has been kept as to the most elementary facts of life seems to her to explain 'why women are what they are – the wonder is they're no worse' (p. 110). She hopes that the conversation at the villa will compensate in time for the narrowness of Rachel's upbringing: 'Talk was the medicine she trusted to, talk about everything, talk that was free, unguarded, and as candid as a habit of talking with men made natural in her own case' (p. 143). Helen's remark directly echoes a comment which Woolf made in a letter to her brother Thoby of May 1903, and thus reveals the degree to which Helen speaks for her author on this subject.[28] Moreover, Helen's point of view is later corroborated by the narrative when we are told that Rachel's conversation with Ralph 'which had no boundaries' does indeed deepen and enlarge 'the strangely small bright view of a girl' (p. 367). The fact that Helen's opinions coincide with subsequent events in the novel encourages the reader to take her point of view seriously, and to respond to her as, to some degree, authoritative. In this way, then, Woolf can control the reader's reaction to her narrative without appearing to do so. It is through Helen that Woolf puts across the idea that Willoughby idealises his dead wife in order that he may use her to justify his selfish ambitious schemes 'for combining this and that and building up a solid mass of industry' (p. 96).[29] Willoughby's feelings about Theresa mask the fact that 'he had not been particularly kind to her while she lived, *as Helen thought*' (p. 96; my italics).[30] Helen recognises that Willoughby uses women, much as he makes use of the natives employed by his shipping firm (p. 232), to bolster his own self-esteem (p. 96).

Woolf puts the feminist debate into the mouths of her fictional characters in the course of the dinner scene following the Dalloway's arrival on board the *Euphrosyne*. During this episode it becomes apparent that Richard Dalloway shares Willoughby Vinrace's opposition to the idea of female suffrage. Given that – through Helen – Woolf encourages the reader to respond to Willoughby's views with a fair degree of scepticism, one is inclined to react to Richard Dalloway in much the same way. Moreover, Woolf employs caricature to direct the reader's response to both Richard and Clarissa.[31] The outrageousness of the Dalloway's world-view, that is, comes across in their remarks. Beneath Richard's authoritarian statement, 'may I be in my grave before a woman has the right to vote in England' (p. 44), for example, lies, one suspects, the fear that his own status in society – like that of Willoughby Vinrace – would be undermined were he to forfeit the worship of charming, but ignorant, women like his wife.

Clarissa is herself as susceptible to the suffragists' criticisms as her husband. Her unwillingness to offer the slightest criticism of Richard helps to perpetuate the kind of society in which his preposterous values prevail.[32] Through Clarissa, Woolf illustrates the argument which she was later to put forward explicitly in *Three Guineas* that many women would rather exercise 'indirect influence' over their husbands than have the right to vote themselves.[33] In this respect Clarissa conforms to that ideal of woman epitomised in the nineteenth century by Ruskin's 'Of Queen's Gardens'.[34] Woolf – like Margaret Wilcox in Forster's *Howards End* – equates the 'indirect influence' exerted by such women with intellectual prostitution.[35] Women of Clarissa's type meet with strong criticism in Richardson's *Pilgrimage*, because they subscribe to the traditional view of womanhood, dedicating their lives to bolstering the 'masculine' world-view, and at the same time minimising the value of their own response to experience.[36]

Like many of the characters in *The Voyage Out*, Clarissa is drawn, in part at least, from Woolf's own experience, being modelled on her acquaintance, Kitty Maxse.[37] A private comment which Woolf made about her friend (in a letter to Violet Dickinson) is equally applicable to her fictional character:

I should feel more confidence in her schemes for setting the

Empire on its legs again if they were ever exactly the *opposite* of 'what Leo thinks' (as she always begins her sentences).[38]

Instead, though, of criticising Clarissa openly in her novel – as she attacks Kitty in her letter – Woolf allows her fictional character to condemn herself out of her own mouth through her ridiculous thoughts and remarks.[39] Clarissa's attitude to her husband is summarised in her reflections as she lies awake on board the *Euphrosyne:*

> I often wonder . . . whether it is really good for a woman to live with a man who is morally her superior, as Richard is mine. It makes one so dependent. I suppose I feel for him what my mother and women of her generation felt for Christ. . . . (p. 55)[40]

Given the outrageousness of Richard's view of Clarissa – and indeed of all women – there is no need for Woolf explicitly to direct the reader's response to his remarks either. Clarissa's tendency to idealise Richard, 'pompous and sentimental' egoist as, according to Helen, he is (p. 89), has the effect of discouraging self-criticism on her husband's part. To his wife's words of self-denigration Richard responds with the remark, 'You're a pretty creature, anyhow' (p. 54), and in belittling his wife's intellect is thus able to boost his own self-confidence.

In commenting on his childhood to Rachel, Richard remarks that 'There's nothing like coming of a large family. Sisters particularly are delightful' (p. 59). The attraction of sisters lies, of course, in the fact that instead of competing with men on their own terms, they are confined to the role of 'ministers' to men. When Richard makes the pronouncement that Jane Austen's merit is that 'she does not attempt to write like a man' (p. 66), he reveals an underlying fear at the idea of competing with women on equal terms.[41] In this instance, Clarissa's undiscriminating acceptance of her husband's point of view – 'I'm afraid he's right. . . . He generally is – the wretch' (p. 67) – serves to allay his fear.

Richard reveals the extent to which he uses his wife to bolster his own position when he explains the basis of their relationship to Rachel. Here, once again, Woolf makes use of a fictional scene and character to illustrate a particular set of ideological positions.

In outlining his attitudes to Rachel, Richard at the same time lays bare his character to the reader:

> I never allow my wife to talk politics. . . . For this reason. It is impossible for human beings, constituted as they are, both to fight and to have ideals. If I have preserved mine, as I am thankful to say that in great measure I have, it is due to the fact that I have been able to come home to my wife in the evening and to find that she has spent her day in calling, music, play with the children, domestic duties – what you will; her illusions have not been destroyed. She gives me courage to go on. (pp. 70–1)

The most palpable of Clarissa's illusions is, of course, her belief that her husband is a 'great man'. It is only through fostering his wife's ignorance of political issues that Richard is able to hide his own fallibility from her. His opposition to the idea of women's suffrage and his assertion that he has never come across a woman who understands 'what is meant by statesmanship', nor would he ever like to meet 'such a woman' (p. 72) stems in fact from a need to mask the implicit injustice of his own social position.

Ann Douglas's description of the society portrayed in Harriet Beecher Stowe's *Uncle Tom's Cabin* captures the essence of the relationship between Richard and Clarissa Dalloway: 'women, protected at home from the harsh and desensitizing forces of the competitive world, were to use the moral suasion of example and mild precept to turn their men to more humane (or feminine) ways; women were never directly to oppose men, no matter how stupid or brutal they might be'.[42] This idea is illustrated through figures like Mrs Shelby and Mrs Bird in *Uncle Tom*. Barbara Taylor discusses the implications of this ideal of woman as the 'moral vanguard' in *Eve and the New Jerusalem*:

> A morality more convenient and yet more contradictory would be hard to imagine. Having confined all those virtues inappropriate within the stock market or the boardroom to the hearts of their womenfolk, middle-class men were then left free to indulge in all those unfortunate vices necessary for successful bourgeois enterprise. The fate of women and Christian selflessness having been thus bound together, the dependency and social powerlessness of the first became a virtual guarantee of

the social irrelevance of the second: once God had settled into the parlour, Mammon had free range in public life – and the exclusion of women from virtually all areas of public existence guaranteed that this tidy division was maintained.

Taylor goes on to argue that 'Female complicity in conventional definitions of womanly virtue could be secured only by ensuring that those who voiced opposition were automatically placed outside the pale of respectable womanhood.'[43] It is this very process which is at work when, in Bennett's *The Old Wives' Tale*, Sophia Baines's parents object to the idea that she should earn her own living on the grounds that it would be 'unwomanly' for her to do so.

Woolf uses the comic scenes between Richard and the naïve Rachel to reveal the limitations of Richard's world-view. Whilst he can respond to his wife's adulation, Rachel's serious, if ill-expressed, criticisms of his attitudes remain unintelligible to him. Richard's egotism prevents him from responding to Rachel except in terms of a young woman attractive to himself. Rachel's tentative experiment in self-expression – 'You see, I'm a woman' – earns, for example, the sententious reply, 'How strange to be a woman! A *young and beautiful* woman . . . has the whole world at her feet' (p. 84; my italics). Richard's obtuseness and inability to understand or sympathise with Rachel are, in part at least, the product of his wife's consistent habit of self-effacement. In this respect, as we shall see, he resembles Mr Hilbery in *Night and Day*.

Rachel's initial response to Richard and Clarissa attests to the fact that it is quite possible to take even such manifestly ridiculous individuals seriously. In case the reader should be inclined to do so, Woolf uses those scenes in which Helen corrects Rachel's response to the Dalloways to make clear to us how we should react to them.

Another amusing scene, in which Woolf puts her social criticisms across obliquely, is that in which the company on board the *Euphrosyne* discuss the British Navy over lunch. Once again Woolf uses Helen to cast an ironic light on the conversation of the other characters. In response to various fatuous remarks about 'valour and death, and the magnificent qualities of British admirals' (p. 75) Helen comments 'that it seemed to her as wrong to keep sailors as to keep a Zoo, and that as for dying on a battle-field, surely it was time we ceased to praise courage' (pp. 75–6).[44] Richard's contempt for Helen – a contempt to which Clarissa all too readily subscribes (p. 52) – can be directly related to the fact that she believes neither in his world nor in its values. Through Helen, Woolf expresses her own dislike of the self-importance of politicians, with their misplaced interest in 'great events'.[45] Whereas Richard considers Mr Vinrace to be 'the kind of man we want in Parliament – the man who has done things' (p. 81), Helen feels that 'A man who's made a fortune in trade . . . is bound to be twice as bad as any prostitute' (p. 377). Terence Hewet's comments on the subject later in the novel also reflect Woolf's own point of view:

> There's no doubt it helps to make up for the drudgery of a profession if a man's taken very, very seriously by every one. . . . What a miracle the masculine conception of life is – judges, civil servants, army, navy, Houses of Parliament, lord mayors – what a world we've made of it! . . . It's the man's view that's represented, you see. Think of a railway train: fifteen carriages for men who want to smoke. Doesn't it make your blood boil? If I were a woman I'd blow some one's brains out. (pp. 253, 258)[46]

Rachel, too (albeit less coherently), subscribes to her author's belief that the individual is more important than political machinery (p. 72).[47]

The Voyage Out is, it has been noted, a version of the *Bildungsroman*, in which the reader is educated alongside the heroine. At the opening of the novel, then, Rachel comes across as extremely naïve and immature. With her fascination for *Who's Who* and its 'biographies' of 'great men' (p. 93), she finds Richard enchanting, his conversation is rich in 'Wonderful masculine stories' (p. 85). Although she has suffered neglect as a girl, she is as yet unable to make the connection between the worship of 'masculine' values and her own deprivation. The link between these two factors is to be made for Rachel – and, of course, the reader – by Terence Hewet.[48] Rachel mistakes Richard Dalloway's desire for her body for an interest in her mind. To the least perceptive of readers, on the other hand, it is apparent that as far as Richard is concerned women have no minds. That the Dalloways share this view is illustrated by their concern, above all, not (like Mrs Elliot) to have a child, but rather to produce a son (p. 53).[49] Under Hewet's influence, Rachel comes to recognise the equal rights of the two sexes, and the injustice implicit in the aggrandisement of the one to the detriment of the other. Terence remarks, in one of those comments about the future which are to take on pathos in the light of Rachel's death, 'We must have a son and we must have a daughter' (p. 360), and the two agree that their son 'should be taught to laugh at great men, that is, at distinguished successful men, at men who wore ribands and rose to the tops of their trees. He should in no way resemble (Rachel added) St John Hirst' (p. 361).

Part of the reader's enjoyment of the scenes between Rachel and Richard Dalloway stems from the fact that one recognises the naïvety with which Rachel is taken in by the older man (though at the same time one cannot but admire her for a childlike faith in other people which it would be impossible for the more sophisticated Helen to hold.) As Rachel becomes more experienced, under the influence of Helen and Terence, not even she can remain blind to the grotesque anti-feminist stance adopted by St John Hirst. Indeed, it is largely through her acquaintance with Hirst that Rachel is awakened to the outrageousness of the assumption that women are naturally inferior to men. The reader is encouraged to participate in this process of enlightenment.

Woolf's portrait of Hirst is, like much of the novel, drawn from her own direct experience. The most obvious model for St John is Lytton Strachey, but the letters which Woolf wrote as a young woman abound in scornful references to this type of university man, who has 'won prizes without number' and is 'consequently unable to talk'.[50] To be aware of this fact is to recognise the skill with which Woolf maintains her balanced, impersonal approach in the novel. Her portrait of Hirst is remarkable not for its anger or bitterness, but rather for a good-natured, humorous sympathy.[51] This humour reaches its heights, perhaps, in the scene at the hotel dance in which Hirst reveals to Rachel – and, of course, to the reader – his despicable views about women, whilst remaining under the illusion that he is attempting to make reasonable conversation. Hirst's sense of his own inadequacy, coupled with his vanity, leads him to adopt a contemptuous tone towards Rachel. His obtuse analysis of Rachel's character – like William Rodney's ridiculous assessment of Katharine Hilbery in *Night and Day* – speaks for itself. There is no need, then, for Woolf explicitly to point out the absurdity of Hirst's position. Rachel, he feels, 'had obviously never thought or felt or seen anything, and she might be intelligent or she might be just like all the rest' (p. 180). Rachel, who remains initially blind to the contempt which her own father and Richard Dalloway feel for women, cannot mistake such a feeling in Hirst's crude and egotistic outburst. She finds the clumsy arrogance of his remarks deeply offensive:

> You see, the problem is, can one really talk to you? Have you got a mind, or are you like the rest of your sex? You seem to me absurdly young compared with men of your age. . . .
> About Gibbon . . . D'you think you'll be able to appreciate him? He's the test, of course. It's awfully difficult to tell about women . . . how much, I mean, is due to lack of training, and how much is native incapacity. (pp. 180–1)

Through Rachel's response to Hirst, Woolf shows how offensive anti-feminist comments can be to individual women, without revealing in her tone that she herself has often been deeply hurt by such remarks. Her indulgent approach to Hirst in fact serves her cause far more effectively than would an angry and indignant authorial outburst against him. She makes use of subsequent scenes between Hirst and Helen Ambrose to encourage the reader, like Helen, to sympathise with him – even as we accept his limitations – implicitly attributing his initial fear of, and hostility towards, Rachel, to the fact of his own sexual uncertainty. Hirst's respect is reserved for older women like Helen Ambrose and his mother, for whom there's 'something to be said . . . though she is in many ways so deplorable' (p. 189). In the course of their conversation at the hotel dance, Hirst remarks to Helen: 'You're the only woman I've ever met who seems to have the faintest conception of what I mean when I say a thing' (p. 189). Her attraction lies in the fact that she is secure enough to be able to absorb Hirst's insecurity, and she can sympathise with, tolerate, and even soothe, his vanity: 'She suspected that he was not happy, and was sufficiently feminine to wish to receive confidences' (p. 190).[52] Helen's relationship with Hirst clearly anticipates that between Mrs Ramsay and Charles Tansley in *To the Lighthouse*.

Hirst is obsessed with his own personality, and, like Willoughby Vinrace and Richard Dalloway, needs to draw upon a woman's sympathy in order to sustain his self-confidence. (Sympathy is a virtue which Woolf explicitly connects with the 'feminine' consciousness, contrasting it with egotism, which she sees as an essentially 'masculine' fault.)[53] In conversation, Hirst typically brings the talk round to the state of his own mind and body (p. 241), remaining quite impervious to the emotional needs of others. This is manifest, for example, during that scene in which he talks with Helen in the garden at the villa. Throughout their conversation, Hirst takes no interest whatsoever in the work with which Helen is occupied (p. 244), being engaged in framing remarks about Rachel ('is she merely a kind of footstool' – p. 244) and about the simplicity of women in general (p. 245). That Helen possesses the 'feminine' virtue of sympathy is revealed in her willingness to minister to his egotism by asking him about Cambridge and encouraging him to discuss with her his future (p. 246).

Hewet recognises the extent of Hirst's egotistical demands for sympathy when he remarks to Rachel:

> I assure you . . . not a day's passed since we came here without a discussion as to whether he's to stay on at Cambridge or to go to the Bar. It's his career – his sacred career. And if I've heard it twenty times, I'm sure his mother and sister have heard it five hundred times. (p. 253)

None the less he remains, like Helen, essentially sympathetic to Hirst. Rachel's bitter anger at the crude caricature of her own life which Hirst puts forward during the dance at the hotel abates when Hewet encourages her to explain its basis (pp. 182–3). He is 'determined that Rachel should not store the incident away in her mind to take its place in the view she had of life' (p. 182). Hewet is able to sympathise at once with Rachel and Hirst, and to recognise the positive aspects of both their world-views, and in this respect he shares his author's dislike of violent partisanship. He tries to explain Hirst's point of view to Rachel and through him Woolf encourages us to sympathise with Hirst:

> You can't expect him to be at his best in a ballroom. He wants a cosy, smoky, masculine place, where he can stretch his legs out, and only speak when he's got something to say. For myself, I find it rather dreary. But I do respect it. (p. 183)

It is part of Woolf's strategy in *The Voyage Out* to avoid the type of virulent attack upon a character like Hirst which would betray her own feminist position and thereby put the unsympathetic reader on the defensive.

Hirst responds initially to the idea of Terence's engagement to Rachel much as Mr Hilbery, in *Night and Day*, reacts to the news that Katharine intends to marry Ralph Denham. Sensing the growing intimacy between the lovers during their river journey, he is overcome by a sense of his own loneliness, and draws towards Helen for sympathy (p. 340). Like Mr Hilbery, then, he sees the engagement in terms of his own loss rather than the happiness of the lovers: 'His feelings about Terence and Rachel were so complicated that he had never yet been able to bring himself to say that he was glad that they were going to be married' (p. 381). Woolf's treatment of Hirst in *The Voyage Out* is, however, more subtle than her caricature of Mr Hilbery in *Night and Day*. The tendency in her depiction of all the characters in the earlier novel is to give them the benefit of the doubt, and to emphasise their positive qualities as well as their negative. She aims, at all costs, to avoid reducing her central characters to conventional and obvious caricatures, little more than pawns in a theoretical discussion of feminism. To depict her characters in such simplistic terms would be to weaken the force of the novel's 'argument'. Thus, although Hirst, for example, is in some respects an egotist, his more attractive traits assert themselves in the course of the narrative, notably during Rachel's illness, but also in that scene in which he determines to congratulate his friends on their engagement (p. 382). The awkwardness of Hirst's speech during this scene implies a depth of feeling which is not necessarily present beneath the more conventional messages of congratulation which the lovers receive from their acquaintances at the hotel (p. 358).

Woolf uses Terence Hewet to cast a faintly ironic light on the essentially sympathetic character of Helen. Hewet considers it 'a strange and piteous flaw in her nature' (p. 296) that Helen is willing to make a compromise of her marriage by indulging Ridley. He recognises, then – and draws the reader's attention to the fact – that Helen, although she does not take the role of 'minister' to men to the same ridiculous lengths as Clarissa Dalloway, is not averse to adopting the traditional sympathetic 'feminine' stance. Unlike Clarissa, however, Helen is aware of this trait in her own character. When Hirst asks her rather pathetically, 'I suppose you've never paid any one a compliment in the course of your life', she replies, 'I spoil Ridley rather . . .' (p. 246). That this is the case is illustrated at the start of the novel, when she enlists Mrs Chailey's help in finding Ridley a comfortable room in which to work (pp. 26–7). Professor Ambrose's complaints ('Did I come on this voyage in order to catch rheumatism and pneumonia' – p. 27) anticipate the remarks which St John later makes about his health in order to win Helen's sympathy (p. 241). Helen is not above commenting to Rachel that 'If one can give men a room to themselves where they will sit, it's all to the good' (pp. 40–1). Indeed, she has, we are told, a certain admiration for the 'masculine' approach to experience:

> Supposing, for instance, that England made a sudden move towards some unknown port on the coast of Morocco, St John knew what was at the back of it, and to hear him engaged with her husband in argument about finance and the balance of power, gave her an odd sense of stability. She respected their arguments without always listening to them, much as she respected a solid brick wall, or one of those immense municipal buildings which, although they compose the greater part of our cities, have been built day after day and year after year by unknown hands. She liked to sit and listen . . .   (p. 373)[54]

The narrator remarks that Helen is not one to encourage 'those habits of unselfishness and amiability founded upon insincerity which are put at so high a value in mixed households of men and women' (p. 143). None the less, life at the villa in Santa Marina undoubtedly centres around the figure of Ridley Ambrose, and is dictated according to his needs:

> As it was, every one was conscious that by observing certain rules, such as punctuality and quiet, by cooking well, and performing other small duties, one ode after another was satisfactorily restored to the world, and they shared the continuity of the scholar's life.   (p. 200)

Ridley, like Mr Ramsay – and indeed St John Hirst – is obsessed by the fear that his academic achievement remains unrecognised. Like Mrs Ramsay, Helen tries to convince her husband of the value of his work, although her private opinion emerges unexpectedly, perhaps, in a remark which she makes to Mrs Flushing: 'my husband spends his life in digging up manuscripts which nobody wants' (p. 234). At the first sign of a crisis of confidence on her husband's part, though, Helen is quick to remind him of his fame and popularity (p. 111).[55] However, she tempers her loving admiration for her husband with humour, and it is this, above all, which differentiates her from Clarissa Dalloway. One cannot imagine Clarissa remarking to Richard, 'I think you're the vainest man I know' (p. 112). In fact it is largely through Helen that Woolf encourages the reader to appreciate the comic side of Ridley, whereas Clarissa's view of her husband is completely at odds with the idea that we form of him from the rest of the novel.

Ridley avoids that outward manner of pompous self-importance characteristic of Richard Dalloway, but his pretended indifference to such questions as that of woman suffrage is in some ways more insidious than Richard's fairly obvious contempt for, and hostility towards, women. When Clarissa questions Ridley on the subject of the vote, he remarks, 'I don't care a fig one way or t'other . . .' (p. 44). However, his claim to neutrality in fact masks a specific set of assumptions about the status and behaviour of women. (Ridley finds Mrs Flushing 'distinctly unsympathetic' (p. 235) largely because he is 'scrupulously fastidious as to the dress and behaviour of ladies' (p. 239).)[56] Indeed, Ridley expects Helen to live up to his conception of womanhood, in much the same way that Willoughby – like his sisters (p. 220) – makes the dead Theresa conform to his ideal of womanliness. When Helen makes a 'wordly-wise' remark to the young people during lunch at the villa, Ridley cuts her short in protest: 'He hated even the semblance of cynicism in women. "Nonsense, nonsense," he remarked abruptly' (p. 379).[57]

The fact that Ridley takes no pains at all to accommodate himself to Helen's character makes his prescriptions for her behaviour presumptious in the extreme. Like Richard Dalloway, he expects his wife to conform to his own standards, making little effort to understand or sympathise with hers. During Rachel's illness, his predominant feeling is one of jealousy for the sympathy which his wife traditionally bestows upon himself (p. 410). Ridley, like Willoughby Vinrace, has a certain amount in common with Woolf's own father.[58] Like her portrait of Mr Ramsay in To the Lighthouse, however, Woolf's treatment of Ambrose remains essentially sympathetic. She avoids any hint of personal animosity, maintaining a balanced tone in her depiction of a character modelled on someone who, through his demands for 'feminine' sympathy, made her own life and that of her sisters at times extremely difficult.

Helen's gift of sympathy is shared by several women at the hotel, as Terence points out to Rachel. Woolf uses Terence to direct not only Rachel's but also the reader's response to these women. When Rachel is inclined to disparage the elderly ladies, Hewet, in contrast, remarks, 'what a nice woman Miss Allan is; you can't deny that; and Mrs Thornbury too' (p. 360). Mrs Thornbury's chief virtue is her capacity for universal and impartial sympathy. She is able to share Miss Allan's interest in Crete (p. 131), Mrs Elliot's distress over her childlessness (p. 134), Arthur Venning's interest in flying (p. 155), and Rachel's enjoyment of the dance at the hotel:

> 'You love it too, Miss Vinrace,' she asked, looking at Rachel with maternal eyes. 'I know I did when I was your age. How I used to beg my mother to let me stay – and now I sympathise with the poor mothers – but I sympathise with the daughters too!'
> She smiled sympathetically, and at the same time rather keenly, at Rachel. (p. 185)

Introducing Mrs Flushing at the villa, Mrs Thornbury automatically assumes the role of 'interpreter, making things smooth all round' (p. 233), and later, when Hirst mocks Rachel for her inability to appreciate Gibbon, she unexpectedly intervenes, 'either because it was her mission to keep things smooth or because she had long wished to speak to Mr Hirst, feeling as she did that young men were her sons' (p. 238). It is from motives of sympathy that Mrs Thornbury keeps the news of Rachel's death hidden from her husband, recognising that it 'would only disturb him' (p. 439), and it is she who, in encouraging Hirst to spend the evening after Rachel's death amongst the visitors at the hotel, helps him to put his feelings about Rachel and Terence into a broader perspective.

Echoing Emma Woodhouse's treatment of Mrs and Miss Bates, Rachel is inclined to dismiss Mrs Thornbury and her friends as trivial, stupid old women (p. 360). She is tempted, for example, to ignore Mrs Thornbury's invitation to tea, claiming that she would rather have her 'right hand sawn in pieces' than be subjected to 'the eyes of all those women!' (p. 377). Although

Rachel finds Mrs Thornbury and her circle merely tedious, the narrative reveals that she is by no means stupidly conventional, as Rachel would believe, thereby vindicating Terence's point of view. Mrs Thornbury admires Miss Allan for earning her own living (p. 133), for example, and will not subscribe to Mrs Elliot's conservative definition of motherhood (p. 133). Indeed, like Terence she advocates women's education and liberation (p. 390), arguing that it is possible for women to enjoy the same opportunities as men and yet to 'remain women' and 'give a great deal to their children' (p. 391).[59]

Hewet's role as Rachel's lover and teacher recalls Mr Knightley's relationship with Emma or Ralph Touchett's with Isabel Archer.[60] In all these novels the reader is encouraged to sympathise with the heroine and thereby to share in her intellectual development. In so far as the lover-teacher's point of view is vindicated by the course of events in the novel, it can be identified with that of the author. Moreover, because Terence – like the narrator – sympathises with the heroine, the reader responds to his world-view as normative. Through Terence, then, Woolf can direct the reader's response to her novel without intervening in her own voice in the text.

Hewet not only recognises the 'feminine' virtue of sympathy in others, but also practises it himself.[61] This sympathy leads him to share his author's tolerance towards all the novel's characters. It is, for example, Terence who points out that the dry, and apparently soulless, Mr Pepper has an old aunt of whom he is extremely fond (p. 184). Woolf uses Evelyn Murgatroyd to emphasise Terence's 'feminity'. Evelyn tells Rachel, 'I had a long talk with Terence the other night. I felt we really were friends after that. There's something of a woman in him' (p. 302), and to Terence himself she remarks, 'You look as if you'd got a nice sister, somehow' (p. 223). Evelyn's response to Terence is borne out in the narrative, when Woolf relates that, in talking with Rachel, Terence instinctively adopts 'the feminine point of view' (p. 253). Hirst is scornful of the way in which Terence turns the conversation during tea at the villa, when he senses that it might offend the ladies (pp. 239, 243). Hewet is, though, no less aware than Rachel (p. 359) or Hirst that the good manners of polite society are artificial. He simply recognises that if one is to communicate at all with the majority of people, it must be through accepted patterns of behaviour (p. 360). Like Mrs Thornbury, he wishes to 'make things smooth'.

Terence shares Woolf's hatred of the mental 'chalk-marks' which simplify and distort characters and experiences, and which Woolf associates with the 'masculine' point of view.[62] He explains his position to Rachel:

> I'm not like Hirst . . . I don't see circles of chalk between people's feet. I sometimes wish I did. It seems to me so tremendously complicated and confused. One can't come to any decision at all; one's less and less capable of making judgments. (p. 264)

Hewet refuses to subscribe to Hirst's reduction of their common acquaintances to a series of 'types', a 'party of old women', or to his idea that 'You could draw circles round the whole lot of them.' (pp. 124, 123). He cannot concur with the kind of generalisation which Mr Thornbury makes when he asserts that 'No young man likes to have it said that he resembles an elderly spinster' (p. 130). During the preparations for the dance at the hotel he makes it 'his business to conciliate the outsiders as much as possible' (p. 175). His sympathetic attitude elicits gratitude and confidences from the outwardly uncommunicative characters whom he approaches (p. 175), thereby vindicating his own attitude and that of the author.

It is primarily through Terence, then, rather than a female character, that Woolf puts across and illustrates the 'feminine' point of view in her novel. Tactically, this is a good way of dissociating his views from her own private opinions. Terence's fullest attempt to articulate the feminist position to Rachel – and, of course, the reader – comes in the scene in which the two look down on the sea from the cliff above the villa. During this episode, Terence reveals an interest in, and sympathy with, Rachel's worldview (p. 255) which is at the opposite pole from Hirst's summary dismissal of her character (at the hotel dance), as quite without interest or significance. Hewet finds girls 'interesting to talk to' (p. 218) and cannot assent to Hirst's view that women are 'stupid' (p. 122) and their bodies disgusting (p. 216). His attempt to appreciate what it is like to be a young woman is as sympathetic as that of Hirst or Richard Dalloway is obtuse. When Rachel, in an echo of Mrs Dalloway's remarks to her husband, tells Hewet, 'You're finer than I am; you're much finer' (p. 345) Terence – unlike Richard Dalloway – refuses to accept his lover's adulation.

Since he is attracted by Rachel's personality, he has no wish to
reduce her to a flattering reflection of his own image.[63] Through
Terence's relationship with Rachel, Woolf illustrates the practical
implications of his views about women and society. Hewet envisages their marriage as one in which Rachel, unlike Clarissa or
Susan Warrington, will remain free, 'like the wind or the sea'
(p. 298; see also pp. 95, 261, 343).

In *The Voyage Out*, Woolf emphasises the importance not only of
her heroine's life but of the lives of all her female characters.[64]
(She uses Rachel's death – like the death of Mrs Ramsay in *To the
Lighthouse* – to bring home the value of Rachel's life to fictional
characters and readers alike.) Two interrelated devices in particular
enable Woolf to draw attention to the importance of women's lives
in her novel, whilst avoiding overt didacticism. On the one hand,
she creates 'dramatic' scenes in the manner of Austen in which
particular women reveal their powers of sympathy for others, a
sympathy which is in marked contrast with the egotism manifested
by many of the male characters. At the same time she uses those
episodes in which Terence discusses woman's social position with
Rachel to place the lives of these particular women in a more
general theoretical context, educating the reader alongside her
heroine in the process. During their conversation on the cliff-top
at Santa Marina Terence makes a number of remarks about
women's lives to Rachel which clearly echo Woolf's own point of
view as it is expressed outside the novel:

> There it was going on in the background, for all those thousands
> of years, this curious silent unrepresented life. Of course we're
> always writing about women – abusing them, or jeering at them,
> or worshipping them; but its never come from women them-
> selves. I believe we still don't know in the least how they live,
> or what they feel, or what they do precisely. If one's a man, the
> only confidences one gets are from young women about their
> love affairs. But the lives of women of forty, of unmarried
> women, of working women, of women who keep shops and
> bring up children, of women like your aunts or Mrs Thornbury
> or Miss Allan – one knows nothing whatever about them. They
> won't tell you. Either they're afraid, or they've got a way of

treating men. It's the man's view that's represented, you see. (p. 258)[65]

This speech of Terence's provides the reader with a clue, if one were needed, as to how to respond to the various characters in the novel, and to the attitudes to, and beliefs about, women embodied in Woolf's narrative.[66]

Through Terence's conversation with Rachel, Woolf introduces into the novel the argument which she was later to put forward in *A Room*, that women are misrepresented in literature because they are always depicted from a man's point of view.[67] Hewet's outburst prompts Rachel to reconsider her own life with her aunts and to recognise that it is these women, and not her father, 'who influenced her really' (p. 259). In contrast with the 'masculine' approach to experience, what Rachel comes to appreciate in the lives of her aunts is that they 'are always doing things' (p. 259), 'minute acts of charity and unselfishness which flowered punctually from a definite view of what they ought to do' (p. 260). Their world is governed not by an arbitrary system of public rewards and punishments, but by an inner integrity, a cultivated moral sense.

Given that we sympathise and identify with Terence and Rachel we are inclined to re-examine the feminist questions which their conversations raise without feeling that Woolf herself is putting pressure on us to do so. She encourages us on the contrary to believe that we are responding independently to the events and characters in her novel.

Terence's theories about women are borne out in the lives of specific characters in *The Voyage Out*.[68] His idea of the selfless spinster, for example, is realised in the novel through the figure of Miss Allan, who has much in common with Lucy Craddock in *The Years*. Although Miss Allan's achievement in writing a history of English Literature gains her little public recognition of the kind afforded to Ridley Ambrose, she avoids both the tendency to egotism manifested by Ridley, and the false modesty exhibited by Hughling Elliot, the Oxford don. Elliot represents that type of academic strongly criticised by Woolf outside the novel who tries to 'ingratiate himself with the young' by belittling his profession (p. 193).[69] In contrast, Miss Allan, although she recognises that her employment is primarily 'a question of bread and butter'

(p. 193), takes a just pride in her work, and has a firm belief in its value:

> She was indeed very proud that she had finished her book, for no one knew what an amount of determination had gone to the making of it. Also she thought it was a good piece of work, and considering what anxiety she had been in about her brother when she wrote it, she could not resist telling them a little more about it. (p. 387)

Miss Allan's conviction of the worth of her profession means that, unlike Ridley and St John, she needs neither external encouragement in the form of assurances of her 'greatness' (p. 248), nor to be continually asserting her own merits (p. 179). Indeed, her indifference on the subject comes across in a remark she makes to Rachel: 'I always consider myself the most ordinary person I know. It's rather distinguished to be as ordinary as I am' (pp. 311–12). Like Mary Datchet in *Night and Day*, Miss Allan combines a 'masculine' ability to pursue a profession diligently and competently with a 'feminine' capacity for sympathising with others. Anticipating Joan Denham in the same novel, she takes upon herself the responsibility for the welfare of her family, reacting, for example, to the news that her brother is facing financial difficulties in New Zealand with the thought that her own trip to South America is 'an extravagance and not the just and wonderful holiday due to her after fifteen years of punctual lecturing and correcting essays upon English literature' (p. 210). Miss Allan is, moreover, as sensitive to the needs of her acquaintances as to the problems within her own family. She could be said to vindicate Terence's view that 'All the most individual and humane of his friends were bachelors and spinsters' (p. 295). Woolf's treatment of Miss Allan, like Austen's portrayal of Miss Bates, or Brontë's of Miss Aines (in *Shirley*), implicitly undermines the popular notion of the spinster as an appropriate object of pity and ridicule – a notion which gained currency in the nineteenth century through numerous fictional portraits of unattractive old maids.[70] Miss Allan is, we are told, 'possessed of an amount of good-will towards others, and in particular towards the young, which often made her regret that speech was so difficult' (p. 314). Her benevolence comes across in that scene in which she entertains Rachel in her room, although Rachel herself is, at this point, in no state to appreciate it.

The 'masculine' world-view which Hewet describes to Rachel is, the novel suggests, upheld by the Church. Like other 'masculine' egotists in *The Voyage Out* the clergyman, Mr Bax, assumes that the domain of sympathy is one inhabited entirely by women. He argues that 'the humblest' can help in his scheme for improving the world:

> the least important things had an influence (here his manner became definitely priestly and his remarks seemed to be directed to women, for indeed Mr Bax's congregations were mainly composed of women, and he was used to assigning them their duties in his innocent clerical campaigns).   (p. 282)[71]

Mr Bax, then, subscribes to the view that 'life exists more fully in what is commonly thought big than in what is commonly thought small'[72], 'what is commonly thought small' being, in this instance, the lives of women.[73]

In her portrayal of Susan Warrington, Woolf shows how the 'masculine' interpretation of experience can effect the lives of individual women.[74] As a woman Susan is – like the unmarried daughter who keeps house for Mr Pepper's friend, Jenkinson (p. 10) – automatically sacrificed to the needs of her family. Susan's description of her life-style at home in Wiltshire reveals that the same perpetual demands are made upon her sympathy as upon the exploited daughters in *Night and Day* – Katharine Hilbery, Euphemia Otway and Elizabeth Datchet. Like the immature Rachel Vinrace, though, Susan evinces unqualified admiration for the father who makes use of her for his own selfish ends:

> There's the ordering and the dogs and the garden, and the children coming to be taught . . . and my tennis, and the village, and letters to write for father, and a thousand little things that don't sound much; but I never have a moment to myself . . . and father has to be very careful about chills in winter which means a great deal of running about'.   (pp. 318–19)

One is reminded of Rachel's ingenuous remark that 'Father generally wanted to be quiet when he came home, because he works very hard at Hull' (p. 254).

It is not only Susan's father who takes advantage of her position of dependence as an unmarried woman; her aunt also exploits

Susan on these grounds. Susan's life-style at the hotel is dictated entirely by the elderly woman's needs. Her days are devoted to Mrs Paley's comfort (p. 129), and her evenings are governed by her aunt's sleeping patterns (p. 117). As she remarks to Arthur Venning, 'that's my life' (p. 139). Echoing Mr Woodhouse's treatment of his daughter in *Emma*, Susan's aunt and father take it for granted that her tastes will coincide with their own. When Mrs Paley chooses to take tea in the garden, it is assumed that Susan, like Katharine Hilbery in *Night and Day*, will superintend the occasion, running to fetch cups for thirsty late-comers (pp. 137, 139) and accepting her aunt's complaints about the heat with equanimity (p. 137). Of all the women in the novel, Susan most obviously epitomises Woolf's notion of 'The Angel in the House'. She is quick to cede the unlooked-for pleasure of a visit to the town with Arthur Venning (p. 139), when it becomes clear that the project conflicts with her aunt's plans for the evening:

> The party broke up, and Susan, who had never felt so happy in her life, was just about to start for her walk in the town with Arthur, when Mrs Paley beckoned her back. She could not understand from the book how Double Demon patience is played; and suggested that if they sat down and worked it out together it would fill up the time nicely before dinner.   (p. 141)

Susan's experience implicitly illustrates another of the feminist arguments which Woolf was to put forward in *A Room*, namely that many women marry in order to escape the pressures of home life. The prospect of such an escape certainly contributes to the happiness with which Susan accepts Arthur's proposal of marriage. She is overjoyed at the 'amazing good fortune' which decrees that she can now 'join the ranks of the married women' and need no longer 'hang on to groups of girls much younger than herself' nor anticipate 'the long solitude of an old maid's life' (pp. 162–3) like that of Miss Allan.[75] Susan regards marriage as a universal positive, because in her own case its advantages seem manifest:

> She had been vaguely uncomfortable at home for two or three years now, and a voyage like this with her selfish old aunt, who paid her fare but treated her as servant and companion in one, was typical of the kind of thing people expected of her.   (p. 212)

The announcement of Susan's engagement coincides with a marked improvement in her aunt's attitude towards her. Mrs Paley becomes 'really grateful for an hour of Susan's company where she had been used to exact two or three as her right' (p. 212).

With Susan Warrington, Evelyn Murgatroyd illustrates Terence's argument that women tend to be the victims in a 'masculine' society. Evelyn is, on the whole, despised in the world of the novel, if not for the circumstances of her birth, then at least for the social unorthodoxy which they may be said to have produced. She refuses to accept the role of 'young lady' assigned to her by the 'masculine' world (p. 159), being interested, like Mary Datchet in *Night and Day*, in socialism, 'the White Slave Traffic, Women [sic] Suffrage, the Insurance Bill, and so on' (p. 303).

Through Evelyn, Woolf expresses many of her own reservations about conventional society. Evelyn is, for example, like Hewet (pp. 295–6), mistrustful of the limitations imposed by marriage upon the two partners. Being engaged has, Evelyn notes, had a bad effect upon Susan and Rachel: 'It was that slowness, that confidence, that content which she hated, she thought to herself. They moved so slowly because they were not single but double' (p. 392).[76]

Although she shares some of her author's views, Evelyn is treated with a certain degree of sarcasm in the novel, epitomised, perhaps, in Woolf's comments on her behaviour towards Hirst during the picnic expedition: 'The full and romantic career of Evelyn Murgatroyd is best hit off by her own words, "Call me Evelyn and I'll call you St John" ' (p. 149). Woolf, however, by no means fully endorses the criticisms of Evelyn put forward by specific characters in the novel. Pre-eminent amongst Evelyn's transgressions against the codes of the novel's society is her inability, like Susan and Rachel, to confine her attentions to one man. Terence implicitly criticises her for this when he asks, 'Do you never flirt?' (p. 228). The irony of such a criticism is that Terence himself has been accustomed to make love to different women (p. 217).[77] Rachel, however, remains quite undisconcerted by his remark: 'In the first place, I've never been in love with other women, but I've had other women' (p. 343). The discrepancy between the kind of behaviour expected of Hewet and that permitted to Evelyn supports the novel's more general criticism of the way in which a male-dominated society dictates standards of behaviour for its women. *The Voyage Out* dramatises many of the criticisms of society's double-standard which Woolf was later to put forward in 'Women and Fiction'. In that essay she argues, for example, that whereas George Eliot's public was scandalised by her relationship with G. H. Lewes, Tolstoy's extravagant youth was accepted as no more than useful experience for the writer.[78]

The symbol of the double standard in *The Voyage Out* is, of course, the prostitute, who could be seen as its ultimate victim.[79] With her knowledge of her own mother's history and of the price which, as a woman, she has paid for being unmarried (p. 225), Evelyn is quick to recognise the injustice whereby prostitutes – though not their clientèle – are condemned.[80] She remarks to Rachel:

> I'm certain that if people like ourselves were to take things in hand instead of leaving it to policemen and magistrates, we could put a stop to prostitution . . . in six months. . . . We ought to go into Piccadilly and stop one of these poor wretches and say: 'Now, look here, I'm no better than you are . . . and if you do a beastly thing it does matter to me.' (pp. 303–4)

Evelyn's naïve idealism makes her an easy prey for the kind of sarcasm which Hirst, for example, levels at her (p. 375). Through Evelyn, however, Woolf is able to draw attention to the issue of prostitution, whilst avoiding overt didacticism in her novel, and at the same time she reveals the valuable side of Evelyn's own personality. (Paradoxically, whereas Hirst is quite prepared to besmirch Evelyn's character, he recognises that the prostitute is a victim of society's double standard (p. 376).)[81] Early in the novel, Woolf remarks that Helen Ambrose dislikes the kind of fiction 'whose purpose was to distribute the guilt of a woman's downfall upon the right shoulders' (p. 144). In *The Voyage Out*, Woolf has no wish to produce such a novel, preferring to make her feminist point obliquely. None the less, her novel, like Shaw's *Mrs Warren's Profession*, illustrates the complicity of society as a whole in the degradation of its victims.[82]

Woolf's treatment of Evelyn is typical of her approach throughout *The Voyage Out*. The persuasiveness with which she puts her feminist ideas across in the novel can be related to the skill with which such ideas are absorbed into its ' dramatic' form.[83] Woolf arouses the reader's interest in the novel's fictional charac-

ters, and thereby encourages us to respond sympathetically to the
issues which are embodied in their story.

(c) PATTERN IN THE NOVEL

I suspect your criticism about the failure of conception is quite
right. I think I had a conception, but I don't think it made itself
felt. What I wanted to do was to give the feeling of a vast tumult
of life, as various and disorderly as possible, which should be
cut short for a moment by the death, and go on again – and the
whole was to have a sort of pattern, and be somehow controlled.
The difficulty was to keep any sort of coherence, – also to give
enough detail to make the characters interesting – which Forster
says I didn't do.[84]

In *The Voyage Out*, Woolf intended to draw attention to the fact
that, as she believed, there is a pattern to be discerned beneath
what might seem to be the most chaotic and meaningless of
events. Through such an emphasis in the novel, Woolf implicitly
denies that Rachel's death is merely arbitrary, and at the same
time, therefore, urges the ultimate value of her heroine's life. The
pattern inherent in her narrative serves, moreover, to suggest a
corresponding order and meaning in the whole of human
experience.[85]

Like her treatment of feminism, Woolf's examination of the idea
that there is a correlation between pattern in art and in life is
focused, in *The Voyage Out*, through Terence Hewet. Woolf uses
Terence to establish the values by which her novel should be
judged, rather than intervening explicitly to this purpose in the
text.[86] Terence is very much his author's spokesman on the subject
of the novel:

As for the novel itself, the whole conception, the way one's
seen the thing, felt about it, made it stand in relation to other
things, not one in a million cares for that. And yet I sometimes
wonder whether there's anything else in the whole world worth
doing. (p. 262)[87]

Like Woolf, Terence is not so much interested in the traditional chronological narrative of suspense and resolution at the level of plot, as in the need for aesthetic unity in the novel. 'There's no difficulty', he remarks, 'in conceiving incidents; the difficulty is to put them into shape' (p. 264).[88] Terence explains to Rachel – and through him Woolf makes clear to the reader – that his aim in writing a novel is to capture something of the significance which he finds in the whole of experience: 'Things I feel come to me like lights. . . . I want to combine them. . . . Have you ever seen fireworks that make figures? . . . I want to make figures' (p. 266; Woolf's ellipses). The explanation which Hewet gives to Rachel of the meaning which he finds in experience resembles Woolf's account of the inspiration behind *The Waves*. Through Terence, then, Woolf is able to make her own intentions as a novelist plain, without addressing the reader directly in her own voice in the novel:

> According to him, too, there was an order, a pattern which made life reasonable, or, if that word was foolish, made it of deep interest anyhow, for sometimes it seemed possible to understand why things happened as they did. Nor were people so solitary and uncommunicative as she believed. She should look for vanity – for vanity was a common quality – first in herself, and then in Helen, in Ridley, in St John, they all had their share of it – and she would find it in ten people out of every twelve she met; and once linked together by one such tie she would find them not separate and formidable, but practically indistinguishable, and she would come to love them when she found that they were like herself.   (p. 366)[89]

Of the four principal characters' autobiographical sketches in *The Voyage Out*, Hewet's alone constitutes an implicit attack upon the traditional narrative of facts of the kind to be found, for example in *Who's Who*. Like René in *The Years*, Hewet is unable to reduce his own complex life to a simple chronological sequence of 'important events'. He is more interested in the feelings which underlie such events, the things which, by tradition, people don't say. In this respect, of course, he speaks for his author:

> 'I am the son of an English gentleman. I am twenty seven,' Hewet began. 'My father was a fox-hunting squire. He died when I was ten in the hunting field. I can remember his body

coming home, on a shutter I suppose, just as I was going down
to tea, and noticing that there was jam for tea, and wondering
whether I should be allowed – '
    'Yes; but keep to the facts,' Hirst put in.   (p. 167)

Later in the novel, Woolf lends authority to Hewet's approach
when she remarks that he is 'far more highly skilled in the art of
narrative than Rachel'. He is able to relate 'not only what
happened, but what he had thought and felt' (p. 366). In Woolf's
own mind, the conventional 'factual' narrative is linked with the
idea of 'masculine' egotism and obtuseness. Men like Richard
Dalloway and Hirst are unable to appreciate the value of that
experience which takes place 'between the acts' of history or
biography. Hewet's rejection of the traditional conception of
biography is consistent, then, with both his own and his author's
'feminine' approach to experience.[90]
    Rachel's love for Terence, like Arthur's for Susan (p. 395), leads
her, at times, to view her own and other people's lives in a new
perspective, so that she finds in her own experience that order in
which Hewet believes:

> Perhaps, then, every one really knew as she knew now where
> they were going; and things formed themselves into a pattern
> not only for her, but for them, and in that pattern lay satisfaction
> and meaning. When she looked back she could see that a
> meaning of some kind was apparent in the lives of her aunts,
> and in the brief visit of the Dalloways whom she would never
> see again, and in the life of her father.   (p. 385)

With Rachel's illness and death, however, Terence's trust in life's
underlying significance is, at least temporarily, undermined. His
own experience is too closely bound up with Rachel's for him to
be able to place her death in a universal perspective. Instead, he
can only feel the immense injustice of his situation, summed up
in his comment: 'This has not happened to me. It is not possible
that this has happened to me' (p. 430). After Rachel's death, the
role of spokesman for the idea of order in experience is taken over
from Terence by Mrs Thornbury, who in this respect anticipates
Eleanor in *The Years*. In contrast with Miss Allan who, on hearing
that Rachel has died, feels that 'There did not seem to be much
point in it all' (p. 434), and Evelyn who finds the death 'wicked'

and 'cruel' (p. 436), Mrs Thornbury argues that 'the older one grows . . . the more certain one becomes that there is a reason. How could one go on if there were no reason' (p. 436). She recognises the value of her own life and 'all that she would have missed had she died at Rachel's age' but she feels that Rachel's death can none the less be fitted into a scheme of things which is essentially positive. Moreover, she believes that once Terence can outgrow the pain of Rachel's death, he too will be able to find a meaning in it:

> There was undoubtedly much suffering, much struggling, but, on the whole, surely there was a balance of happiness – surely order did prevail. Nor were the deaths of young people really the saddest things in life. . . . [Woolf's ellipsis]
> And in time Terence would come to feel – . . .   (p. 439)

Mrs Thornbury's belief in the coherence of experience is illustrated through the structure of the novel itself, with its pattern of recurrent themes and ideas.

In reading *The Voyage Out* for the first time it is easy to assume that it is a conventional novel of courtship and marriage, and to take it for granted that the various problems encountered by specific characters, and particularly the heroine, will be resolved when, at the end of the novel, she is united with the man whom she loves. Even as Woolf describes Rachel's illness, the reader to some extent shares Terence's belief that it is no more than a temporary setback: 'he never lost the sense that these thoughts somehow formed part of a life which he and Rachel would live together' (p. 422). Woolf, indeed, encourages the reader to share Terence's confidence in Rachel's ultimate recovery. Following Dr Lesage's first visit to the villa, for example, she remarks that: 'Owing perhaps to the change of doctor, Rachel appeared to be rather better next day. Terribly pale and worn though Helen looked, there was a slight lifting of the cloud which had hung all these days in her eyes' (p. 422). Clutching at this hint from the author, the reader anticipates a detailed account of Rachel's convalescence, culminating in her happy union with Terence. Consequently, when Rachel dies, the surprise which we feel is a fainter image of the shock experienced by Terence. In *The Voyage Out*, Woolf tackles the problem posed by the fact that the central characters in our lives can and will die.[91] Part of Woolf's purpose in the novel is to assert that there is a meaning to be discovered even in a world where such things happen. As in *The Waves*, she wishes 'to show that the theme effort, effort, dominates: not the waves: & personality: & defiance'.[92]

It is not, then, through the superficial events of her novel that Woolf suggests that human experience is ordered and harmonious, but rather through its underlying pattern.[93] As in *The Years* and, to a lesser extent, *Night and Day*, in *The Voyage Out* the argument that there is a pattern to be found in experience is supported by Woolf's careful structuring and ordering of her own material. Her letter to G. L. Dickinson of 27 October 1931 on the subject of *The Waves* shows that Woolf considered that she could best emphasise her belief in an inherent order in experience by achieving a comparable pattern in her own works of fiction:

> Many people say that it is hopelessly sad – but I didnt mean that. I did want somehow to make out if only for my own satisfaction a reason for things. That of course is putting it more definitely than I have a right to, for my reasons are only general conceptions, that strike me as I walk about London and then I try to fit my little figures in. But I did mean that in some vague way we are the same person, and not separate people. The six characters were supposed to be one. I'm getting old myself – I shall be fifty next year; and I come to feel more and more how difficult it is to collect oneself into one Virginia; even though the special Virginia in whose body I live for the moment is violently susceptible to all sorts of separate feelings. Therefore I wanted to give the sense of continuity, instead of which most people say, no you've given the sense of flowing and passing away and that nothing matters. Yet I feel things matter quite immensely. What the significance is, heaven knows I cant guess; but there is significance – that I feel overwhelmingly. Perhaps for me, with my limitations, – I mean lack of reasoning power and so on – all I can do is to make an artistic whole; and leave it at that. But then I'm annoyed to be told that I am nothing but a stringer together of words and words and words.[94]

This passage brings to mind a remark which Leslie Stephen made about his wife Julia: 'although she had no definite religious creed, she did believe that things were somehow right at bottom. So, perhaps, in some sense do I'.[95] Beneath the superficial events of

The Voyage Out lies a structure of repetitions whose presence in the novel enables Woolf not only to avoid intervening in her own voice in her text, but also to suggest an inherent significance to human experience.[96] Repeated references to specific ideas – which can be classified loosely under the headings 'chaos and order', 'death', 'the future' and 'illness' – contribute to our sense of an underlying pattern in *The Voyage Out*.

Chaos and Order

The dichotomy between order and chaos is one which makes itself felt in *The Voyage Out* not only in the life of Terence Hewet – when Rachel dies – but throughout the narrative. At the start of the novel, for example, Helen Ambrose feels that all meaning has gone from her life because she is leaving her children in London (p. 2). Order is restored to her world, however, as the life-style of the *Euphrosyne* asserts itself, only to be banished again with the unexpected arrival of the Dalloways (p. 40). A further disturbance comes with the storm at sea which, like the tempest at the end of the novel, can be linked with Rachel's illness and death in that each temporarily interrupts life's ordinary rhythms. Just as, at the end of the novel, the fact of Rachel's death is absorbed into the routine of life at the hotel, so, too, order reasserts itself on board the *Euphrosyne* as the storm dies away. The passengers on the ship return from 'the strange underworld, inhabited by phantoms' and begin 'to live among tea-pots and loaves of bread with greater zest than ever' (p. 80).

In the course of the novel, various characters become aware of a conflict between order and chaos in the world around them. As Helen walks home after taking tea at the hotel, she feels that 'terrible things' are happening beneath the 'likings and spites, the comings together and partings' of daily experience: 'It seemed to her that a moment's respite was allowed, a moment's make-believe, and then again the profound and reasonless law asserted itself, moulding them all to its liking, making and destroying' (pp. 321, 322). For Hirst, the ferocious and arbitrary cruelty of experience is symbolised in the chaos of the South American jungle: 'God's undoubtedly mad. What sane person could have conceived a wilderness like this, and peopled it with apes and alligators' (p. 336). Helen replies that, on the contrary, it *is* possible to recognise a plan and a meaning in the natural world: 'She bade him look at the way things massed themselves – look at the amazing colours, look at the shapes of the trees' (p. 337). Helen's argument, then, supports Mrs Thornbury's (and, of course, Woolf's) view – a version of the argument from design – that if one submerges the particular in the general, an overall pattern can be discerned in experience. (This point of view is illustrated by the jungle itself, which opens out into a beautiful natural clearing in which the native village is situated. The 'gentleness and order of the place' suggest to the observers 'human care' (p. 342).) When Rachel dies, however, Terence finds it impossible to explain her death satisfactorily. That she should die is, he feels, arbitrary and senseless; it cannot be seen as part of a universal and benevolent plan.

During Rachel's illness, Terence finds himself able for a few brief moments, as he stands in the garden of the villa, to forget her situation. He has a glimpse of 'the real world, the world that lay beneath the superficial world, so that, whatever happened, one was secure' (p. 418). Terence is surprised by this short period of forgetfulness, just as he is later amazed that he should ever have been able to ignore the latent suffering and pain in the world. As Mr Flushing remarks to Mrs Thornbury, 'people seem to forget that these things happen, and then they do happen, and they're surprised' (p. 438).[97] The novel as a whole, however, stresses the importance of being able to forget. It is only when the individual can distance him or herself from the cause of their suffering, that the meaning returns to life, as it returns to Helen when she forgets her grief over her children.[98] Most of the characters in the novel have experienced the death of a close friend or relative, but have nevertheless been able, in time, to place these deaths in some sort of perspective. The novel's ending suggests that the 'stir of life' is strong enough to absorb such emotional shocks and that society as a whole is able to affirm itself against the chaos of death.[99] It is for this reason that Terence finds comfort, during Rachel's illness, in the newspaper, 'which with its news of London, and the movements of real people who were giving dinner-parties and making speeches, seemed to give a little background of reality to what was otherwise mere nightmare' (p. 408). Similarly, when Hirst returns to the hotel after Rachel's death, he finds his suffering alleviated when it is absorbed into the complex of lives which makes up the society there. Despite his theory of 'chalk-marks', Hirst welcomes the sympathetic presence of the visitors to the hotel whom, like Rachel, he has previously derided: 'The movements and the voices seemed to draw together from different parts of the room, and to combine themselves into a pattern before his eyes; he was content to sit silently watching the pattern build itself up, looking at what he hardly saw' (p. 456).

Death

I walked along the Cliff yesterday, and found myself slipping on a little ridge just at the end of a red fissure. I did not remember that they came so near the path; I have no wish to perish. I can imagine sticking out ones arms on the way down, and feeling them tear, and finally whirling over, and cracking ones head. I think I should feel as though I saw a china vase fall from the table; a useless thing to happen – and without any reason or good in it.[100]

Although the reader shares Hewet's shock at the unexpectedness of Rachel's death, this death is in fact carefully anticipated in the novel.[101] Woolf never explicitly discusses the idea of death in her own voice in the narrative, but she draws attention to it through her systematic use of repetition. The structure of *The Voyage Out* is, then, extremely carefully worked out, but in this novel, as in *The Years*, Woolf skilfully maintains the illusion that the events which she narrates are 'natural' or 'real'.

The idea and the implicit threat of death is, in fact, all-pervasive in *The Voyage Out*. (Early in the novel, for example, William Pepper refers to the fact that his friend Jenkinson 'has had the misfortune to lose his wife' (p. 10). Helen Ambrose is aware that her brother-in-law, Willoughby, whose wife is also dead, 'seldom spoke of the dead, but kept anniversaries with singular pomp' (p. 20). On the day after the dance at the hotel, Mrs Thornbury receives a letter telling her that 'Poor old Mrs Fairbank' has died (p. 209). When Helen comes upon Rachel asleep in her room on the ship, her niece has the air of one who is dead; 'lying unprotected she looked somehow like a victim dropped from the claws of a bird of prey' (p. 35). Similarly, describing William Pepper asleep in the hotel, Woolf remarks that his 'lean form' is 'terribly like the body of a dead person' (p. 120). When Hewet, during the picnic, deliberately simulates the posture of a dead person, we are told that 'His body, lying flat among them, did for a moment suggest death' (p. 170).

Hewet's description of his own father's death (p. 167) comes to mind at the end of the novel. So, too, does Woolf's comment about the conversation Helen holds with Hirst at the hotel, during which the two characters speak 'of matters which are generally only alluded to between men and women when doctors are present, or the shadow of death' (p. 190).)

Woolf links the ideas of separation and dying in *The Voyage Out.* The parting between the Dalloways and the passengers on board the *Euphrosyne* anticipates the enforced separation which Rachel's death will later bring about. As she leaves the ship, Mrs Dalloway remarks: 'That's the tragedy of life – as I always say! . . . Beginning things and having to end them' (p. 87). This is also Rachel's tragedy, and the vague sadness which all the characters feel at the departure of the Dalloways is a fainter image of the acute sorrow which they feel when Rachel dies:

> A feeling of emptiness and melancholy came over them; they knew in their hearts that it was over, and that they had parted for ever, and the knowledge filled them with far greater depression than the length of their acquaintance seemed to justify. (p. 88)

In the same way, Rachel's slight acquaintances at the hotel feel a deep sadness at her death, and even the selfish Mrs Paley is drawn to remark (echoing a comment she makes earlier in the novel – p. 213) that 'She ought not to have died' (p. 441). A second separation which anticipates Rachel's death occurs when Mr Pepper leaves the villa. With his abrupt departure for the hotel, Helen is overcome by a sense of life's inconclusiveness, and finds it 'sad that friendships should end thus' (p. 107).[102] Her friendship with Mrs Elliot also comes to a sudden end, so that, as far as Helen is concerned, Mrs Elliot might as well be dead (p. 269).

The opening to Chapter 8 of *The Voyage Out* seems to contain a covert reference to the latter part of the novel:

> The next few months passed away, as many years can pass away, without definite events, and yet, if suddenly disturbed, it would be seen that such months or years had a character unlike others. (p. 108)

Several other remarks in the novel also implicitly point ahead to

Rachel's death. One thinks, for example, of Helen Ambrose's angry response to the method of Rachel's up-bringing: 'My brother-in-law really deserves a catastrophe – which he won't get' (p. 110), which is contradicted in an unexpected way when Rachel dies. Similarly, the generalisation which Woolf makes in connection with the atmosphere at the hotel one hot afternoon – 'Disastrous would have been the result if a fire or a death had suddenly demanded something heroic of human nature. but tragedies come in the hungry hours' (p. 136) – proves applicable to Rachel's death. Rachel has a premonition of her own death as she sits in her room at the villa one morning and thinks that 'in time she would vanish, though the furniture in the room would remain' (p. 145).[103] Woolf's comment about the *Euphrosyne* setting forth on her voyage ('The sea might give her death or some unexampled joy' – p. 29) also has a hidden reference to Rachel.

Arthur's remark about his love for Susan is equally applicable to the events at the end of the novel:

> One goes along smoothly enough, one thing following another, and it's all very jolly and plain sailing, and you think you know all about it, and suddenly one doesn't know where one is a bit, and everything seems different from what it used to seem. (pp. 160–1)

The presence of Arthur and Susan in the novel serves to emphasise the apparent arbitrariness of human experience; Terence's fiancée dies, Arthur and Susan remain together. Rachel reflects upon life's chanciness as she sits on the hillside during the picnic and bends back a piece of grass, feeling 'how strange it was that she should have bent that tassel rather than any other of the million tassels' (p. 164). The audacity of Woolf's approach in *The Voyage Out* is that she makes her central character – that is, the focus of sympathy in the novel – the victim of chance, allowing her to die, whilst relatively peripheral characters remain alive.

Mrs Thornbury is convinced that the deaths of young people are not the most tragic things in life, 'they were saved so much; they kept so much' (p. 439). Her belief seems to be borne out by Mrs Paley's experience. Lamenting the fact that if she were to die nobody would miss her, Mrs Paley thinks of the two people whom alone she considers to be finer than herself, both of whom died in their youth. One is her brother 'who had been drowned before her eyes', the other her greatest friend 'who had died in giving birth to her first child' (p. 213).[104] (Helen has a great admiration for Rachel's mother who – like Mrs Paley's brother and her friend – died young.) Dr Lesage corroborates the view that a young person's death is somehow less tragic than that of an old person (p. 428) when he tells Hewet and Hirst about an eighty-five-year-old patient he has been treating who 'had a horror of being buried alive' (p. 427), and goes on to remark that 'It is a horror . . . that we generally find in the very old, and seldom in the young.' When Rachel turns over the music on the piano at the hotel, she notices that the predominant tone of the pieces throughout the evening has been one of 'passionate regret for dead love and the innocent years of youth; dreadful sorrows had always separated the dancers from their past happiness' (p. 194). Through her death, Rachel is spared this kind of suffering and disillusionment.[105]

Rachel's death is anticipated in the fragment of conversation which Hewet overhears as he stands outside the villa, 'If I were to die tomorrow . . .' (p. 220; Woolf's ellipsis), and also in Rachel's comment on her spinster aunts, 'And yet they feel things; they do mind if people die' (p. 259). A remark made by Miss Allan similarly takes on new significance when Rachel dies: 'Don't you think it would be very annoying if you tasted ginger for the first time on your death-bed, and found you never liked anything so much' (p. 310).

The idea of death permeates the episode of the voyage up-river to the native village. When Mr Flushing and Helen discuss the journey beforehand, it seems to them that it is 'neither dangerous nor difficult' (p. 323), but can be made 'without damage done to mind or body' (p. 323). In retrospect it appears possible that their confidence has been misplaced.

In the course of the journey, Mr Flushing points out to his companions 'a hut where Mackenzie, the famous explorer, had died of fever some ten years ago, almost within reach of civilisation' (p. 339), and Mrs Flushing asks eagerly, 'Did they find his dead body there' (p. 341). Her lively curiosity as to the details of Mackenzie's death is in strong contrast with the anger and distress which she experiences when Rachel dies. Like Helen (p. 411), Mrs Flushing is overcome by a feeling of 'indignation with somebody' whose victim Rachel seems to be (p. 438).

On arriving at the native village in the jungle, Helen is struck by the vulnerability of the group of English people around her:

She became acutely conscious of the little limbs, the thin veins, the delicate flesh of men and women, which breaks so easily and lets the life escape compared with these great trees and deep waters.   (pp. 349–50)

The characters in the novel are as defenceless as the moth which shoots from light to light in the hall of the hotel, 'causing several young women to . . . exclaim, "Some one ought to kill it" ' (p. 216). Helen regrets that in undertaking the journey the group have 'exposed themselves', her sense of their insecurity being symbolised in the image of 'a boat upset on the river in England, at midday' (p. 350). The river inspires in her 'anxieties for Ridley, for her children, for far-off things, such as old age and poverty and death' (p. 340). The river journey could be said at one level to represent 'life's journey' (though, of course, the novel's symbolism, like that in To the Lighthouse, remains intentionally vague and open-ended).[106] Whilst it may be more obviously dangerous to take a voyage up river than to stay at home, to live at all is to expose oneself to the apparent caprices of fate.[107] Given that Rachel does die, Helen proves right to have felt presentiments of disaster both on setting out on the voyage in the Euphrosyne (p. 7), and on taking upon herself the responsibility for her niece (p. 98).

Despite the emphasis on the idea of death throughout the narrative, and notwithstanding his own assertion that being dead is not 'awful' but 'quite easy to imagine' (p. 170), Terence is deeply shocked at what he considers the unexpectedness of Rachel's death. It is not until Dr Lesage remarks that Rachel 'has a chance of life' (p. 424), that the implications of her illness become clear to Terence: 'Suddenly he saw it all. He saw the room and the garden, and the trees moving in the air, they could go on without her; she could die' (p. 424). Rachel's death imparts a new reality to the concept of mortality which has been discussed so dispassionately by various characters in the course of the novel.

Through the numerous references to dying in The Voyage Out, Woolf encourages the reader to place Rachel's death in a general perspective. The 'reason or good'[108] which may be said to emerge from this particular death are to be found in the unity and sympathy which it evokes amongst the characters who remain alive. Linked through their common fear and hatred of death, the disparate individuals in the novel achieve a deeper communion than is normally possible. The picnic excursion earlier in the novel serves to illustrate just how difficult it is to bring together a group of heterogeneous individuals.[109] As Terence sets out on the expedition with Hirst, he wonders 'why on earth he had asked these people, and what one really expected to get from bunching human beings up together' (p. 147). Terence's picnic is (like Mrs Dalloway's party, or Mrs Ramsay's dinner) an attempt not only to bring people together but to unite them. His achievement remains partial, however, when compared with the way in which Rachel's death draws out the common humanity in her friends and acquaintances. Experience of bereavement and fear of death is something which they all share. The response which Rachel's death elicits from all the characters in the novel vindicates Hewet's inclination to give them the benefit of the doubt. Early in the novel he remarks to Rachel of Hirst, for example, that 'There's a great deal more in him than's ever been got at' (p. 184). The sympathetic side of Hirst's character, which normally remains hidden beneath his superficially vain and self-absorbed manner, emerges in response to Rachel's illness and Terence's need for support. In this way, Woolf reveals the positive aspects of an event which might seem to have no meaning or justification.[110] In the face of Rachel's death, not only Hirst's but even Ridley's attention is diverted from his books to the lives of other people, and he finds it 'impossible to sit alone in his room' (p. 427). The grief which all the characters in the novel experience when Rachel dies contradicts, then, Helen's cynical assertion that they are simply emotional vultures:

> Directly anything happens – it may be a marriage, or a birth, or a death – on the whole they prefer it to be a death – every one wants to see you. They insist upon seeing you. They've got nothing to say; they don't care a rap for you; but you've got to go to lunch or to tea or to dinner, and if you don't you're damned.   (p. 378)

In fact Rachel's death meets with a universally sympathetic and sensitive response from the characters at the hotel.

Alongside the many references to dying in *The Voyage Out* we find recurrent allusions to 'the future' and particularly to Rachel's future. Like the various remarks about death in the novel, these apparently unconnected comments take on a new significance when Rachel dies. With this event, indeed, the novel must be read in a new way.

The Future

The effect of Rachel's death at the end of The Voyage Out is to invest earlier references to her future with a deep pathos.[111] One thinks, for example, of the comment which Vinrace makes to Helen about Rachel, at the start of the novel – 'we expect great things of her' (p. 16) – or the remark Helen Ambrose makes to Mrs Chailey: 'If ever Miss Rachel marries, Chailey, pray that she may marry a man who doesn't know his ABC' (p. 27). Rachel is destined to know neither the joys nor the sorrows of marriage. Like the ship in which she sets out on her spiritual voyage, she will remain 'a bride going forth to her husband, a virgin unknown of men' (p. 29). The comment which she makes to Clarissa Dalloway – 'No. I shall never marry' (p. 64) – proves all too true. The happiness which Rachel and Hewet anticipate for their marriage, which is summed up in the simple phrase 'We will go for walks together' (p. 344), is never to be realised. Nor is their determination never to behave like the Ambroses after they are married (p. 379) to be tested. Rachel's description of Hewet as 'the man with whom she was to spend the rest of her life' (p. 345) is pathetically accurate. In retrospect, there is a deep poignancy, too, in Hewet's jubilant remark: 'It does seem possible . . . though I've always thought it the most unlikely thing in the world – I shall be in love with you all my life, and our marriage will be the most exciting thing that's ever been done' (p. 365). The excitement of their relationship is in fact to be preserved at the cost of Rachel's life. Nevertheless, Rachel is, as Mrs Thornbury suggests, spared through death much suffering and disappointment. Examining his fiancée's face, Terence wonders to himself 'how it would look in twenty years' time, when the eyes had dulled, and the forehead wore those little persistent wrinkles which seem to show that the middle-aged are facing something hard which the young do not see' (p. 367). When Rachel becomes engaged, Helen, similarly, wonders 'what would happen in three years' time, or what might have happened if Rachel had been left to explore the world under her father's guidance' (p. 372). To ask this question is to reflect, as Evelyn does, upon the chanciness of human existence; the fact that, in slightly different circumstances, Rachel's death 'need never

have happened' (p. 436). In dying, however, Rachel escapes from
the type of sorrow and disenchantment suffered, for example, by
the women in Bennett's *The Old Wives' Tale*. The young couple's
confidence in the future success of their relationship is never to
be tried. As she considers the prospect of 'June in London' with
Terence, Rachel remarks: 'And we're certain to have it too . . . It
isn't as if we were expecting a great deal – only to walk about and
look at things' (p. 369). Her optimism is countered not by the
death of love, but by death itself. There is, then, no opportunity for
her relationship with Terence to lapse into the kind of unromantic
alliance of roles which is the basis of Susan's relationship with
Arthur (p. 295).

There is a pathos in the fact that both Helen and Mrs Thornbury
envy Rachel and Terence the 'great, unknown future that lay
before them' (p. 373). Mrs Thornbury remarks to Rachel, 'You
think yourself happy now, but it's nothing to the happiness that
comes afterwards' (p. 389), and she speaks enthusiastically of 'the
things you young people are going to see' (p. 390). She imagines
that Rachel 'must want to see her father – there would be a great
deal to tell him' (p. 394). The news which in fact awaits Mr Vinrace
at the villa is that of his daughter's death.

After arguing with Terence on the way down to the hotel, Rachel
thinks to herself, 'how often they would quarrel in the thirty, or
forty, or fifty years in which they would be living in the same
house together, catching trains together, and getting annoyed
because they were so different' (p. 386). Their essential difference
manifests itself in a more surprising way, however, when, through
death, they are separated.

Illness

The apparently coincidental references to illness in *The Voyage Out*,
like the remarks on 'chaos and order', on 'death' and on 'the
future', prove, with Rachel's illness and death, to be part of the
novel's careful structure. The sea-sickness suffered by the passengers on board the *Euphrosyne*, for example, anticipates Rachel's
fever later in the novel. In each case, illness takes over the mental
and physical life of its victims. Rachel's feelings during the storm
at sea are very similar to her subsequent experience of delirium:

Rachel had just enough consciousness to suppose herself a

donkey on the summit of a moor in a hail-storm, with its coat blown into furrows; then she became a wizened tree, perpetually driven back by the salt Atlantic gale. (p. 78)

Helen's brief visit to Clarissa's sick-room anticipates the prolonged period which she will later spend in nursing Rachel (p. 79). The gesture with which Richard Dalloway gets up when he is unwell, finds himself still ill, and returns to bed (p. 80), is echoed when Rachel gets out of bed in her room at the villa, only to find that 'it would be far more intolerable to stand and walk than to lie in bed' (p. 401). Richard remarks that 'It's humiliating to find what a slave one is to one's body in this world' (pp. 81–2). The ultimate proof of this remark comes in the fact of Rachel's death.

Mr Pepper's caustic farewell to the company at the villa, ('If you all die of typhoid I won't be responsible' (p. 107)), is unexpectedly fulfilled when Rachel dies. Through the various references to illness in the novel, Woolf raises the question of the apparent arbitrariness of suffering. There seems, for example, to be no reason why Rachel should die of fever, whilst Hughling Elliot recovers under the ministrations of Dr Rodriguez (pp. 388–9).[112] Similarly, there is no obvious explanation as to why Mrs Flushing's brother should have 'had fever for twenty-six days once' (p. 415) or why Mrs Thornbury should have had typhoid for six weeks on her honeymoon in Venice (p. 389) and yet have recovered, whilst Rachel dies.[113]

Paradoxically, the repeated references to illness and death in The Voyage Out help to invest the novel's events with significance. On the one hand, they serve to suggest that suffering is an aspect of our common humanity which encourages sympathy and unity in the human race as a whole. (For example, although Hughling Elliot does not die, the anxiety which his wife endures while nursing him (p. 389) links her with Helen Ambrose and her distress during Rachel's illness.) On the other hand, the structure of repetitions in the novel implies that there is an underlying pattern to the whole of human experience, although that pattern may not be clear to particular individuals.

Incidental Repetitions

Alongside thematic repetitions in the novel, more incidental echoes are to be found which, whilst they do not serve to draw attention to important ideas, are yet instrumental in suggesting that there is an order beneath experience. (For example, the tropical river which catches Rachel's imagination (p. 98) and which she and Helen describe to Mr Pepper in an attempt to dissuade him from breaking his journey at Santa Marina (pp. 105–6) also figures in Helen's embroidery (p. 30). The deer in this embroidery anticipate those subsequently seen by the company on board the river steamer (p. 342), and are also brought to mind when Rachel describes the deer in Richmond Park to Terence (p. 257). The phrase which Rachel uses to express her anger at Mrs Chailey's 'dishonesty': 'Lies! Lies! Lies!' (p. 25) is echoed in her exclamation of disgust at the letters of congratulation which she receives from the hotel visitors: 'Oh, what lies – what lies' (p. 359). When Woolf remarks of Mrs Chailey that she 'limped because of the rheumatism in her feet, but it appeared to her mere waste of time to take any notice of the unruly flesh of servants' (p. 429), she recalls the fact that the three most fastidious gentlemen in the novel, Mr Pepper (p. 8), Ridley Ambrose (p. 27) and St John Hirst (p. 237) all make a considerable fuss about their rheumatism.) Although trivial in themselves, taken collectively these examples of repetition have the effect of suggesting a pattern beneath the apparently heterogeneous human lives in the novel. If, then, one considers *The Voyage Out* a microscope of the 'real world', the novel's complex structure of repetitions does indeed suggest a parallel order to the whole of experience.

In reading Austen's *Emma*, one is struck by the skill with which the author plans and constructs her novel. With the dénouement, the reader has, like Emma herself, to reread the novel's events in the context of his or her increased knowledge. (The procedure is one familiar to readers of James's fiction.) In *The Voyage Out* Woolf develops this technique further. With Rachel's death, one is obliged to reread what has seemed to be a comic novel about love and marriage as a novel about life and death. In *The Voyage Out*, that is, Woolf – in contrast with Austen – tackles the problem of human suffering head-on, dramatising the problem of evil in the life of Rachel Vinrace. Through the novel's carefully worked out structure of echoes and repetitions, however, she is able to capture something of the significance and value which, for her, is present beneath what might appear to be the most arbitrary of experiences and obscure of lives.

The Voyage Out is a work, then, which cannot easily be subsumed into the argument that Woolf is a purely modernist writer. Her first novel in fact draws heavily upon fictional conventions and established narrative forms. Yet, woven into what is an essentially 'realist' novel we find many of the ideas which were later to pervade modernist works like To the Lighthouse and The Waves. In The Voyage Out, rather than reacting violently against the 'realist' tradition in fiction, Woolf chooses to exploit its potential to the full, stretching its boundaries as far as she can without actually breaking her fictional illusion. In so doing, she produces a novel which is at once 'realistic', because many of the devices which she uses are familiar to the reader, and at the same time original, since she uses these devices to put across ideas which are very much her own. We have noted that Woolf found James's Wings of the Dove 'unrealistic' because, she argued, the excessive ingenuity of that novel draws attention away from the fictional characters to the person of the author. Whilst such a criticism would seem equally applicable to Woolf's own modernist fiction, and particularly The Waves, it does, at the same time, suggest the motivation behind her choice of narrative method for The Voyage Out.

3

Night and Day

(a) INTRODUCTORY

The previous chapter focused upon two methods whereby Woolf introduces ideas which are of particular interest to her into *The Voyage Out*, whilst avoiding overt didacticism. I took as my examples her interest in feminism and her belief in an inherent pattern in experience, suggesting that the former is dramatised in the novel through the lives of her fictional characters, whilst the latter is illustrated through the novel's underlying pattern of repetitions. Repetition in the novel also serves to draw attention obliquely to a number of ideas which are of importance to Woolf. The present chapter traces a similar narrative method in Woolf's second novel, *Night and Day*.[1]

Many of the characters in *The Voyage Out* – feminists and anti-feminists alike – have their counterparts in *Night and Day*. Moreover, Woolf's exploration of the contrast between 'masculine' egotism and 'feminine' sympathy is common to both novels. In each novel, the idea of 'feminine' sympathy is linked with that of the exploitation of women. Whilst Terence Hewet is the most obviously 'feminine' man in *The Voyage Out*, in *Night and Day* it is Ralph Denham who illustrates Woolf's belief that it is possible for men to be as sympathetic as women, suggesting that the 'feminine' nature is not an innate sexual characteristic, but the product of social conditioning. The contrast between Ralph and William Rodney in *Night and Day* has much in common with that between Hewet and St John Hirst in *The Voyage Out*.

(b) FEMINISM

In *Night and Day*, as in *The Voyage Out*, Woolf puts forward feminist ideas whilst avoiding overt propaganda by dramatising such ideas in the lives of her fictional characters. The novel could be said to work on two levels; the humorous and relatively superficial, and the serious and more penetrating. At one level, Woolf's light-hearted caricature serves to place in a critical perspective both the traditional view of women embraced by characters like Mr Hilbery, William Rodney and Mr Clacton – *malgré lui* – and the blinkered attitudes of over-zealous philanthropists such as Mrs Seal, Mr Clacton and, to a lesser extent, Mr Basnett.[2] Woolf treats these characters in much the same way as the Dalloways in *The Voyage Out*. At a deeper level is to be found Woolf's exploration of the concept of androgyny, or of the contrasting 'masculine' and 'feminine' natures, and the way in which these may complement one another. The ideal of androgyny is one which Woolf puts forward in *A Room* when she argues that the minds of the great writers are 'woman-manly or man-womanly': 'Some collaboration has to take place in the mind between the woman and the man before the art of creation can be accomplished. Some marriage of opposite has to be consummated.'[3] In *Night and Day*, Mary Datchet alone appears to have attained a balance of the 'masculine' and the 'feminine' within her personality, akin to that achieved by Miss Allan in Woolf's first novel.[4] That Mary's character is in some sense exemplary is suggested at the end of the novel, when Katherine sees in the light radiating from Mary's window 'a sign of triumph shining there for ever, not to be extinguished this side of the grave'.[5] The absence of caricature in Woolf's portrayal of Mary also lends authority to her world-view. The device of treating certain characters humorously and others seriously in the novel serves, then, to direct the reader's response to the narrative. At the same time, however, it creates certain problems. Woolf's caricature of specific figures in *Night and Day* may well strike the reader as too schematic. (The conflict between 'realism' and caricature is one which I will discuss in some detail towards the end of this chapter.)

Anti-feminists

> I daresay I am hard on the men compared with the women. But you see men are at their worst with women – perhaps their best, but certainly their worst.[6]

William Rodney's relationship with Katherine affords Woolf the opportunity to expose – through caricature – the outrageousness of the position traditionally afforded to women by some of the men who profess to love and worship them. Her portrayal of William is, however, like that of St John Hirst in *The Voyage Out*, notable for its lack of bitterness. She once remarked to Lytton Strachey: 'dialogue was what I was after in this book'[7] and in *Night and Day*, as in *The Voyage Out*, she allows a character like William Rodney to condemn himself out of his own mouth. Through William's ludicrous remarks about Katharine, and about women in general, Woolf is able, under cover of entertaining the reader, to drive home a serious feminist point. The novel is rich in his hilariously pompous comments about the place of women in society. Through the scene in which he reads his paper on Elizabethan metaphor, Woolf establishes Rodney as an individual of recognisably limited intelligence. In this way, she implicitly encourages the reader to respond to his outspoken comments about women with a good deal of scepticism. In the course of the novel, moreover, the fact that Katharine emerges as a character whose complex personality can hardly be understood within the narrow terms of William Rodney's conception of life serves to cast further doubt upon the validity of his world-view. None the less, William is, like St John Hirst, treated with tolerant humour in the novel. Woolf's good-tempered and essentially sympathetic portrayal of the anti-feminists in *Night and Day* is considerably more persuasive than a bitter attack upon them would be. Rodney's extavagant remarks on the subject of women and marriage can, after all, be left to speak for themselves.

The way in which Woolf allows Rodney to reveal his own limitations to the reader is manifest, for example, in the scene in which he and Katharine walk beside the river, after the meeting in Mary's room. Rodney concludes an egotistic outburst upon the difficulties which he experiences as a writer with the remark: 'If I could write – ah, that would be another matter. I shouldn't bother you to marry me then, Katharine' (*Night and Day*, p. 62). Oblivious to the insult implicit in this comment – as Hirst is ignorant of the way in which he hurts Rachel during the dance at the hotel – he goes on to reply to Katharine's question about whether he would recommend marriage for herself: 'Certainly I should. Not for you only, but for all women. Why, you're nothing at all without it; you're only half alive; using only half your faculties; you must feel that for yourself' (p. 63). The point of view which Woolf puts forward through Rodney is one which was sanctioned not only by many Victorian men, but also by their wives and daughters. It is summed up by Elizabeth Gaskell in a passage from *The Life of Charlotte Brontë*:

> When a man becomes an author, it is probably merely a change of employment to him. . . . another merchant or lawyer, or doctor, steps into his vacant place, and probably does as well as he. But no other can take up the quiet regular duties of the daughter, the wife, or the mother, as well as she whom God has appointed to fill that particular place: a woman's principal work in life is hardly left to her own choice; nor can she drop the domestic charges devolving on her as an individual, for the exercise of the most splendid talents that were ever bestowed.[8]

Like Rollo Spencer in Rosamund Lehmann's *The Weather in the Streets*, Rodney accepts without question that whilst for a woman love is the only legitimate occupation, for a man it is a secondary diversion from the more serious affairs of life.[9] On several occasions, moreover, he quite unashamedly suggests that whilst a man's literary judgements are the product of reason a woman's are merely the expression of feeling – a view, incidentally, to which Cassandra Otway is quite happy to subscribe. Rodney's belief in the inferiority of women is, ironically enough, itself based upon vague intuitions rather than convincing rational arguments. Like Richard Dalloway, he illustrates the idea that the temptation to disparage women in order to bolster one's own self-esteem is one to which the man of limited intelligence all too easily – and often unconsciously – falls prey.

Rodney's idea of Katharine is in large part the product of his prejudicial view of women in general; an attitude which leads him to denigrate Katharine even as he imagines that he worships her. He remarks to Ralph Denham, for example, that Katharine leads 'one of those self-centred lives – at least, I think them odious for a woman . . . She can understand you when you talk to her. But she's a woman, and there's an end of it.' (p. 68). As the narrative progresses it becomes clear that on the one hand few lives could be less self-centred than Katharine Hilbery's and on the other that she is considerably more intelligent than William. Rodney's slighting remarks about Katharine therefore shed more light upon

his own character, and its restrictions, than upon that of his
fiancée.

Woolf makes use of Ralph Denham and Henry Otway to cast a
critical light upon William Rodney, and in doing so, she avoids
attacking him in her own voice in the novel. Both Ralph and Henry
find Rodney's attitude to Katharine antipathetic in the extreme. A
scene like that in which William talks to Henry in the latter's
room at Stogden House enables Woolf to criticise William's naïve
misrepresentation of Katharine obliquely. Henry is angered by
William's readiness to place Katharine in the same class as the
society women whom he meets each year at Bolham Hall. He
reacts coldly, therefore, to William's description of his manner of
entertaining these women:

> 'You talk to them about their children, if they have any, or
> their accomplishments – painting, gardening, poetry – they're so
> delightfully sympathetic. Seriously, you know I think a woman's
> opinion of poetry is always worth having. Don't ask them for
> their reasons. Just ask them for their feelings. Katharine for
> example – '
> 'Katharine,' said Henry . . . 'Katharine is very unlike most
> women.'   (p. 214)

In fact, Rodney's conception of Katharine has very little to do with
her personality as it is revealed in the novel as a whole. He sees
her in terms of a suitable wife for himself and as 'a perfect mother
– a mother of sons' (p. 258). Like Ibsen's Helmer, Rodney seeks
a child-wife in marriage, rather than an intellectual equal. The
novel traces the process whereby Katharine, like Nora, realises
that her first duty is not to any husband or child, but to herself.[10]
The reader is educated by being caught up in this process. As with
Woolf's treatment of Rachel in *The Voyage Out*, we are encouraged,
through our interest in Katharine's dilemma, to consider the
position of middle-class women in society. In the course of the
novel, Woolf emphasises the powerful effect which Katharine's
personality has upon characters like Ralph Denham and Henry
Otway. Thus she implicitly criticises Rodney's inability to recognise her as an individual in her own right at all. It becomes clear
that he is enamoured not of Katharine Hilbery, but of the wife of
William Rodney.[11] Rodney's attitude can be related to his 'masculine' egotism, a characteristic which Woolf places in *Night and*

Day, as in *The Voyage Out*, at the opposite pole from 'feminine' sympathy.

Egotism is a fault which William Rodney and Mr Hilbery have in common. The relationship between Katharine and her father illustrates what was to become a central argument in the polemical essay *Three Guineas*, namely, that certain men exploit the concept of purity in women in order to keep them in a subject and dependent position in society. Bernard Shaw attacks the 'ideal of womanliness' in the chapter of the *Quintessence of Ibsenism* entitled 'The Womanly Woman'. He remarks that, 'of all the idealist abominations that make society pestiferous, I doubt if there be any so mean as that of forcing self-sacrifice on a woman under pretence that she likes it; and, if she ventures to contradict the pretence, declaring her no true woman'.[12] In *Three Guineas*, Woolf illustrates this argument with reference to the case of Sophia Jex-Blake towards the end of the last century.[13] Her father, Woolf argues, bitterly opposed the idea that she should earn her own living, on the grounds that it would not be 'ladylike' or 'womanly' for her to do so. His argument was that his daughter was not obviously in material want, and that, moreover, if she were to marry a man of whom he approved, he himself would be happy to provide her with a fortune.[14] Woolf argues that his real motive for opposing Sophia's desire to work was not that for her to do so would be 'unwomanly', but rather that it would release her from financial – and, therefore, emotional – dependence upon himself. She suggests that the father's wish to keep his daughter in economic subjection to himself is the product of his jealousy over her, and she relates this theory to Freud's concept of 'infantile fixation'.[15]

Mr Hilbery's relationship with Katharine in *Night and Day* serves to dramatise this idea that the father's ostensible concern for his daughter's purity may in fact mask a more sinister – if unconscious – motive. Mr Hilbery's invocations of outraged decency at the news that Katharine has broken her engagement to William Rodney seem to be, in part at least, a cover for his own jealousy over his daughter's love for Ralph Denham.[16] When Katharine informs her father of her engagement to Ralph, Mr Hilbery finds himself 'surprised by a pang of acute jealousy. She might have married Rodney without causing him a twinge. This man she loved' (p. 529). Instead of congratulating Katharine, Mr Hilbery, we are told:

never looked at his daughter, and strode out of the room, leaving in the minds of the women a sense, half of awe, half of amusement, at the extravagant, inconsiderate, uncivilized male, outraged somehow and gone bellowing to his lair with a roar which still sometimes reverberates in the most polished of drawing-rooms.   (p. 530)

If the conventional male, represented by Rodney and Mr Hilbery, consciously or unconsciously keeps women in a subject position, he is often encouraged to do so by women themselves. Mrs Otway, for example, in advising Katharine about her forthcoming marriage, takes it for granted, like Clarissa Dalloway in *The Voyage Out*, that a successful marriage depends upon the complete submission of the woman to her husband (pp. 221–3). Mrs Milvain, like Mr Hilbery, disguises her own emotional needs behind her commitment to an obselete set of social conventions on sexual matters. The novel suggests that throughout society men and women alike are responsible for perpetuating woman's subservient position. Even the girl at the zoo from whom Ralph and Katharine buy buns for the animals chooses to take the money from Ralph, deciding 'from conventional reasons, that it was the part of the gentleman to pay' (p. 390).

Through Katharine's history, Woolf dramatises her belief that moral dogmatism, of the kind which Mr Hilbery invokes in an attempt to prevent his daughter from breaking her engagement to a man whom she does not love, proves inadequate to deal with the complexities of human experience. Mr Hilbery's allegiance to the established moral code manifests itself early in the novel, when he prevents Katharine from visiting her cousin Cyril and his lover (p. 110). Katharine finds his attitude difficult to justify. In the same way, when he learns that Katharine intends to break off her engagement, Mr Hilbery has recourse to a rigid moral code in an attempt to deny the importance of his daughter's feelings (p. 496). Although he finds the position of tyrannical authority which he assumes over Katharine strangely inadequate, he can envisage no obvious alternative to it. The alternative which the narrative itself offers – and which Mrs Hilbery, in particular, embodies – is that of sympathy. Unlike her husband, Mrs Hilbery has the imagination to transcend an inflexible moral code when it proves inappropriate to an individual situation.

William Rodney's relationship with Katharine, like Mr Hilbery's, serves to illustrate the limitations of moral dogmatism. Both men are the victims of their own narrow-minded commitment to public opinion. Rodney's conventionality first manifests itself in the scene in which Ralph watches him walking home with Katharine after the meeting in Mary's room. Ralph notes that 'The couple in front of them kept their distance accurately' (p. 60). It becomes clear later in the same scene that Rodney is by no means convinced of the propriety of walking home with Katharine at all (p. 64). The history of his relationship with Katharine traces the process whereby she persuades him – and, by implication, the reader – of the need to lay aside obsolescent conventions and inadequate moral dogmas. She recognises that social codes exist to serve human needs rather than to govern them.

When Katharine suggests that William should meet Cassandra under the guise of his supposed engagement to herself, the idea meets with 'a discomfited silence' because 'By all his codes it was impossible to ask a woman with whom he had just broken off his engagement to help him become acquainted with another woman with a view to his falling in love with her' (p. 342). Even when William accepts that it is in his own interest to throw aside certain conventions, he is less happy when Katharine follows suit (p. 436). None the less, the personal happiness which Katharine's unconventionality proves to have brought to at least four characters at the end of the novel validates her point of view and that of her author.

Feminists

Woolf's exploration in *Night and Day* of the way in which the oppression of women becomes an accepted social norm remains light-hearted throughout. She avoids that over-insistence which might alienate the reader both through its militancy, and also through destroying our belief in her fictional characters. Her humorous treatment of the more narrow-minded feminist campaigners in the novel serves – paradoxically – to strengthen, rather than to undermine, her own feminist position. Through her caricature of Mrs Seal and Mr Clacton, Woolf implicitly attacks the aggressively opinionated attitudes adopted by some of the participants in the suffrage campaign.[17] She anticipates possible criticisms of her novel's feminist perspective by drawing attention

– through caricature – to the weak spots in the movement as a whole. In so doing, she awakens the reader's interest in feminism, making us the more receptive to the serious 'discussion' of androgyny which centres, in *Night and Day*, around Mary Datchet. This discussion gains credibility through its juxtaposition with Woolf's parody of the less acceptable elements in the feminist organisations.

In her account of Leonard Courtney's attempt to bring together the two groups of suffragists who opposed one another over the question of the Contagious Diseases Act, Ray Strachey focuses upon the way in which many suffragists used their political campaign for private ends:

> The solid ground of their differences had melted away, and there was no valid reason for separation; but, of course, as always happens with human undertakings, vested interests (of the most innocent nature), and personal animosities (of the most ladylike kind) had grown up. Honorary secretaries were unwilling to give up the arduous task of writing letters and keeping minutes; honorary treasurers clung to the privilege of making up deficits out of their own private purses; committee members did not like the idea of sitting round the same table together, and Mr Courtney's task was hard.[18]

Woolf had little sympathy for the type of feminist which Ray Strachey here describes,[19] but rather than introduce an explicit attack on the officiousness of philanthropic society members into her text, and thereby destroy the 'realist' illusion, she allows the mild caricature of Mrs Seal and Mr Clacton to speak for itself.[20] The suffrage office episodes reveal that Mrs Seal uses her work to fill a void in her emotional life. Indeed, she could hardly be said to lead a life apart from that of 'the cause'.[21] Mr Clacton, on the other hand, whilst professing to be a feminist, exploits his position in the office to exercise power over the women with whom he works. In the course of the novel it becomes clear that he considers women inferior to men. He imagines that Mary's original ideas must have been suggested to her by the 'group of very clever young men' with whom she mixes. When she adopts an authoritative manner towards him, he is taken aback and envisages 'a time even when it would become necessary to tell her that there could not be two masters in one office' (p. 280).

Mr Clacton represents those individuals who hide all the old prejudices behind a façade of radicalism. He adopts a consistently patronising manner towards Mrs Seal (p. 278), although – as Ralph's remark to Katharine about the inadequacy of both Mary's colleagues suggests (p. 92) – he has no reason to be superior. The fact that before the committee meeting he decorates the table with a vase of chrysanthemums 'in deference to the taste of the lady members' (p. 171) suggests that his notion of the relationship between the sexes has more in common with that of Mr Hilbery or William Rodney than he would care to admit.

Perhaps Woolf's chief criticism of Mrs Seal and Mr Clacton, however, is one which she repeatedly voices elsewhere against philanthropists, namely, that all too often dedication to a 'cause' is accompanied by a lack of sympathy for individual human beings. Mary's colleagues both manifest 'the reformer's love of humanity, which has so much of hatred in it as well as love'.[22] When Mary becomes unhappy they react not with personal sympathy, but with anxiety lest this should interfere with her efficiency as a worker (p. 280). Mrs Seal is incapable of responding to other people except in terms of 'the cause'. She is disappointed when Ralph arrives for tea in the office, because she is expecting the printer to call, and she is quite unable to respond adequately to Katharine, seeing her exclusively in terms of a potential convert to suffragism (p. 86).

Woolf links the philanthropist's lack of sympathy with his or her inability to respect the other person's point of view. Mrs Seal, for example, espouses the kind of political partisanship which Eleanor deplores in *The Years*, as is obvious in her anger when the vote is once again denied to women:

'It's all so *simple*.' She referred to a matter that was a perpetual source of bewilderment to her – the extraordinary incapacity of the human race, in a world where the good is so unmistakably divided from the bad, of distinguishing one from the other, and embodying what ought to be done in a few large, simple Acts of Parliament, which would, in a very short time, completely change the lot of humanity.   (p. 277)[23]

Mrs Seal's desire to impose her own point of view upon society as a whole is, Woolf implies, singularly like William Rodney's or Mr Hilbery's desire to exert power over women. *Three Guineas* makes clear that facism and sexism are inseparably linked in Woolf's own mind for this very reason.[24] What Mrs Seal shares with Mr Basnett is a desire to limit legitimate experience to that encapsulated in her own world-view. In Mr Basnett's company, Katharine Hilbery feels that 'the number of things that could properly be thought about was strictly limited' (p. 378).

Ralph Denham unfairly attributes to Mary the type of blinkered response to experience manifested in the lives of her feminist colleagues. When she refuses his insincere offer of marriage, he responds with a bitter personal attack: 'you can't judge people by what they do. You can't go through life measuring right and wrong with a foot-rule. That's what you're always doing, Mary; that's what you're doing now' (p. 266). In fact Woolf uses Mary in the novel to cast an ironic light upon the limited perspective of over-zealous and bigoted philanthropists. The process whereby Mary comes to reject her colleagues' outlook serves a similar function in the novel to Katharine's rejection of William Rodney and his values or Rachel's gradual repudiation of all that the Dalloways stand for, in *The Voyage Out*. Just as Katharine's history serves to illustrate the limitations of moral dogmatism, Mary's story reveals the dangers of political intolerance. Mary recognises the validity of Ralph's criticisms of the suffrage workers, 'meting out right and wrong' (p. 266), being all too aware of the temptations inherent in the life of the suffrage office. She realises that to use her position there to achieve personal emotional security, rather than as a means to a political end, is to adopt a false position akin to that of her colleagues. The world of the office can all too easily become one of escape from the complexities of not only political, but also emotional, issues. Mary acknowledges this temptation during the committee meeting which follows her encounter with Ralph in Lincoln's Inn Fields. Within the narrow terms of the meeting she feels that she knows 'exactly and indisputably what is right and what is wrong' (p. 173), but she also understands that such a feeling is deceptive. To draw personal satisfaction from her ability to bring the other members round to her way of thinking (p. 174), is to betray her own deeper sense that to interpret experience in black-and-white terms is to simplify it beyond recognition. Later in the novel, thinking of the way in which she uses her own political opinions to serve private ends, Mary feels that:

They weren't, rightly speaking, convictions at all. She could not see the world divided into separate compartments of good people and bad people, any more than she could believe so implicitly in the rightness of her own thought as to wish to bring the population of the British Isles into agreement with it. (p. 271)[25]

When Katharine remarks that she would like to have a profession in order to be able to beat other people down, Mary replies that, 'One doesn't necessarily trample upon people's bodies because one runs an office' (p. 54). None the less, it could be argued that it is her recognition of the way in which she is tempted to do just this that leads her to resign her position in the suffrage office.

In *The Voyage Out* Woolf makes use of Terence Hewet's relationship with Rachel to educate the reader and direct our response to the narrative. Mary's relationship with the other characters – and particularly Ralph – has a similar function in *Night and Day*. Mary's theories are, like Terence's, borne out in her actions. Ralph's relative unpopularity in the office can be related, Woolf suggests, to the fact that he is 'too positive, at this stage of his career, as to what was right and what wrong' (p. 130). Through good-natured mockery, Mary is in the process of making Ralph less opinionated and 'less dictatorial at home' (p. 131).[26] Like Woolf, Mary believes that 'there's no such thing as right and wrong; no such thing, I mean, as judging people' (p. 292). She puts this belief into practice in that she is primarily self-critical rather than censorious of other people. Mary turns her experience with Ralph and Katharine to positive account, using it to enrich her own personality. She differs from Mrs Seal, moreover, in that she refuses to deny the value of the personal happiness which she has lost, thereby avoiding the temptation to make her political commitments into a substitute for emotional satisfaction.[27] Nor does she fall into the trap of suggesting that the life-style of a wife and mother is somehow inferior to that of a political activist. On the contrary, she emphasises the validity of motherhood as a profession in its own right. It is Mary who points out to the 'clever young man', Mr Basnett, that 'No one works harder than a woman with little children' (p. 378). When he asks Katharine Hilbery whether she is in search of employment, Mary replies that 'Marriage is her job at present' (p. 379).

Discussing with Ralph the new society which Mr Basnett is in the process of setting up, Mary once again acknowledges the need to respect other points of view. She remarks to Ralph, 'I'm inclined to agree with you; we ought to try to be more conciliatory. We're absurdly strict. It's difficult to see that there may be sense in what one's opponents say, though they are one's opponents' (p. 412). Mary's point is borne out in the narrative. For example, Mr Hilbery describes to his wife and daughter how as a young man he offered to speak at a public meeting. As the meeting progressed, however, and he listened to the speeches of his fellow-enthusiasts, he gradually became converted to the opposite point of view, and was in fact unable to speak at all (p. 100). Mr Hilbery's open-mindedness in the political sphere parallels his daughter's attitude to established morality. Katharine cannot endorse the conventional response to her cousin Cyril's situation because it is by no means obvious to her that in choosing to live with the woman he loves Cyril has done anything wrong (p. 113). Similarly, she sees the arrangement whereby her own engagement to William is dissolved in the name of their mutual happiness as 'all perfectly right' (p. 477). Through Katharine, Woolf educates the reader as to the importance of tolerance and sympathy in the emotional sphere, whilst she uses Mary to advocate the same qualities in the domain of politics.

The 'Masculine'/'Feminine' Distinction

In *Night and Day*, Woolf explores the concept of androgyny which she was to put forward more explicitly in *A Room*.[28] Various relationships in the novel illustrate the way in which the 'masculine' and the 'feminine' natures may complement one another, but it is Mary's character which most successfully combines these two qualities. Like Miss Allan in *The Voyage Out*, she manifests both toughness of mind and sympathy:

> She had contracted two faint lines between her eyebrows, not from anxiety but from thought, and it was quite evident that all the feminine instincts of pleasing, soothing, and charming were crossed by others in no way peculiar to her sex.   (p. 43)

Ralph Denham puts this another way when he remarks of Mary's personality that 'It's the combination that's odd – books and stockings' (p. 45). To her fellow-suffragists in the committee-room she evinces a union of 'gentleness and strength, an indefinable promise of soft maternity blending with her evident fitness for honest labour' (p. 172). Mary's androgynous nature makes her the most capable of self-sufficiency amongst the novel's protagonists.

At the start of Night and Day, when Woolf contrasts Ralph with his sister Joan ('whereas he seemed to look straightly and keenly at one object, she appeared to be in the habit of considering everything from many different points of view – pp. 22–3), it seems that they represent the 'masculine' and 'feminine' natures respectively. As the novel progresses, however, it becomes clear that there is a strong 'feminine' element in Ralph's character, a gift for sympathy, which he appears to have learned in part from Mary, who is 'in process of turning him from Tory to Radical' (p. 131). Ralph, indeed, resembles Terence Hewet in his capacity for sympathising with others. As Rodney walks home with Ralph, following the scene on the Embankment with Katharine, he feels inclined to confide in Denham, finding in him, as he thinks, 'all the good masculine qualities in which Katharine now seemed lamentably deficient' (p. 66). This scene is echoed when, towards the end of the novel, Rodney meets Ralph outside the house in Cheyne Walk, and again finds the other man's silence 'oddly suggestive of the good masculine qualities which he much respected' (p. 420). What Rodney in fact seems to be responding to in Ralph is a 'feminine' ability to sympathise which complements Rodney's own 'masculine' egotism. This sympathy comes across when Ralph soothes Rodney's vanity by expressing an interest in his play (p. 71), just as Cassandra is to do later in the novel (p. 362). The relationship between Ralph and Rodney in Night and Day corresponds, then, to that between Hewet and Hirst in Woolf's first novel. Ralph's 'femininity' is illustrated by his reluctance to pursue a conventional career. He belies Mrs Milvain's argument that no man 'Is really happy unless he succeeds in his profession' (p. 156). Unlike Rodney, Ralph cannot regard marriage as a second-best to success in public life.

Katharine Hilbery's character seems to Mary to elude conventional sexual stereotyping. At times Katharine appears to be very much the egotist, yet 'in her voice, in her face, in her attitude, there were signs of a soft brooding spirit, of a sensibility unblunted and profound, playing over her thoughts and deeds, and investing her manner with an habitual gentleness' (p. 285). The idea that Katharine is not conventionally 'feminine' is borne out by Woolf's description of the gesture with which she settles into an armchair in Rodney's flat as 'rather masculine in its ease' (p. 139). Rodney himself finds the 'carelessness of her attitude . . . rather masculine than feminine' (p. 300). When he tries to account for the failure of their relationship, he traces it to 'something temperamental. I think you're a trifle cold, and I suspect I'm a trifle self-absorbed' (p. 302). Another way of putting this would be to say that they are both, at times, egotists. Rodney however, regards the element of egotism in Katharine's nature as a fault, because he accepts that it is a woman's role to efface her own personality and to be, above all, sympathetic to men.

Woolf describes Katharine's nature as 'manly' in comparing her with her cousin Cassandra:

> Where Katharine was simple, Cassandra was complex; where Katharine was solid and direct, Cassandra was vague and evasive. In short, they represented very well the manly and the womanly sides of the feminine nature.   (p. 362)

Cassandra, in an attempt to explain their incompatibility to Katharine and Rodney, remarks to William, 'you've asked her for sympathy, and she's not sympathetic' (p. 440). When Katharine has tea with Mary in the suffrage office, the latter notices this absence of sympathy in her visitor; Katharine, she feel, lacks the disposition to 'make things easy' (p. 86). Henry Otway also responds to this trait in Katharine's character. Woolf describes Henry as 'rather an egotistical young man' (p. 207), yet when the two cousins are together, he automatically assumes the 'feminine' role. When, for example, Katharine visits his room in Stogden House, it is Henry who places the coal on the fire,

> drawing a chair up to the grate, and laying aside her cloak. Her indifference to such details often forced Henry to act the part generally taken by women in such dealings. It was one of the ties between them.   (p. 206)

Similarly, when Rodney stays behind in the room to talk to Henry, following Katharine's departure, it is Henry who adopts the 'feminine' stance of sympathetic listener. He shares Ralph's anxiety to sooth William's vanity, praising the latter's expert horsemanship in an attempt to 'help Rodney in his effort to recover his complacency' (p. 212).[29]

Cassandra's compatibility with Rodney can be related to her willingness to adopt a consistently sympathetic 'feminine' role in his company. As Katharine listens to her cousin talking about William, she discovers the secret of her own failure with him:

> She had never asked him to teach her anything; she had never consented to read Macauley; she had never expressed her belief that his play was second only to the works of Shakespeare. (p. 485)[30]

Alongside the novel's 'discussion' of 'masculinity' and 'femininity' there is an emphasis in Night and Day, as in The Voyage Out, upon the importance of sympathy to the smooth running of society, and a suggestion that traditionally the onus of sympathy has been placed upon women. In many cases the extent of society's demand for sympathy from women is such that it can only be described as exploitation.

Although Mrs Hilbery is at times, like her husband, treated humorously in the narrative (there was some indignation at the time of publication at her resemblance to Lady Ritchie),[31] her 'feminine' gift of sympathy comes across as a positive, unifying force in the novel as a whole. In this respect, she anticipates Mrs Ramsay in To the Lighthouse. The novel opens with a drawing-room scene in which the whole responsibility for entertaining the assembled company falls, despite Mr Hilbery's presence, upon his wife. It is Mrs Hilbery who deftly smooths over Ralph's awkward entrance half-way through the proceedings (p. 2), just as it is she who, detecting the awkward silence between Ralph and Katharine, attempts to draw Ralph into the conversation (p. 6). Woolf makes it plain that although Mrs Hilbery may be ignorant in 'masculine' terms, the strength of her personality is not be to underrated. Unable as she is to differentiate between the Battle of Trafalgar and the Spanish Armada (p. 5), she is gifted with a sensitivity to the needs of other people in which her husband, for all his intellect, is totally lacking:

> She had never learnt her lesson, and had constantly to be punished for her ignorance. But as that ignorance was combined with a fine natural insight which saw deep whenever it saw at all, it was not possible to write Mrs Hilbery off among the

dunces; on the contrary, she had a way of seeming the wisest person in the room.   (p. 39)[32]

Mrs Hilbery can, however – her individual merits notwithstanding – be regarded, like Mrs Ramsay and Clarissa Dalloway, as the feminists' most insidious opponent, in that she panders to the popular idea of the woman as sympathiser to men.[33] Discussing marriage with Katharine, Mrs Hilbery asks: 'What is nobler . . . than to be a woman to whom everyone turns, in sorrow or difficulty? How have the young women of your generation improved upon that, Katharine?' (p. 117). Mrs Hilbery, like Eleanor in *The Years*, is 'the soother, the maker-up of quarrels'.[34] In adopting this role unquestioningly she helps to perpetuate the kind of society in which many men prove singularly inadequate at sympathising with others, depending upon women to perform this function on their behalf. There is an absurdity in the fact that the whole duty of entertaining Mr Hilbery's guests should fall upon his wife. The extent to which Mr Hilbery has opted out of all social accountability becomes apparent towards the end of the novel, when his wife's temporary absence from Cheyne Walk – like Mrs Ramsay's death in *To the Lighthouse* – precipitates an atmosphere of emotional confusion amongst the rest of the family.

Mr Hilbery's reaction to the news that Katharine has broken off her engagement to Rodney is to ask 'why have I not been told of this . . . ?' (p. 494), 'Why am I left to hear of these events for the first time from my sister?' (p. 503). The answer is to be found in Mr Hilbery's own character. Having formed the habit of delegating all responsibility for the emotional needs of the household to his wife and daughter, Mr Hilbery has himself become blind to the presence of such needs, and incapable of responding to them properly. This is manifest quite early in the novel, when he sheepishly avoids having to break the news of cousin Cyril's 'misdemeanours' to his wife (p. 112) and the burden of explanation falls, in consequence, upon his daughter. When Katharine explains to her father that she is no longer engaged to Rodney, Mr Hilbery's reaction is again to try to place the burden of sympathy on someone else. 'No doubt,' he thinks, 'there was some quarrel, some whimsey on the part of William, who, though a good fellow, was a little exacting sometimes – something that a woman could put right' (p. 494), and he concludes that 'it would be better to wire to his wife, to send for one of his sisters' (p. 495). Mr Hilbery, then, banishes the lovers from sight in the hopes that this will put them from his mind. He remains, none the less, to some extent aware of the inadequacy of his response to the situation. He finds the authoritarian stance which he adopts towards Katharine distasteful (p. 506) and is to a certain extent troubled by the fact that he has no idea what she is thinking (p. 506). He turns in desperation to the novels of Sir Walter Scott in an attempt to escape from the unfamiliar demands of his position as Katharine's father (p. 505).

With Mrs Hilbery's return to Cheyne Walk, the soothing power of sympathy at once begins to make itself felt. Mrs Hilbery's sensitivity to Katharine's needs (like Mrs Ramsay's sympathy for her son James), is infinitely greater than her husband's. Woolf describes the relief which her mother's return brings to Katharine:

> In truth, she found an extraordinary pleasure in being thus free to talk to some one who was equally wise and equally benignant, the mother of her earliest childhood . . .   (p. 510)

As the novel draws to a close there is a suggestion that Mrs Hilbery in fact knows her daughter's mind better than Katharine does herself. She has recognised from the start the potential compatibility between Ralph and Katharine; her absence in Stratford, the reader is encouraged to suspect, is a move to precipitate their union.

The irony of the Hilberys' relationship is that, for all her vagueness, Mrs Hilbery is very much in command. She deliberately ignores her husband's ridiculous over-reaction to Katharine's broken engagement, although he is under the illusion that his wife has simply 'confused the meaning of his instructions' (p. 527). Mrs Hilbery is thus able at once to get her own way, and to placate her husband. With her sensitivity to his personality, she has only to appeal to his vanity with the question: 'Oh, Trevor, please tell me, what was the date of the first performance of *Hamlet*' (p. 528), and harmony is restored to the household. Like Mrs Ramsay, Mrs Hilbery is prepared to exert 'indirect influence' over her husband, whilst publicly ceding nominal authority to him. Ralph recognises, none the less, that it is she, and not her husband, who is the moral head of the household. When she brings Ralph back to Cheyne Walk after his temporary banishment, he notices that 'She had become suddenly serious and composed, mistress in her own house. The gesture with which she dismissed him had a dignity that Ralph never forgot' (p. 520).

For Mrs Hilbery, as for Mrs Ramsay, the role of soother and peacemaker amounts to a vocation. Katharine, on the other hand, like Lily Briscoe, resents the demands which society perpetually makes upon her sympathy. Through Katharine, therefore, Woolf places Mrs Hilbery's attitudes in a critical perspective. During the opening scene of the novel Katharine, like her mother, is aware of the need to draw Ralph into the conversation. She recognises that 'he would not be easily combined with the rest' (p. 3), but she refuses to sacrifice her own integrity to a young man's egotism:

> They were further silenced by Katharine's rather malicious determination not to help this young man, in whose upright and resolute bearing she detected something hostile to her surroundings, by any of the usual feminine amenities.   (p. 6)[35]

Later in the scene, Katharine – like Lily – relents, providing an opportunity for Ralph to escape from her mother's enthusiastic clutches (p. 15).

To William Rodney it is manifest that Katharine's role in life should be to sympathise with other people. After quarrelling with Katharine on the Embankment, Rodney thinks bitterly: 'She'd leave me not a moment's peace – and she'd never understand me – never, never, never' (p. 65). He regards Katharine's life as 'odious' and 'self-centred' because she is not prepared to devote her whole time and energy to bolstering his self-approval. Although Katharine shies away from the traditional 'feminine' role of appeaser and entertainer, she often adopts this role automatically. As she walks along the street with Ralph after having tea with Mary, Katharine feels a wish to be alone with her own thoughts, but none the less she does 'her duty by her companion almost unconsciously' (p. 92). Again, when Ralph arrives unexpectedly at Rodney's flat during an emotional exchange between Katharine and William, it is Katharine who, by making the first move, restores comparative order to the situation: 'Years of training in a drawing-room came at length to Katharine's help, and she said something suitable' (p. 309). On many occasions Katharine's conditioning as peacemaker gets the better of her natural antipathy to this role. It is this conditioning which leads Katharine to suppose that marriage necessarily demands self-sacrifice on the part of the woman, and that she has no right to expect personal happiness from it. She concludes, therefore, that it is probably right for her to marry William:

> She would come to feel a humorous sort of tenderness for him, a zealous care for his susceptibilities, and, after all, she considered, thinking of her father and mother, what is love. (p. 107)

Katharine's discussion of marriage with her mother and Mrs Otway only serves to corroborate this view. Mrs Otway argues that no woman should contemplate marrying unless she is prepared to submit to her husband (pp. 221, 223), her own willingness to comply having been evident from the first moment of her engagement, when she accepted an emerald ring with gratitude, although she had secretly hoped for a diamond. In Mrs Otway's company, Katharine feels that she is probably wrong to expect more from marriage than her aunt does:

> it seemed to her that she could satisfy William as these women had satisfied their husbands; she could pretend to like emeralds when she preferred diamonds. (p. 225)

The scene with William on the way back from Lincoln, however, serves to convince Katharine that to submit to him 'as her mother and her aunt and most women, perhaps, had submitted' would involve 'treachery to him' (p. 255). Mary Datchet finds the same kind of dishonesty in Ralph's insincere proposal of marriage. Both women come to accept the validity of Mrs Hilbery's romantic belief that marriage must be an expression of mutual love. For Katharine to agree to marry Rodney out of a sudden sympathy for his loneliness is to betray both him and herself. The terms in which Katharine accepts Rodney's proposal ('I will marry you. I will try to make you happy' – p. 259) suggest that she is opting for the 'feminine' role of 'minister' to men in spite of her better self. A marriage between Katharine and Rodney would bring about a polarising of their respective personalities, after the pattern of Mr and Mrs Hilbery. (This is, indeed, the model to which Rodney and Cassandra seem destined to conform at the end of the novel.) Marriage to Denham, on the other hand, leaves both characters free to develop 'masculine' and 'feminine' characteristics; they are free, that is, to become fully androgynous.

In contrast with Katharine, Cassandra Otway, like her mother, unequivocally accepts that women should be the servants of social harmony. Although Katharine tells William that Cassandra is 'what they call a Feminist' (p. 371), this is not borne out by her cousin's behaviour. Cassandra's initiation into the society of Cheyne Walk excites in her a desire to emulate her female relatives' 'femininity'. As she enters the drawing-room on her first evening with the Hilberys, her expression becomes 'very gentle and sympathetic, as if she, too, were full of solicitude for the world which was somehow being cared for, managed and deprecated by Aunt Maggie and Aunt Eleanor' (p. 370). During the visit to the zoo, Cassandra seizes upon the opportunity to exercise her 'new-born feminine susceptibility, which urged her to charm and conciliate the other sex' (p. 391), and towards the end of the novel, as she drinks tea with William in the Hilberys' drawing-room, Cassandra attempts to allay his discomfort at his ambiguous situation. Her instinct tells her 'that an appeal to his affection, at this moment, would be extremely ill-judged', but as she sits quietly beside him sipping her tea, William is soothed by the sight of her adorable 'feminine attitude' (p. 464). Cassandra's willingness to uphold a system in which it is taken for granted that men will make limitless demands for sympathy upon women is never openly criticised by Woolf. The novel as a whole, however, illustrates the pernicious effect of such an assumption upon individual women in society. With *The Voyage Out*, *Night and Day* reveals just how destructive the self-sacrifice which society traditionally and unashamedly demands of its women can be. (The union between Rodney and Cassandra at the end of the novel is therefore disappointing in so far as it has the effect of minimising the importance of the examination of the way in which many marriages are little more than alliances of roles, which Woolf makes elsewhere in the narrative.)

In the course of the novel, Woolf makes clear the extent to which Mr Clacton (and Mary too) enjoys patronising Mrs Seal. In conversation with Mary, however, Mrs Seal mentions certain 'domestic circumstances' (pp. 85, 177) which, she says, made it impossible for her to devote herself to 'the cause' as a young woman. The implication of her remarks is that she is one amongst many daughters, like Susan Warrington in *The Voyage Out*, whose lives have been swallowed up in the demands of their relatives. Consequently, she has been deprived of the formal education which has equipped Mary, for example, to hold her own in a committee room.

Mrs Seal's experience is shared by the many unmarried women who are shown to be exploited in *Night and Day*. Just as Mr Clacton despises Mrs Seal for being, as he thinks, incapable of rational thought, Ralph Denhan mocks his sister for suggesting that the word *amo* comes from Greek. Joan Denham resembles Mrs Seal in that her education has been neglected through 'domestic circumstances'. Like Mrs Hilbery, however, she combines a lack of traditional knowledge with a deep capacity for sympathy. The awkward scene around the tea table in Highgate, towards the end of the novel, becomes relaxed and harmonious when Joan appears (p. 399), much as the atmosphere in the Pargiter household in the 1880 section of *The Years* lightens with Eleanor's return from work. In the case of both young women, personal happiness has been sacrificed to the family's needs. Considering his sister Joan's situation, Ralph Denham feels 'how unfair it was that all these burdens should be laid on her shoulders' (p. 24).

Euphemia Otway's position at home mirrors that of Ralph's sister. Her youth and energy have been devoted to appeasing her father's vanity and responding to his perpetual demands for sympathy:

> Already, at the age of thirty-five, her cheeks were whitening as her mother's had whitened, but for her there would be no memories of Indian suns and Indian rivers, and clamour of children in a nursery.   (p. 217)

The Reverend Datchet – like Sir Francis Otway – assumes that his daughter will dedicate her life to creating a peaceful domestic environment in which he can pursue his own interests uninterrupted. Indeed, Mary Datchet's relative liberty could be said to have been bought at the price of her sister's servitude. It is, moreover, won through the kind of emotional battle with her father which Woolf describes in *Three Guineas*. When Katharine expresses envy of Mary's independent life-style, the latter replies:

> It means, chiefly, a power of being disagreeable to one's own family, I think. I have that, perhaps. I didn't want to live at

home, and I told my father. He didn't like it. . . . But then I have a sister, and you haven't, have you.   (p. 55; Woolf's ellipsis)

Through Katharine Hilbery's narrative Woolf makes more explicit what is only implied in her treatment of Susan Warrington in *The Voyage Out*. Katharine represents those women to whom Woolf refers in *A Room*, who are tempted to make a loveless marriage in order to escape from the tyranny of their relatives' perpetual demands for sympathy.[36] It is assumed that Katharine – like Kitty Malone in *The Years* – will entertain her parents' elderly friends over the tea table; a position which Ralph recognises from the first to be 'not without its difficulties' (p. 5). She is expected to act as unpaid curator of her grandfather's mementos (pp. 7, 334), in much the same way that Kitty is obliged to show the Malones' friends around Oxford. Through her parents' expectations of her, Katharine is – like Kitty – forced into a wholly antipathetic role in the household. It is convenient for the Hilberys to subscribe to the idea that Katharine is 'the most practical of people', since as such she bears the whole burden of 'Ordering meals, directing servants, paying bills' and generally attending to the more ardous and wearisome household duties (p. 38). In a passage which echoes *Three Guineas*[37] Woolf points to the injustice of Katharine's position as unpaid family servant:

> Katharine, thus, was a member of a very great profession which has, as yet, no title and very little recognition, although the labour of mill and factory is, perhaps, no more severe, and the results of less benefit to the world. She lived at home.   (p. 39)[38]

It is partly because Katharine's own profession remains unrecognised that she envies Mary Datchet. She complains to Mary, 'I want to assert myself, and it's difficult. If one hasn't a profession' (p. 54).[39] Ralph is quick to notice that Katharine suffers from the fact that she is without an identity of her own (p. 10). When people do take an interest in her, it is not as Katharine Hilbery, but as 'the poet's granddaughter' (p. 87), the collaborator in her mother's biography of the 'great man' (p. 55). Mrs Hilbery exploits Katharine's willingness to take the onus of entertaining from her own shoulders (p. 333), just as she abuses Katharine's good-will when she abdicates to her daughter the responsibility for the 'life' of Richard Alardyce. The relationship between mother and daughter has affinities with that between Casaubon and Dorothea in *Middlemarch*. Like Casaubon, Mrs Hilbery is engaged in a monumental, yet futile, literary task whose gigantic proportions threaten to absorb the whole of Katharine's youth. Like Dorothea, Katharine feels a smothered resentment at the way in which her dependent posisiton is exploited:

> She had suddenly become very angry, with a rage which their relationship made silent, and therefore doubly powerful and critical. She felt all the unfairness of the claim which her mother tacitly made upon her time and sympathy, and what Mrs Hilbery took, Katharine thought bitterly, she wasted. (p. 117)

Mr Hilbery is, presumably, joking when he remarks to the editor, Mr Peyton, 'our children . . . have their uses' (p. 374), but it is true that Katharine has been conditioned to believe it her duty to devote her own life to her parents' well-being and peace of mind. There is a pathos (as Mrs Hilbery recognises) in the reassurances which she gives her mother about her prospective marriage to William, 'It will make no difference. I shall always care for you and father most' (p. 146).

Talking with Katharine after the meeting in Mary's room, Ralph Denham remarks, 'I don't see why you shouldn't go to India' (p. 94). His question is answered in the course of the narrative. Katharine may belong to a higher social class than Ralph, but she is financially and emotionally bound to her parents and to the lifestyle which they dictate for her.[40] In the light of her position at home, marriage to Rodney seems to offer a means of escape. As Katharine listens to her female relatives discussing the case of cousin Cyril, she is overcome by a sense of weariness at the discrepancy between 'their own version of the becoming' (p. 125) and her own very different world-view. Finding her life at home a travesty of her private aspirations, Katharine concludes that 'Perhaps it would be better if I married William' (p. 126). She articulates her position in an imaginary conversation with Henry Otway, in which she attempts to justify her engagement to Rodney:

> But why I'm marrying him is, partly, I admit – I'm being quite honest with you, and you mustn't tell any one – partly because I want to get married. I want to have a house of my own. It

isn't possible at home. It's all very well for you, Henry; you can
go your own way. I have to be there always. Besides, you know
what our house is. You wouldn't be happy either, if you didn't
do something. It isn't that I haven't the time at home – it's the
atmosphere.   (pp. 202–3)[41]

Through a passage like this, which falls quite naturally into place
in the narrative, Woolf dramatises the arguments which she was
later to put forward in *A Room* and *Three Guineas*. What Katharine
lacks is 'a room of her own' – like the room to which Jacob Archer
is entitled – in which she would be free to pursue her own interests
apart from the pressures of her family.[42] Katharine envies Mary
her bed-sit because 'in such a room one could work – one could
have a life of one's own' (p. 286). (Katharine's situation parallels
that of Joan Denham. Whilst Joan's brother has a private room in
which he is free to come and go as he pleases, Joan's whole waking
life is devoted to the public duties of visiting needy relatives and
sorting out her own family's complex affairs. As Ralph notes, she
never has 'time for anything decent' – p. 27.) Katharine makes the
mistake of thinking that a loveless marriage to William Rodney
will bring her privacy and freedom: 'When her mind took this
turn her marriage seemed no more than an archway through
which it was necessary to pass in order to have her desire' (p. 226).
Through William's conversation with Henry Otway, however,
Woolf makes it quite clear that in marrying Rodney Katharine will
in fact take on more demands for sympathy. William assumes that
Katharine's married life will be devoted not to such private interests as mathematics and astronomy, but to 'children – a household
– that sort of thing' (p. 215).[43] Katharine's naïvety over her
prospective marriage to William recalls Isabel Archer's misconcep-
tion of her relationship with Gilbert Osmond in James's *Portrait of
a Lady*. Unlike Isabel, however, Katharine avoids walking into the
trap which, with the help of society, she has prepared for herself.

   Woolf explored many of the central ideas of *Night and Day* in
a manuscript draft which Susan Dick has entitled 'Phyllis and
Rosamund', dated 'Wed. June 20–23rd 1906'. The draft describes
a typical day in the lives of two out of a family of five daughters
living in London. Like Katharine Hilbery the girls are forced to
make a 'profession' out of living at home with their parents: 'To
see them in a drawing-room full of well dressed men and women,
is to see the merchant in the Stock Exchange, or the barrister in

the Temple. This, every motion and word proclaims, is their native air; their place of business, their professional arena.' [44] In 'Phyllis and Rosamund', as in *Night and Day*, Woolf contrasts the life-style of the conventional 'daughter of the house' with that of the 'modern woman'. A dialogue between Phyllis and the artist, Sylvia Tristram, anticipates Katharine Hilbery's conversations with Mary Datchet and Ralph Denham:

> 'What do you do?' she demanded suddenly, in order to get to business at once.
> 'What do I do?' echoed Phyllis. 'O order dinner and arrange the flowers!'
> 'Yes, but what's your trade,' pursued Sylvia, who was deter-mined not to be put off with phrases.
> '*That's* my trade; I wish it wasn't! Really Miss Tristram, you must remember that most young ladies are slaves; and you mustn't insult me because you happen to be free.'
> . . .
> 'I can't see why you shouldn't do what you like as we do,' said Sylvia, looking round the room.
> 'Do you think we could have people like this? Why, we can never ask a friend, except when our parents are away'
> 'Why not?'
> 'We haven't a room, for one thing: and then we should never be allowed to do it. We are daughters, until we become married women.'[45]

Like Katharine Hilbery, Phyllis Hibbert is tempted to marry simply in order to gain, as she thinks, 'freedom and friends and a house of her own'.[46] To compare the manuscript draft of 'Phyllis and Rosamund' with *Night and Day* is, however, to recognise the skill with which Woolf integrates her theoretical preoccupations into the published novel. The characters in 'Phyllis and Rosamund' on the other hand are – like those in the fictional sections of *The Pargiters* – too obviously mouthpieces for Woolf's private concerns.

Given Woolf's evident sympathy, in *Night and Day*, for those 'odd women' (Gissing's phrase) who are society's scapegoats, her portrayal of Katharine's elderly female relatives is mildly surprising. The chapter on *The Years* which follows will suggest that when, in *Mansfield Park*, Austen chooses to ridicule the child-less Mrs Norris, she is adopting an essentially 'masculine' stance in her novel, and the same could be said of Woolf's caricature of these women. Woolf suggests that Mrs Milvain's prurient interest in other people's affairs can be related to the fact that she is 'elderly and fragile'. Her 'childlessness seemed always to impose these painful duties on her, and to revere the family, and to keep it in repair, had now become the chief object of her life' (p. 121). The pathos of Mrs Milvain's situation emerges, however, in spite of such comments. Notwithstanding the narrator's essentially flippant approach to her, within the context of the novel's 'discussion' of woman's place in society Mrs Milvain must be seen as a victim.

(c) THE METHOD OF *NIGHT AND DAY*

To describe *Night and Day* as a 'dramatic' work is to draw attention to the fact that much of the novel is made up of dialogue, of 'scene-setting' and of 'stage-directions'; passages, sentences, phrases, adjectives and adverbs, that is, which describe the fictional characters' appearance, actions, gestures, facial expressions and tone of voice from an external point of view.[47] Particular characters' private thoughts, moreover, are often – as in a play – expressed in public form. For example, Mrs Hilbery's reaction to the news of Katharine's engagement to Rodney is conveyed through an extract from a letter to Mrs Milvain (pp. 146–8).[48] Similarly, Katharine's thoughts about her prospective marriage to William are given through an imaginary conversation with her cousin Henry (pp. 202–3).

Night and Day remains very different, of course, from, for example, Ivy Compton-Burnett's fiction, which is rendered almost entirely in dialogue. Interspersed among such passages in Woolf's novel are sections of authorial comment which tell us facts about her characters' histories, their attitudes, beliefs and feelings, which it would be extremely difficult to convey through conversation alone. None the less, Woolf is at pains in this novel – like James in *The Awkward Age* – to disguise her own authority, and thus to create the impression that the reader is witnessing a scene which he or she judges for themselves. For example, she often uses one character's reaction to another to tell us something about them both; we see Katharine as she appears to Ralph or Mary, Mrs Hilbery as she seems to Katharine. Like James, Woolf exploits phrases such as 'it seemed', 'as if', 'as though', 'probably', 'perhaps', 'indeed', 'no doubt', 'certainly', in order to qualify her analysis of the thoughts and attitudes which underlie a particular character's external behaviour. In so doing, she avoids making unequivocally authoritative statements about her characters' inner lives. Woolf uses this device to create the illusion that she is judging the novel's characters from without. In this way, she encourages us to 'believe in' her fictional characters as autonomous individuals, and therefore to accept unconsciously the 'argument' which is dramatised through their narrative.

In a diary entry for 6 November 1919 Woolf notes E. M. Forster's reaction to *Night and Day:* 'None of the characters in N. & D. is lovable. He did not care how they sorted themselves out.'[49] Another way of putting this would be to say that in her second novel Woolf fails to draw the reader into the kind of sympathetic relationship, and sense of identification, with her central characters which we experience in *The Voyage Out.* One weakness in *Night and Day* is that although Woolf avoids obviously intervening in her own voice in the novel, the variety of styles employed has the effect of drawing attention to the presence of the author behind her narrative, and thereby disrupting the illusion of 'realism'.

Alongside the more traditional passages in *Night and Day* (many of which recall in their irony and caricature the work of Wells, Galsworthy and Bennett), one finds innovative sections which anticipate the poetic style of *The Waves* typically associated with Woolf.[50] At times Woolf adopts a 'masculine' approach in her narrative which is deeply rooted in literary tradition. This is particularly evident in the rather formal introductory passages to specific chapters. [51] These opening sections – whose style brings to mind that of Austen or George Eliot – strike the reader, like many individual phrases in the novel, as 'borrowed' or 'literary', rather than peculiar to Woolf. In juxtaposition with such 'ready-made' phrases are experimental passages which anticipate the idiosyncratic style of Woolf's later novels, but which are not sufficiently integrated into the text. Through such passages, Woolf hoped to infuse poetry into 'the flatness of N. & D.'.[52] Whereas in a work like *The Waves* she adheres to the poetic mode throughout, in *Night and Day* she injects isolated experimental

passages into an essentially 'traditional' text, notably in those
scenes in which Katharine (and, at times, Ralph), tries to find 'the
centre of things; sometimes one may call it reality, again truth,
again life'.[53] The language of these episodes is strongly contrasted
with the more conventional style of the rest of the novel. (Specific
sentences also stand out in *Night and Day* because they anticipate
the syntax of Woolf's later fiction. One example might be the
description of Mary's reflections as she sits in front of the Elgin
Marbles: ' "For", she thought to herself, as she gazed fixedly at
some information printed behind a piece of glass, "the wonderful
thing about you is that you're ready for anything" ' (p. 80).
Another example is to be found in Katharine's thoughts as she
contemplates her marriage to William: 'For, "Oh dear," she
thought, looking into a tobacconist's window, "I don't care for
any of them" ' (p. 284). There is a hint of Woolf's later style, too,
in Denham's response to the fact that Katharine is late for their
meeting at Kew: 'The world, he assured himself, since Katharine
Hilbery was now half an hour behind her time, offers no happiness, no rest from struggle, no certainty' (p. 348).)

At the opposite pole from the experimental sections of *Night and
Day* whose style anticipates Woolf's mature poetic novels are those
passages which involve melodrama and caricature. Many of the
novel's characters, for example, are identified by simple physical
characteristics.[54]

The contrast between the poetic sections of *Night and Day* and
the novel's relatively melodramatic love-plot has the effect of highlighting the presence of the author behind her text. This is particu-
lary true of the scene in which Cassandra emerges upon William
and Katharine from her hiding-place behind the drawing-room
curtains (pp. 438-9),[55] of Mr Hilbery's histrionic response to the
news of Katharine's broken engagement (p. 494) – although here,
of course, part of the humour lies in the fact that Mr Hilbery tries
unsuccessfully to adopt the role of tyrannical father familiar to him
from literature – and of the final reconciliation scene around the
tea-table at Cheyne Walk (pp. 524–30).

Woolf argued that *Night and Day* suffers from the fact that it is
a testing-ground for her later novels. In a discussion of Defoe, she
suggests that:

We have only to reflect how seldom a book is carried through on
the same impulse of belief, so that its perspective is harmonious

throughout, to realize how great a writer Defoe was. One could number on one's fingers half a dozen novels which set out to be masterpieces and yet have failed because the belief flags; the realities are mixed: the perspective shifts and, instead of a final clarity, we get a baffling, if only a momentary, confusion.[56]

Whilst the modern critic probably would not want – as Percy Lubbock does in *The Craft of Fiction* – unequivocally to endorse Woolf's view that there is a direct correlation between the stylistic consistency of a novel and its aesthetic value, it would be fair to say that such consistency may contribute to the persuasiveness of a novel's 'argument'. In *Night and Day*, the method of *To the Lighthouse* or *The Waves* conflicts with that of *The Years*, thereby drawing attention to the narrative process and disrupting the 'realist' illusion.

One could argue that *Night and Day* stands in much the same relation to Woolf's mature works of fiction – and particularly *The Years* – as her originally unpublished essay-novel, *The Pargiters*. In both these lesser works Woolf learned, as she puts it, 'what to leave out: by putting it all in'.[57] The unevenness of style in *Night and Day* undoubtedly impedes Woolf's polemical purpose, since in highlighting the presence of the author behind her text, it inhibits the reader's unconscious assimilation of the ideology implicit in the narrative.

(d) REPETITION IN THE NOVEL

Her mind, passing from Mary to Denham, from William to Cassandra, and from Denham to herself . . . seemed to be tracing out the lines of some symmetrical pattern, some arrange-ment of life, which invested, if not herself, at least the others, not only with interest, but with a kind of tragic beauty. (pp. 331–2)

Like *The Voyage Out* and *The Years*, *Night and Day* contains a complex underlying structure of repetitions. Despite the fact that Woolf fails to sustain a uniform style throughout the novel, she manifests considerable skill at integrating these patterns of repetition into her text, in such a way that they at once remain unobtrusive and at the same time draw attention obliquely to ideas which are of particular importance to her, and in this respect *Night and Day* anticipates her penultimate novel, *The Years*. In particular, the relationships between the various lovers in the novel are tightly linked through thematic and verbal repetition.

The Double Love-Plot

For example, Woolf describes how various characters in the novel become oblivious to the world around them as they contemplate the person whom they love. (Ralph Denham, walking with Mary across the fields to Lincoln, forgets his surroundings as he thinks about Katharine (p. 235). Mary herself becomes distracted as she stands in front of a statue of the Duke of Bedford thinking of Ralph (p. 274), and Rodney, leaving Cheyne Walk after spending the evening with Cassandra, appears to Katharine 'a little strange, as if he were walking in his sleep' (p. 383). In the course of the novel several characters are shown to be so preoccupied with their own thoughts that they fail to recognise someone they know. (When Ralph, for example, passes Katharine in the street, she is murmuring a sentence from Dostoevsky to herself, and remains unaware of his presence (pp. 132–3). Later, when Mary comes upon Ralph walking near his office, she walks past him without his having noticed her. It is only when she comes back and taps him on the shoulder that he sees her (pp. 165–6). Towards the end of the novel, Rodney tells Cassandra that he has seen Katharine in the street, but she has failed to recognise him (p. 480). 'She looked', he says, 'like some one walking in her sleep' (p. 481).) A further parallel is to be found in the way in which the various lovers are interrupted in the course of their 'tête-à-têtes'. (When Ralph visits Katharine for the second time at Cheyne Walk, their conversation is no sooner started than it is broken up by the arrival of Katharine's aunts (p. 152). Later Katharine remarks to Ralph, 'You will come again, I hope. We always seem . . . to be interrupted' (p. 161). There is an echo of this scene at the end of Chapter 24, when Mrs Hilbery comes upon her daughter and William alone together, and feels obliged to leave them, 'as if she forced herself to draw the curtain upon a scene which she refused all temptation to interrupt' (p. 346). The irony is that Mrs Hilbery's interruption falls immediately after Katharine and William have agreed that they will pretend that they are still happily engaged in order to cover up William's 'courtship' of Cassandra. Later in the novel, Woolf describes how Katharine's frequent absences from Cheyne Walk expose Cassandra and William 'to interruptions which almost destroyed their pleasure in being alone together' (p. 481). After Mrs Milvain's visit to her brother, Mr Hilbery feels an obligation to speak with his daughter although, like his wife, he feels sure that he has 'interrupted some happy hour of hers with Rodney' – p. 493.) On several occasions different conversations are interrupted by a sudden rapping at the door. (When Ralph visits Mary before the meeting in her room, he is disappointed to hear a knocking outside which he fears will bring their private conversation to an end (p. 46). As Katharine and William discuss the latter's feelings for Cassandra, their tense exchange is interrupted by Ralph knocking at the door (p. 307). And when Katharine visits Mary in order to find out Ralph's address, the hostile scene between the two women is interrupted by a 'loud knocking at the door' – p. 473.)

After the meeting in Mary's room, Ralph follows Katharine and William along the street, and observes that 'when a pedestrian going the opposite way forced them to part they came together again directly afterwards' (p. 60). The scene is echoed when Ralph and Katharine walk along the street together after having tea with Mary in her office, 'parting and coming together again' (p. 93). Katharine feels some initial irritation at finding Ralph at her side when she would rather be alone. In a similar way, Ralph is annoyed with himself for agreeing to accompany Rodney to his rooms after Mary's meeting (p. 66), and Rodney, too, is put out when he comes upon Ralph outside Katharine's house and feels obliged to walk with him although he has 'no wish for company' (p. 420).

The scene in which Ralph follows Katharine out of Mary's office (pp. 90–1) has a parallel in that in which the two leave Rodney's flat together (p. 311). In each case, the abandoned lover is overcome by a feeling of anger and disappointment. The problem of jealousy, and the need to rise above it, is a dominant one in the novel. (When Katharine tells Mary that she has met Ralph, Mary remarks, 'I believe I'm jealous' (p. 380), and when Rodney is repulsed by Cassandra, his jealousy over Katherine's relationship with Denham returns (p. 436). Cassandra herself becomes jealous when she finds that Rodney is taking a 'proprietary' rather than merely a 'friendly' interest in Katharine's welfare (p. 481). The jealousy which the lovers experience is shared by Mr Hilbery, whose solicitousness for his daughter is far from disinterested – p. 529.) Various individuals in the novel have to learn to control their unrequited love and to transform it into friendship. (When Katharine leaves Rodney's flat with Ralph, she turns to look back at Rodney, 'trusting to this last glance to seal their compact of good friendship' (p. 311), and meets instead with an angry stare. Later, however, when Katharine shows herself willing to help Rodney in his 'courtship' of Cassandra, he accepts her offer of friendship: ' "We will help each other," he said, repeating her words, seeking her eyes in an enthusiasm of friendship' – p. 345.)

Each of the lovers must make a choice between 'helping' or 'hurting' the people with whom he or she is involved. (Ralph is ashamed of the critical tone which he adopts towards Mary when he finds her irritating, and feels 'with remorse that he had been hurting her' (p. 136). Henry Otway recognises in his cousin Katharine a 'determination to hurt' Rodney through her speech and behaviour (p. 210). (Henry himself has earlier found himself 'divided between an impulse to hurt her and an impulse to be tender to her' – p. 207.) In each case Ralph or Katharine is reacting with annoyance to the fact that they cannot reciprocate the love which others feel for them. Following the visit to Lincoln, Rodney comes to the conclusion that there is something in Katharine's character which 'made it impossible for her to help hurting people' (p. 296), and again, during the visit to the zoo, he is struck by what he considers Katharine's 'delight in hurting' him (p. 393). Rodney himself hurts Katharine, however, when, in the course of their evening together at his flat, he asserts 'that for him she was without romance' (p. 303). Nevertheless, Katharine responds generously to the opportunity for helping Rodney by bringing him together with Cassandra under the secrecy of her own supposed engagement (pp. 307, 339, 342, 343, 345, 375). Ralph Denham feels a wish to hurt Katharine when he talks with her in Kew Gardens, frustrated as he is by the engagement he believes to exist between her and Rodney (p. 355). When Katharine describes her pact of friendship with Ralph to Mary, the latter is anxious to protect Ralph from Katherine's ability to hurt him (p. 381), and when Ralph himself visits Mary in order to tell her about his love for Katharine, we are told that 'The distance between them hurt her terribly' (p. 414). None the less, when Katharine comes to her in distress, Mary wishes to help her (p. 475), just as Ralph wants to help Rodney (p. 421). Katharine finds Ralph's treatment of Mary inexplicably callous (pp. 292, 355), although it exactly mirrors her own behaviour towards Rodney.)

The progress which each character makes from wishing to hurt the loved one to wanting to help him or her is accompanied by a recognition of the need to renounce a special closeness to them. (When Mary realises that Katharine has come to know Ralph better than she herself does, she feels a 'desire for the old unshared intimacy too great to be born without tears' (p. 292). Similarly, Katharine, in furthering Rodney's relationship with Cassandra, finds it for an instant 'impossible to surrender an intimacy, which might not be the intimacy of love, but was certainly the intimacy of friendship, to any woman in the world' (p. 340; see also p. 428). As Mary listens to Ralph's confession of his love for Katharine, she is tempted to 'force him to confide in her', in order that she may 'enjoy once more his intimacy' (p. 414).) In the course of the narrative, the various protagonists have each, at least temporarily, to come to terms with the prospect of living in a loveless world in which there is no possibility of intimacy with the lover-friend. (The effect, for example, which Katharine's announcement of her engagement to Rodney has upon Ralph is to make him feel that the meaning or pulse is gone from his life, leaving it barren and cold (pp. 161–2, 407–8). Similarly, when Mary forces herself to face up to the idea of living in a world without Ralph she recognises that 'her life there would be harsh and lonely almost beyond endurance' (p. 234). Katharine, too, standing alone in her parents' drawing-room whilst William and Cassandra converse animatedly, feels that her own world is now quite devoid of romance, that 'never had life been more certainly an affair of four walls' – p. 373.) Woolf suggests, however, that such experience is necessary to the ill-matched lovers if they are to avoid treachery to one another. (Katharine recognises that to submit to William by marrying him, simply in order to secure the intimacy of friendship, and not of love, would be to betray him (p. 255). Her feeling is symbolised by the gesture with which she withdraws her arm from his on the way back from Lincoln (p. 251). Mary makes a similar gesture in response to Ralph's offer of marriage. She finds an unbearable dishonesty in Ralph's willingness to propose to her when he is in fact in love with Katharine – p. 262.) In the course of *Night and Day* various proposals of marriage are made or accepted in such a way as to suggest that they are insincere. (One such example comes in the way in which, early in the novel, Katharine accepts Rodney's offer of marriage: 'Perhaps it was that no man could expect to have the most momentous question of his life settled in a voice so level, so toneless, so devoid of joy or energy. At any rate William made no answer' (pp. 145–6). Katharine's second acceptance of William, following the scene in the Lincolnshire countryside, is motivated by pity, rather than love, for him, and therefore echoes the insincerity of the earlier episode (p. 259). Mary Datchet refuses Ralph's proposal to her because it is manifestly hollow – pp. 261, 265.)

The relationships between Ralph and Mary, Rodney and Katharine, are frequently likened to that of brother and sister, a comparison which suggests their unsuitability as lovers. (Seeing Mary stroke her brother Christopher's hair, for example, Ralph feels, 'I should like Mary to stroke my head like that' (p. 200). When the two walk to Lincoln together, Mary is pleased by Ralph's readiness to respect her intellect in discussion. It seems to her that he argues 'as fiercely with her as if she were his brother' (p. 229). Later, when Ralph asks her about her plans to go to America, she once more detects 'a brotherly kindness in his voice' (p. 235). Similarly, when Katharine talks to William in his flat after Christmas, she is 'conscious of a most sisterly desire to help him' (p. 303). Later, however, when William describes the position in which his 'courtship' of Cassandra will place Katharine as one 'in which I could not endure to see my own sister' Katharine rejoins impatiently: 'We're not brothers and sisters' – p. 344.) In the course of the narrative, all the protagonists come to recognise the essential difference between such caring brotherly/sisterly relationships and the romantic alliance of lovers.

Echoing Ralph's feelings for Mary, Katharine is tempted to accept William for the sake of the protection and security which his friendship can give her. To marry William even without loving him would, at least, she thinks, save her from the loneliness of life without him (p. 437). In the same way, Ralph feels that were he to accept Mary's love, 'they would clasp each other tight, and her arms would hold him like his mother's' (p. 239). Katharine recognises, however, that if she is not to betray William she must give him up to Cassandra, even at the cost of her own isolation, just as Mary acknowledges the need to renounce Ralph to Katharine. Mary manages to come to terms with her own situation and is therefore able to be of help to both Ralph and Katharine.[58]

When Katharine discusses Ralph with her mother, she describes him as 'fearfully rash – he's always taking risks' (p. 509). The need to take such risks, or, as Mrs Hilbery puts it, 'to have faith in our vision' (p. 513), is one which the various lovers come to accept in the course of the novel. (For example, Mary remarks, in an attempt to quell Katharine's indignation at the way in which Ralph has treated her: 'No, no . . . you don't understand. If there's any fault it's mine entirely; after all, if one chooses to run risks – ' (p. 292). Katharine herself justifies her decision to help bring Rodney and Cassandra together with the comment: 'I've come to the conclusion that there are risks which have to be taken, though I don't deny that they hurt horribly' (p. 345). The pact of friendship which Ralph makes with Katharine at Kew depends upon the understanding that if either party falls in love, 'he or she does so entirely at his own risk' – p. 357.)

Incidental Repetitions

The parallels between the different relationships in *Night and Day* serve to link them and to suggest that there is an underlying significance beneath the apparently arbitrary experiences of the lovers. At another level, they bind together the material of the novel, and to this end they are helped by the presence of more general verbal and thematic repetitions throughout.

Examining her feelings for Ralph, at the start of the novel, Mary decides that 'She did not want to marry at all' (p. 81). This phrase recurs later, when Katharine reacts angrily to her mother's enthusiasm at the idea that her daughter will soon be called Katherine Rodney: 'The alteration of her name annoyed Katharine, and she observed, rather sharply, that she didn't want to marry any one' (p. 103). Similarly, the phrase 'There are different ways of loving' which Mary uses when she realises that she is no longer obsessed with Ralph (p. 474) is echoed when Mrs Hilbery remarks to Katharine: 'Don't marry unless you're in love! . . . But . . . aren't there different ways, Katharine – different – ' (p. 509).

At the begining of the novel, when Ralph describes his family to Katharine, she remarks that it sounds 'rather dull' and he retorts superciliously, 'You would think us horribly dull' (p. 11). His comment is echoed later when Mary thinks about Ralph's prospective visit to Disham and fears that he will find it tiresome. She is drawn to defend her family as 'queer, yes, but not dull', 'eccentric and limited, perhaps, but not dull' (p. 190). Like Ralph (p. 24), Mary cannot help believing that there is 'something very remarkable' about her family. Just as Mary wants Ralph to be impressed by her relatives, so, too, both Mary and Ralph feel a need to impress Katharine Hilbery. When, for example, Ralph attacks Katharine for her subservience to family traditions, he feels 'gratified to find that he had the power to annoy his oblivious, supercilious hostess, if he could not impress her; though he would have preferred to impress her' (p. 10). Similarly, when Katharine visits the suffrage office, Mary is anxious to impress her by the efficiency of the organisation. As Mrs Seal holds forth interminably on the subject of the vote, though, Mary gives up 'all hope of impressing her' (p. 84).

The underlying conflict between the two women's life-styles forms part of the novel's wider 'discussion' of the respective merits of 'earning a living' or 'staying at home'. When Ralph criticises Katharine for her lack of independence with the remark, 'Do you do anything yourself' she replies: 'What do you mean? . . . I don't leave the house at ten and come back at six' (p. 13). The phrase 'ten to six', which recurs throughout the narrative, is used as a short-hand for the public world in which the individual earns his or her own living (p. 77). When Ralph suggests – his criticism of Katharine notwithstanding – that it is demeaning for his sister to have to go out to work, she comments: 'It doesn't hurt any one to have to earn their own living. I'm very glad to have to earn mine' (p. 27). Mary, like Joan, is proud of the fact that she supports herself: 'From ten to six every day I'm at it' (p. 54). She feels that to have stayed in her room 'all day long, in the enjoyment of leisure, would have been intolerable' (p. 75). When Ralph suggests to Rodney, 'I dare say it's just as well that you have to earn your own living' (p. 71), however, the latter replies that he would be quite happy to have the whole day free to spend as he liked. This option does not present itself to the women in the novel. If a woman like Katharine stays at home, she immediately becomes involved in the unpaid, and unrecognised, profession of daughter of the house. Earning a living gives a purpose to one's existence which staying at home cannot provide, as Mary recognises when, watching the 'clerks and typists and commercial men' hurrying to work in the morning, she feels that 'she shared with them the serious business of winding-up the world to tick for another four-and-twenty hours' (p. 75). Through repeated references in the novel to the idea of 'earning a living', Woolf is able, then, to draw the reader's attention to the question of woman's social position, without intervening in her own voice in the narrative.

When Katharine comments to Ralph upon the impossibility of discussing anything with one's own family (p. 356) we are reminded of Ralph's own thought at the start of the novel that it would be much easier to discuss 'happiness' with Miss Hilbery than with any member of his family apart from his sister Joan (p. 26). The question of 'happiness' surfaces at many points in *Night and Day*.[59] It is one which Woolf herself considers in her diary when she asks: 'Happiness – what, I wonder constitutes happiness? I daresay the most important element is work.'[60] Happiness is linked in Woolf's mind, then, with earning one's living.

The idea of the 'great man' – epitomised in the figure of Richard Alardyce – is one which recurs throughout the novel. To the poet's relatives the concept of 'great men', 'great books', 'great writers' and 'the great tradition' is an impressive one.[61] When Ralph first meets Katharine, however, he remarks, 'I hate great men' (p. 13), and suggests that the Victorian ideal of 'greatness' in fact masks the worthlessness of that generation. Ralph's point of view is very close to Woolf's private opinion on the subject.[62] Linked with the 'discussion' of 'great men' in *Night and Day* is that of the various characters' literary aspirations. Woolf suggests that, among the leading English families, it is inevitable that 'when one of them dies the chances are that another of them writes his biography' (p. 31). Hence Mrs Hilbery's role as biographer to her father, despite her manifest ineptitude for the task (pp. 34 – 5). William Rodney is another example of an enthusiastic but ungifted writer (p. 52). Katharine's own dislike of literature is in part a reaction to the mediocrity of her relatives' attempts to emulate her grandfather: 'All my relations write poetry . . . I can't bear to think of it sometimes – because, of course, it's none of it any good' (p. 151).[63] Another dominant idea in *Night and Day* is that of 'propriety'. One of the problems which Mrs Hilbery faces in writing her father's biography is that of 'what to leave in and what to leave out' (p. 35). Richard Alardyce may be a 'great man', but the fact is that he 'left his wife, and after some years of a rather reckless existence, she had died, before her time' (p. 101). There is an irony, in the light of this, in the fact that cousin Cyril's behaviour should be considered likely to dishonour his grandfather's name. Cyril, with his faithfulness to his lover and his work for the 'poor men's college' (p. 121) comes across as an extremely moral character when compared with the 'great man' who is his grandfather. Linked with the question of cousin Cyril is the problem of whether Katharine should marry Ralph or not. Mrs Hilbery finds in her father's unorthodox attitude to his wife a vitality which she considers to be absent from the lives of the younger generation. With characteristic inconsistency, however, she is extremely uncomfortable at the idea that her daughter might choose to live with Ralph (p. 511).

As the examples cited in this section suggest, *Night and Day* contains numerous perhaps rather trivial instances of repetition, whose cumulative effect is, nonetheless, to suggest an underlying pattern to experience, and to emphasise ideas which are of particular importance to Woolf. The novel is, however, disappointing both in the limited scope of its subject-matter – it deals simply with courtship and marriage – and in the fact that the union between Rodney and Cassandra seems to undercut those criticisms of specific social values and attitudes which are written into the relationship between Katharine and Ralph.

It is in her penultimate novel, *The Years*, that Woolf makes the most impressive use of the technique of echo and repetition within an essentially 'realist' narrative, investing the apparently dreary and meaningless events of everyday life with a heightened beauty and significance, and drawing attention obliquely to her own interests and concerns, and to ideas which she has developed throughout her career both as a modernist and as a 'dramatic' novelist.

4
The Years

(a) INTRODUCTORY

Previous chapters have focused upon the way in which, in her 'dramatic' novels, Woolf is careful to create the illusion of authorial absence from her narrative. In *The Voyage Out* and *Night and Day*, that is, she embodies her own world-view in the lives of her fictional characters, and she exploits repetition as a means of unifying her material and of drawing attention indirectly to her own opinions and experience. In writing *The Years*, Woolf once again tackled the problem of how best to introduce theoretical ideas into a work of fiction, building upon the experiments which she had made in her earlier novels.[1] The present chapter will suggest that the 'argument' of *The Years* is more persuasive than that of *Night and Day* because Woolf sustains a uniform tone throughout this novel. In the published work, she transforms the uneven and over-schematic 'essay-novel' *The Pargiters* into the fluent 'realist' narrative which is *The Years*.[2]

(b) *THE PARGITERS* AS 'ESSAY-NOVEL'

Many of the ideas which Woolf used in *The Pargiters* can also be found in *A Room*. In this essay, for example, Woolf uses the imaginary figure, Judith Shakespeare, to explain why the Elizabethan period produced no female writer to rival Shakespeare himself.[3] She builds up a picture of a girl of genius, deprived of any formal education of the kind afforded to her brother William, and called from her furtive attempts to learn something from his schoolbooks to 'mend the stockings or mind the stew and not moon about with books and papers'.[4] Judith Shakespeare, Woolf suggests, was at an early age betrothed to the son of a neighbouring wool-stapler. She cried out that marriage was hateful to her, and for that she was severely beaten by her father. Then he ceased to scold her. He begged her instead not to hurt him, not to shame him in this matter of her marriage. He would give her a chain of beads or a fine petticoat, he said; and there were tears in his eyes. How could she disobey him? How could she break his heart?[5]

Woolf highlights the methods, both financial and emotional, then, whereby a late sixteenth-century father could blackmail his daughter. She emphasises, too, the temptation presented to a young girl of the period by any offer of marriage which would free her from the oppression of the family home, and she contrasts the conditions of home-life for an unmarried woman with those in which her brothers might expect to live. Whilst the former might hope to be provided with enough pin money to keep her clothed, the latter could expect to have money for 'a walking tour, a little journey to France . . . the separate lodging which, even if it were miserable enough, sheltered them from the claims and tyrannies of their families'.[6]

Our opening chapter suggested that Austen, with Shakespeare and Scott, represented, for Woolf, archetypal non-partisan (or 'dramatic') authors. Marilyn Butler has made a strong case for an examination of the form of Austen's novels within their social and literary context, which would suggest that these works would certainly not have been regarded as apolitical by Austen's contemporaries. Butler's argument notwithstanding, one can see why a novel like *Mansfield Park*, to take one example, should have appealed to Woolf. For this novel effectively illustrates many of the feminist points put forward in *A Room*. For example, the process of blackmail whereby a father or guardian might force his daughter or ward to marry an unattractive suitor is illustrated in Sir Walter Bertram's reaction to Fanny Price's refusal to marry Henry Crawford. Consequent upon this refusal is Sir Walter's withdrawal of many of the benefits upon which she has come to rely. Sir Walter exploits the discrepancy between his own wealth and the poverty of Fanny's family at Portsmouth in an attempt to persuade her to accept Henry Crawford. Faced with the prospect of a prolonged period of suffering in her family home, Fanny is seriously tempted to use marriage to Crawford as a means of escape. Marriage in the novel, indeed, frequently comes across as the only possible alternative for a woman to the oppression of home life. Of the two Bertram girls, the elder, Maria, marries the rich and unattractive Mr Rushworth in order to free herself from the restrictive tyrannies of the parental home. The younger, Julia, elopes with Mr Yates so as to avoid the increased limitations upon her life at Mansfield, which she believes will follow upon her sister's elopement with Henry Crawford.[7]

It is, though, not only the young and 'marriageable' women in *Mansfield Park* who are seen to be adversely affected by the restraints imposed upon them by society. In *A Room*, Woolf quotes Greg's belief that the 'essentials of a woman's being . . . are that *they are supported by, and they minister to, men*'.[8] The implications for women of such a view are illustrated, in *Mansfield Park*, through Lady Bertram and Mrs Norris. The former, denied any responsibility in the serious management of house and estate, has lapsed into complete mental and physical lethargy. (In this respect she resembles Marie St Clare in *Uncle Tom's Cabin*.) The latter, in contrast, has developed an excessive interest in those household concerns and economies which mark the limits of her responsibility.[9] The jealousies which arise amongst the young women in the novel can be explained by the fact that marriage is the highest end to which they can aspire. Marriage represents a life of vicarious interest in the achievements of men. Since upper-middle-class women are unable to pursue careers apart from those unpaid ones of wifehood and motherhood, their status as individuals in society is determined according to the husband's financial position. Hence the inordinate emphasis within the society of the novel upon the need for a woman to sell herself to the highest bidder. The consequences of an 'imprudent' marriage are illustrated in the life-style of the Price family at Portsmouth.

Mansfield Park is of particular interest as an embodiment of feminist ideas because the narrator seems to adhere to an anti-feminist attitude in the novel; at times she appears to adopt uncritically an essentially 'masculine' point of view. The 'feminine' viewpoint is discussed by Woolf in *A Room*. Here she praises the fictitious novel *Life's Adventure*, by 'Mary Carmichael', for its original treatment of friendships between women. Traditionally in fiction, Woolf suggests, women are portrayed from a man's point of view.[10] Even when the novelist is dealing specifically with a relationship between two women, he or she can see this relationship only in terms of a rivalry over a third party, who is a man.[11]

In *Mansfield Park*, Austen, far from asserting the feminist implications of her own narrative, seems to adopt and reiterate the
'masculine' attitudes which her society has inherited and perpetuates. This is very much in evidence when she comments upon
and interprets her fictional characters' behaviour in the novel.
For example, although she acknowledges the emotional pressures
placed upon Fanny Price, she attributes the jealousy between
Maria and Julia Bertram over Henry Crawford to their want of
principle, and to their relatives' indifference to their moral
education. The idea that such a jealousy might be the product of
the intense pressure to marry imposed on them by society is one
which emerges in spite of, rather than because of, the narrator.[12]
Austen also adheres to 'masculine' values in treating Lady Bertram
and Mrs Norris as objects of ridicule rather than of sympathy. The
domestic concerns which mark the limits of their experience are
trivialised by the narrative even as they are depicted as woman's
only proper sphere of action and responsibility.[13]

   The reader, then, is receptive to the truth about woman's
position in society which emerges in the course of Austen's narrative because the narrator herself is not obviously committed to
such ideas. (One could, indeed, present a convincing case for
saying that she was fiercely opposed to them.) The fictional
sections of Woolf's own *The Pargiters* have much in common with
Mansfield Park. The opening chapter, depicting family life at Abercorn Terrace in 1880, captures, like Austen's novel, the claustrophobic atmosphere of women's lives in the family home. The
jealousy experienced by Milly and Delia Pargiter – notably over
the question of who is to dine with a young man – corresponds
to the rivalry which exists between the two Bertram girls over
Henry Crawford.[14] However, the reader's inclination to believe in
Delia and Milly is seriously disrupted by Woolf's explicit attempts
to direct our response to them. In reading the essay-section
devoted to this chapter, it becomes obvious that the Pargiter girls
have been created in order to illustrate a particular point. For
example, Woolf remarks:

> That three healthy girls should be sitting round a tea-table with
> nothing better to do than to change the sheets at Whiteleys and
> peep behind the blinds at young men who happen to be calling
> next door may seem incredible. And yet the facts drawn from
> life seem to support that picture.[15]

As soon as we recognise that the fictional incidents exist not for themselves but solely to support a specific narrow theory, the 'realist' illusion is broken. In the course of the interchapters, Woolf makes explicit what has only been suggested in the chapters. In so doing, she deprives the reader of the sense that he or she is judging the characters for themselves, just as one might form an opinion about people who actually live. For example, Woolf provides her own interpretation of the way in which the Pargiter girls respond to the invitation to dinner with Roger Blake (in *The Years* renamed Robin Burke):

> It also roused a certain hostility: Delia felt that Milly, Milly that Delia, was a rival who would intercept this excitement, this stimulus; and the thoughts of each sister at once went to her personal appearance, and to her clothes.[16]

In reading *Mansfield Park*, one becomes aware of a corresponding rivalry, and consequent interest in personal appearance, amongst Austen's women.[17] Nowhere in the novel, though, does Austen deprive us of the sense that this hostility is something which we have observed and recognised for ourselves. She may ridicule certain women for their excessive interest in dress, but she is not obviously concerned to explain to the reader the social causes behind such an interest.[18] A study of the evolution of *The Years* reveals the skill with which, in the published version of that novel, Woolf disguises the personal interest in social injustice which is manifest in *The Pargiters*.

In the unpublished 'essay-novel', however, the narrative voice breaks into the fictional sketches, detracting from their persuasiveness. The author's presence makes itself felt, indeed, not only in the passages of narrative, but also in the dialogue. The characters, that is, frequently seem to be speaking on Woolf's behalf, rather than for themselves. In the second essay, for example, Woolf presents us with a brief scene between Delia's music-master and his mother. During this episode, the musician asks: 'How is it you women can be so musical; and yet, why is it that no woman has ever been a great composer?'[19] The scene, and the characters involved in it, have too obviously been created in order that Woolf can ask this question through them. *The Pargiters* contains many such episodes which are not sufficiently integrated into the text, and consequently are explicable only in terms of Woolf's own theoretical concerns. The extraordinary emphasis, for example, upon Milly's attempts to have a bath at the end of Chapter One is at first sight puzzling. Woolf's desire to underline the 'primitive' conditions of Victorian middle-class family life leads her to adopt an over-insistent tone and so to break the illusion of her fictional scene.[20]

Throughout *The Pargiters*, Woolf's portrayal of fictional characters is clearly affected by her critical interests. There is a tendency – as in *Night and Day* – to over-simplify characters and to polarise their interests and concerns. Lucy Craddock is an obvious example of a figure who seems to exist merely to illustrate a number of theoretical points; the lack of opportunities in education for women, for example, or the way in which intelligent women are despised if they are unattractive to men.[21] Similarly, the Brooke family (in *The Years*, the Robsons), is obviously brought into existence, with the Howard Fripps, as the antithesis to the University figures – the Malones, Edward Pargiter, Dr Andrews – whom Woolf herself despises. Granted that the idealised portrait of Mr Brooke ('he was a working man; he had no manners at all; he was far the nicest man she had ever met' – p. 132) is partly of Kitty's own making, he none the less remains too simplistic an example of the good working man.

Many of the characters in *The Pargiters* have counterparts in Woolf's earlier novels (as in *Mansfield Park*), who illustrate her ideas more persuasively, precisely because they do not seem to have been conceived to this end, but rather to be a product of the author's interest in people for their own sake. Mrs Ramsay in *To the Lighthouse* corresponds to Eleanor Pargiter in that she sacrifices her own life to the emotional demands of her family. This aspect of her character is never explicitly discussed in the novel, however, but makes itself felt in a number of more subtle ways. The immense power of Mrs Ramsay's personality is emphasised through the contrast between her presence in the opening section and her absence in the final one. Her death is depicted in terms of the effect of disintegration which it brings about in the Ramsay family. The question of the justice of Mrs Ramsay's self-sacrifice to society is never actually asked. It is, though, implied through the contrast between Mrs Ramsay and Lily Briscoe. Lily rejects the traditional role assigned to her by society, regarding her art as a higher end to which she can make her own kinds of sacrifices. The consequent contempt in which she is held as a conventionally unattractive, intellectual female by certain male characters in the novel places her alongside Lucy Craddock. Particular scenes in *To the Lighthouse* – the dinner, Mrs Ramsay's visit to the town with Charles Tansley, the episode in which Lily praises Mr Ramsay's boots – illustrate the degree to which the men in the novel rely upon women to bolster their pride and self-confidence. One does not feel, however, that these scenes exist merely to illustrate such points, but rather as portraits of unique and interesting individuals. The scene in *The Pargiters* which focuses upon Rose Pargiter's guilty puzzlement over the question of sex has a far more subtle parallel in *To the Lighthouse*, where the child's confused fears about sex are implicit in James's and Cam's response to the relationship between Paul Rayley and Minta Doyle.[22] They are also present, perhaps, in Jacob Flander's shocked discovery of the couple on the beach, at the opening of *Jacob's Room*. In *The Pargiters* the episode in which Rose encounters the exhibitionist on the way back from Lamley's toyshop is weakened by Woolf's anxiety to explain it to the reader. Edward Pargiter's relationship with Tony Ashton, too, has a more effective counterpart in the friendship between Jacob Archer and his college friends, Timmy Durrant and Richard Bonamy. In the earlier novel, physical attraction is clearly one aspect of the relationship between the young men, but one does not feel that the characters exist simply to illustrate this kind of love.[23] Many ideas which are put forward directly by the narrator of *The Pargiters* remain implicit in Woolf's earlier works of fiction, whose effect depends largely upon the novelist's willingness to suggest, rather than to explicate.

The disruptive effect of the narrative voice is, perhaps, seen at its worst in the Sixth Essay of *The Pargiters*, where Woolf makes it quite clear that her fictional characters are mere puppets for her own views. Purporting here to tell us something about Kitty Malone's state of mind, she lapses after a couple of sentences into the personal voice of *A Room* and *Three Guineas*:

Kitty took it for granted that the laws of conduct were fixed. A woman behaved in one way and a man in another. Ever since she could remember, she had been trained as a woman. And the *Concise Oxford Dictionary*, though published in 1929 – more than fifty years later – still preserves in its definition of womanliness, in a compact form, [the ideal] which governed Kitty's life in 1880; 'Womanly . . . having or showing the qualities befitting a woman . . . modesty, compassion, tact, &c.'[24]

In the course of this passage it becomes clear that Woolf has no interest in sustaining the reader's belief in Kitty Malone as an actual person; she is purely representative. Throughout *The Pargiters* Woolf's intrusions into her text serve to dispel our belief in her fictional characters as interesting individuals.

The relative failure of *The Pargiters* in 'essay-novel' form is, however, an indication not so much of Woolf's limitations as of her strength as a creative artist. For in Woolf's own mind it remained no more than an unsuccessful experiment, not to be published in her own lifetime. Her skill manifests itself in the way in which, through the 'dramatic' method, she transmutes the unpromising material of *The Pargiters* into the published novel, *The Years*.

(c) *THE YEARS* AND THE 'DRAMATIC' METHOD

Let me make a note that it would be much wiser not to attempt to sketch a draft of On Being Despised, or whatever it is to be called, until the P.s is done with. I was vagrant this morning & made a rash attempt, with the interesting discovery that one cant propagate at the same time as write fiction. And as this fiction is dangerously near propaganda, I must keep my hands clear.[25]

The belief 'that one can't propagate at the same time as write fiction' led Woolf to abandon the original conception of *The Pargiters* as an 'essay-novel'. The form of *The Pargiters* is, indeed, completely at odds with the stress which Woolf lays elsewhere on the need for authorial 'anonymity' in 'realist' fiction.[26] Whilst at work on *The Years*, Woolf was increasingly drawn to the 'dramatic' narrative approach as one which enabled her to embody her own theoretical ideas in a 'realist' work of fiction. Her diary entries over this period of composition contain numerous references to *The Years* as a 'dramatic' work. Moreover, she repeatedly describes individual sections of the novel as 'scenes' rather than chapters.[27]

Discussing the novel in her diary for 19 December 1932, she remarks of her method:

> Of course this is external: but there's a good deal of gold – more than I'd thought – in externality. . . . I'm off to join the raggle taggle gipsies oh! The Gipsies, I say: not Hugh Walpole & Priestley – no.[28]

'The gipsies' are represented in Woolf's mind, as we have seen, by Shakespeare and Scott, both of whom she praises for their 'dramatic' approach to characterisation. She recognises the ability of each to create convincing characters not through elaborate analysis, but by an astute use of dialogue. In an interesting discussion of the development of the novel, in a letter to George Rylands of 27 September 1934, Woolf traces its growth out of the drama and its subsequent movement towards introspection and internalisation. She concludes: 'Perhaps we must now put our toes to the ground again and get back to the spoken word, only from a different angle; to gain richness, and surprise.'[29] That this was Woolf's own intention in *The Years* is suggested by a remark she made about Sara and Maggie: 'I want to make both S. & M. bold characters, using character dialogue.'[30]

Woolf's recognition of the novel's 'dramatic' potential places her, it has been noted, firmly alongside Henry James. In her diary she describes the method of the 'Raid Scene' in *The Years* as that of 'character telling a character',[31] and the phrase certainly has a distinctly Jamesian ring to it. The evolution of *The Years*, too, resembles that of James's novels. The tendency of his fiction, in the course of composition, is always towards ambiguity and mystification. That is, he originally conceives his novel as a straightforward narrative in which his own point of view is very much in evidence.[32] In the course of writing the novel, this narrative is refracted through the prism of the fictional characters. The reader's understanding of the novel's action depends, in part at least, then, upon the characters' response to one another, and upon what they say and do. The history of *The Years* follows a similar pattern to this. Woolf takes as her starting point the original 'essay-novel' draft of *The Pargiters* in which the narrator's point of view is quite explicit. In the final version of *The Years*, overt authorial comment has been carefully eliminated, and Woolf gives us in its place a number of characters who appear to think and speak for themselves. (This is not, of course, to say that *The Years* is without implicit authorial directives, such as the revelation of a particular character's thoughts, which enable the reader – probably unconsciously – to place and judge the fictional characters independently of their own opinions of, and reactions to, one another.)

The overall structure of *The Years* – like the history of its composition – has affinities with James's fiction. As is the case with James's *The Golden Bowl*, for example, a pattern seems to emerge in the novel's material of which the characters instrumental in creating it remain unaware.[33] This pattern is integrated into the novel in such a way as to impress the critic at once by its 'naturalness' and its artifice.[34] That Woolf herself intended such an effect is suggested by a reference in her diary to the scene in Hyde Park: 'What I want to do is to reduce it all so that each sentence though perfectly natural dialogue has a great pressure of meaning behind it.'[35] This idea that the author should impose a structural design upon the novel is one which permeates the whole body of Woolf's criticism. It has already been suggested – in the discussion of *The Voyage Out* in Chapter Two – that it was Woolf's intention in particular that the structure of *The Waves* should reflect a pattern which she felt to be inherent in the world, and which is at its most fundamental in the passing of the sun from East to West, and of living forms from birth to death.

Although in this and many other respects *The Years* resembles the earlier novel *The Waves*, superficially they betray a marked contrast of narrative method. In *The Years*, the poetic, metaphorical language of *The Waves* is replaced by the prosaic language of ordinary speech, with all its redundancies and superfluities. Even when Woolf sets out to portray her characters' 'private' thoughts in the later novel, she does so through the colloquial language of conversation. Whereas in *The Waves* the reader must infer public utterances from private images, in *The Years*, as in ordinary intercourse, he or she can only guess at private experience from the public language of thought and speech. In *The Years*, then, Woolf has come to terms with the fact that it is impossible for the writer to capture entirely the uniqueness of individual lives. To do so, one would stand in need of a 'private language', a concept which is in itself incoherent. Whereas in *The Waves* Woolf focuses upon the way in which Bernard comes to recognise this truth, in *The Years* she takes it for granted. It is implicit in her choice of narrative method.

In the previous section the relative failure of *The Pargiters* was connected with the way in which the author's own polemical voice intrudes into the text. A comparison between the early drafts and the published version of the 1880 section of *The Years* reveals the way in which Woolf disguises her own presence in the latter. Opinions which can, in the case of *The Pargiters*, be attributed specifically to the narrator become, in *The Years*, aspects of Woolf's characterisation.

For example, in reading *The Years* our response to the figure of Eleanor is directed partly through the way in which the narrative traces her thoughts, but also by assimilating and comparing the other characters' reactions to her. To the man on whose toe she treads in a bus, she is: 'a well-known type; with a bag; philanthropic; well nourished; a spinster; a virgin; like all the women of her class, cold; her passions had never been touched; yet not unattractive'.[36] To Milly, on the other hand, Eleanor is: 'the soother, the maker-up of quarrels, the buffer between her and the intensities and strifes of family life' (*The Years*, p. 13). Although Woolf avoids commenting explicitly upon Eleanor's character, these two contrasted views of her not only create a sense of Eleanor as an actual person to whom other people can react in different ways, but also implicitly illustrate an important feminist point. As in her treatment of Mrs Ramsay in *To the Lighthouse*, Woolf at once shows how significant Eleanor is to her immediate family, and how easily sneered at by the wider society for whom she performs her voluntary acts of philanthropy. The Eleanor of *The Pargiters* is too obviously modelled on the 'well-known type' of the self-sacrificing Victorian daughter. In contrast, in *The Years*, Woolf's private conception of her characters is filtered, in part at least, through her portrayal of other characters. The description of Eleanor as 'a well-known type; with a bag; philanthropic' tells us as much about the character of the man who sees her as such as about Eleanor herself. Similarly, it is an aspect of Milly's 'younger sister's doglike devotion' (p. 402) that she should idealise Eleanor. Through Milly, Woolf can highlight the positive elements in Eleanor's character without praising her specifically in her own voice. Milly's faith in Eleanor parallels, in this respect, Lily's worship of Mrs Ramsay in *To the Lighthouse*.

Whereas in *The Pargiters* it is Woolf as narrator who emphasises the exact nature of the jealousy which exists between Milly and Delia over the dinner with Roger Blake, in *The Years* it is Eleanor

who notes the animosity between the two sisters. Eleanor's observation at once reveals an aspect of her personality – her sensitivity
– and also indirectly illustrates Woolf's own feminist concerns.
The same effect is achieved by attributing to Eleanor the belief
that Delia's and Milly's lives are too restricted. ('They stay at home
too much, she thought; they never see anyone outside their own
set. Here they are cooped up, day after day' – p. 32.) The idea is
reiterated through Morris's thoughts later in the same scene. He
blames the stifling atmosphere of home life upon his sisters: 'There
he was cooped up with all these women in an atmosphere of
unreal emotion' (p. 46). The repetition of the same phrase draws
attention indirectly to the claustrophobic nature of life in Abercorn
Terrace. The difference, however, is that Morris, unlike Eleanor,
has himself deprived his sisters of the opportunity of a formal
education, through his monopoly, with his brothers, of the family
funds. At the same time he despises them for their consequently
limited outlook and life-style.

Woolf devotes a large proportion of *The Pargiters* to overt
comment upon the nature of middle-class family life in the 1880s.
In *The Years*, specific characters, notably Kitty and Delia, absorb
Woolf's own outlook into their personalities. For example, it is
through Delia's annoyance at the way in which Crosby clears the
tea table that Woolf suggests some of the irritations implicit in the
life of Abercorn Terrace:

> One by one with an exasperating little chink she put the cups,
> the plates, the knives, the jam-pots, the dishes of cake and the
> dishes of bread and butter, on the tray. Then, balancing it care-
> fully in front of her, she went out. There was a pause. In she
> came again and folded the table-cloth and moved the tables.
> Again there was a pause. A moment or two later back she came
> carrying two silk-shaded lamps.   (p. 19)

Here a careful choice of words conveys Delia Pargiter's feelings of
frustration far more effectively than pages of authorial comment.
The adjective 'exasperating', the inversions 'In she came' and 'back
she came', and the repetitiveness of the passage as a whole, all
suggest Delia's sense of boredom and anger at being penned up
at home with her sisters.

Delia's character is, then, the vehicle for a critical approach to
experience in *The Years*. Delia is unable, for example, like Kitty, to

feel the 'appropriate' responses to her mother's death. She stands back from the emotion of Mrs Pargiter's funeral rather as Bloom does in a comparable scene in *Ulysses*.[37] Like Bloom, Delia notices someone across the road peeping at the funeral procession from behind the blinds. At the cemetery, again like Bloom, she remarks on the newness of the coffin that is about to be buried. She shares Bloom's belief that it is more honest to laugh in the presence of death – as her brother Martin accidentally laughs – than to adopt a pious expression for the sake of propriety. It is Delia, too, who remarks to herself as her father comes stumbling violently from his dead wife's room, 'You did that very well . . . It was like a scene in a play' (p. 49). Delia's response to her mother's death in fact corresponds very closely to Woolf's own reaction to the premature death of Julia Stephen,[38] but – as is the case with the parallel incident in *To the Lighthouse* – Woolf's private experience is disguised in the novel.[39] At no point are we told explicitly that Delia's attitude to her father coincides with Woolf's own feelings about Leslie Stephen. Woolf deliberately abstains from commenting upon Abel Pargiter's behaviour, so that the reader remains ignorant as to whether Delia's interpretation of it is 'accurate', or simply a projection of her own feelings on to her father (although our response to the scene is clearly influenced by the way in which both characters are presented in the rest of the novel).

Just as Woolf avoids analysing explicitly Abel Pargiter's state of mind following his wife's death, so too she limits the extent to which she probes the young Rose's thoughts, following her experience on the way back from Lamley's toyshop. She makes no attempt to give a definitive account of Rose's response to the incident, but confines herself to the remark that Rose 'had a profound feeling of guilt; for some reason she must lie about the face she had seen' (p. 42). It is for the reader to respond to the suggestions of this sentence. Similarly, whereas in *The Pargiters* Woolf takes pains to explain the implications of Milly's frustrated attempts to have a bath, in *The Years* she uses the house agent's visit to Abercorn Terrace to criticise implicitly the Pargiter family's life-style. Through this scene Woolf is able to call the reader's attention obliquely to the conditions of Victorian middle-class family life.

Just as Woolf's personal sense of anger at the constraints of Victorian domesticity is channelled through her fictional characters in *The Years*, so too is her dislike of the small-mindedness of academic institutions. Theoretical points which in *The Pargiters*, *A Room* and, particularly, *Three Guineas* are discussed at great length, in *The Years* are dramatised through an apt scene or thought. For example, following the dinner party at the Master's Lodge in the 1880 section, Woolf describes how in leaving the Lodge,

> with a wave of the hand dictated by centuries of tradition, Mrs Larpent drew back her foot, as if she had encroached upon one of the chalk marks which decorate academic lintels and, signifying that Mrs Lathom, wife of the Divinity professor, should precede her, they passed out into the rain.   (pp. 59–60)

Woolf's own view of the petty futility of such academic 'chalk marks' is illustrated in a letter to Julian Bell of 11 March 1936 and also in *Three Guineas*.[40] In *The Years*, however, she deliberately keeps this private opinion submerged, allowing the incident to speak for itself. Kitty's thoughts about her father's dislike of the kind of house in which Lucy Craddock lives are similarly more telling than any overt authorial comment (p. 67). The novel's implicit criticism is far more persuasive than an outburst on the part of the narrator would be. The symbol of the half-fallen tree in the garden at the Master's Lodge is another example of such criticism. It is a tree 'under which Kings and poets had sat drinking three centuries ago, but now it was half fallen and had to be propped up by a stake in the middle' (p. 66). There is a suggested link between the tree and the half-dead academic traditions which Woolf herself abhors. But Woolf is careful not to make the connection explicit. Later, she once again exploits Kitty as a means of putting forward indirectly her own criticisms of male academics' prejudicial attitudes to women. In reply to Lucy Craddock's praise of the great historian, Dr Andrews, Kitty remarks: ' "Well, he doesn't talk history to me" . . . remembering the damp feel of a heavy hand on her knee' (p. 69). In the Fifth Essay of *The Pargiters* Woolf takes it upon herself to elucidate Kitty's comment:

> When Kitty made her unfortunate remark about Henry the Eighth, she was not really consoled or instructed by feeling Dr Andrews' hand upon her knee. Thus, the social intercourse between learned men and girls with original minds in the

eighties was full of difficulties and misconceptions on both sides.[41]

Far from adding to the effect of Kitty's remark, Woolf's commentary in fact undermines it by depriving us of the illusion that we are responding to it independently. The reader does not need to be told the implications of Kitty's comment any more than he or she wants to be informed that the half-fallen tree *stands for* academic institutions.

In an unpublished draft of a scene between Maggie and Elvira (Sara) in which the two sisters discuss Rose's political activities, Woolf puts into the mouths of her fictional characters many of the arguments which she was later to confine to her polemical essay, *Three Guineas*.[42] Maggie, for example, points out to her sister – and, of course, to the reader – the fact that although women may be described as British subjects on their passports, they are excluded from many of the privileges afforded to British men.[43] Like Woolf in *Three Guineas*, Maggie attacks 'gold lace, and Eton and Harrow and muskets'. Elvira imagines a letter which Rose might write to the Prime Minister, in her capacity as social reformer, in which she would say:

Milord Duke . . . What with child birth and chastity, and looking after old gentlemen who have [sic] shot off half their fingers in the wars (like my sister Elea[n]or) and sitting in a dark room for a million years – a room that smells of cabbages . . . (you remember the smell of Abercorn Terrace, Maggie?) we, the undersigned have inherited a tradition, Milord – if not an education, still a civilisation – which in our opinion it would be [a] thousand pities to swop for yours. For wherea[s] – here she should begin a new paragrapgh [sic] with a capital W – ' . . . Whereas the gentlemen of England (see Whittakers Almanac) never stir a finger save for money; and are educated thereto (see Edward my brother teaching undergraduates) we the undersigned have for countless ages worked without pay; Roses [sic] income being precisely twelve pound ten a quarter. Hence her coat and skirt . . .'[44]

In the published version of the novel, Woolf's fictional characters make no such overt political statements. Rather, Woolf's social criticism comes across obliquely in the course of the narrative. This point is illustrated if we compare a manuscript portrait of the Stephens' cook, Sophia Farrell, with her fictional counterpart in *The Years*, Mrs Crosby. In the manuscript, Woolf remarks of the kitchen in which Sophia worked: 'If you look at it today you may wonder – how any human being can have lived there, down in a basement house. . . . The kitchen must have been almost always dark.'[45] In the published version of the novel this argument is put across quite subtly through Eleanor's thoughts as she parts from Crosby in 1913:

> 'I should think you'd be glad to be out of that basement anyhow, Crosby,' said Eleanor, turning into the hall again. She had never realised how dark, how low it was, until, looking at it with 'our Mr Grice', she had felt ashamed.   (*The Years*, p. 232)

In the published version of *The Years*, even when she is 'setting the scene' for her narrative, as in the opening to each chapter, Woolf avoids speaking in her own private voice. These opening passages could be said to correspond to those sections devoted to the chorus in a play. On a first reading, the novel might appear to open with the kind of 'objective' authoritative description which Bernard parodies in *The Waves*:[46]

> It was an uncertain spring. The weather, perpetually changing, sent clouds of blue and of purple flying over the land. In the country farmers, looking at the fields, were apprehensive; in London umbrellas were opened and then shut by people looking up at the sky. But in April such weather was to be expected. (*The Years*, p. 1)

Perhaps the most striking feature of this opening, to the reader familiar with Woolf's work, is its ordinariness. It is made up of the kind of phrases used by millions of people in everyday conversation. A comment like, 'But in April such weather was to be expected' belongs, indeed, to the kind of speech described by Malinowski as 'phatic communion', whose function it is not to impart information but to express community with the listener, and as such is quite the opposite of the idiosyncratic poetic mode characteristic of a self-consciously innovative novel like *The Waves*.[47] As the narrative continues, however, it becomes apparent that the language used is designedly and not accidentally simple. The voice of the interludes is not that of Woolf as author but rather the common voice of society. This becomes explicit as the passage proceeds: 'But in April such weather was to be expected. Thousands of shop assistants made that remark' (p. 1). This technique of appearing to write in her own person, but subsequently disowning her statements, is typical of Woolf's approach throughout the novel. Often the question as to whether she is speaking in her own voice, in that of a particular character, or of society as a whole remains unanswered in the novel.[48] When, for example, she remarks upon how 'Diners-out, trotting over the Bridge in hansom cabs, looked for a moment at the charming vista' (p. 2), the cliché, 'charming vista', seems to belong to the language of conventional, habitual intercourse which Woolf parodies in *The Waves*. It appears, that is, to represent society's opinion of, rather than the author's private response to, the view across Hyde Park.

Woolf's approach in *The Years* can be seen as the antithesis to her technique in *The Waves*. In the earlier work she avoids, as far as possible, introducing hackneyed phrases into her narrative which could lead the reader to judge the world 'inside' and 'outside' the novel in preconceived terms. Through metaphorical language she tries to come as close as she can to capturing that which is unique in individual experience. *The Waves* implicitly – and particularly through the figure of Bernard – condemns ordinary language for its power to dull the user's response to experience. In *The Years*, in contrast, Woolf deliberately focuses upon the social aspects of language and experience. Despite one's essential isolation within a unique personality and history, language enables one at least to some extent to share one's life with other people. It is this corporate aspect of experience which Woolf meant to capture and embody in *The Years*, if we can trust her own retrospective account of the ideas behind the novel:

> But what I meant I think was to give a picture of society as a whole; give characters from every side; turn them towards society, not private life; exhibit the effect of ceremonies; Keep one toe on the ground by means of dates, facts: envelop the whole in a changing temporal atmosphere; Compose into one

vast many-sided group at the end; and then shift the stress from present to future; and show the old fabric insensibly changing without death or violence into the future – suggesting that there is no break, but a continuous development, possibly a recurrence of some pattern; of which of course we actors are ignorant. And the future was gradually to dawn.[49]

The Waves criticises the fact that language takes the place of the experiences which it connotes in the minds of its users. The suggestion is that when experience is made familiar through language something of its intensity is lost. In *The Years*, on the other hand, Woolf concentrates on the fact that experience only becomes recognisable and, therefore, communicable when it is expressed in the terms of an already existing language. Language helps, moreover, to draw attention to a pattern within experience. For example, the cooing of the pigeons in *The Years* can be made familiar and shared when it is translated into the verbal phrase, 'Take two coos, Taffy'. In *The Years*, as in *The Voyage Out* and *Night and Day*, Woolf exploits verbal repetitions and echoes in order to convey to the reading public her own sense that there is a pattern behind, and a significance to, human experience.

(d) REPETITION IN THE NOVEL

She knew exactly what he was going to say. He had said it before, in the restaurant. He is going to say, She is like a ball on the top of a fishmonger's fountain. As she thought it, he said it. Does everything then come over again a little differently? she thought. If so, is there a pattern; a theme, recurring, like music; half remembered, half foreseen? . . . a gigantic pattern, momentarily perceptible? The thought gave her extreme pleasure: that there was a pattern. But who makes it? Who thinks it? (*The Years*, p. 398; Woolf's ellipsis)[50]

Although *The Years* is in certain respects the antithesis of *The Waves*, both novels reflect Woolf's interest in the relationship between the individual and society, and the part which language plays in this relationship. The contrast comes in the language which Woolf herself uses in each novel. In *The Waves* she exploits the poetic, metaphorical potential in language in order to suggest, if not to capture completely, the unrepeatable nature of individual experience. In *The Years*, in contrast, Woolf limits herself as narrator to the language of ordinary speech. The poetry or vision in the later work comes not in the individual word or image, but in the structure of the novel as a whole, with its repetitions and recollections,[51] through which Woolf approaches the idea of *The Waves* from a new direction.[52] Repetition in the novel serves, moreover, like the metaphorical language of *The Waves*, to illustrate the fact that although individuals may share the same language and national (or public) history, these can never have exactly the same significance for two different people. The meaning of a phrase depends, in part, upon the history of the user, and upon the context in which it is used, both of these being unique. For this reason, Woolf's characters are able to participate unconsciously in a repetitive pattern, whilst at the same time retaining their singularity. A diary entry for 21 November 1935 makes clear that this was Woolf's intention for the novel: 'I want to keep the individual & the sense of things coming over & over again & yet changing. Thats what's so difficult: to combine the two.'[53] Like Henry James, Woolf is concerned to maintain the illusion that her characters are independent autonomous beings, whilst at the same time imposing a rigorous artistic pattern upon their thoughts, words and actions.[54] As the previous chapters have suggested, her belief in the need for structure and aesthetic coherence in the novel is bound up with her view that there is an underlying significance to experience as a whole. In the letter to G. L. Dickinson, quoted above, which she wrote shortly after the publication of *The Waves*, Woolf expressed her disappointment at the public's 'misunderstanding' of the novel. *The Years* can be seen as an attempt to make more explicit the idea behind *The Waves* as described in that letter.[55] Woolf hoped that the complex underlying structure of repetitions which gives significance to the apparently unremarkable events of *The Years* would suggest to the reader a corresponding order and meaning beneath the whole of human experience.[56] Although she does not appear to be manipulating the characters in the novel according to a preconceived pattern, a close examination of *The Years* reveals just how 'artificial' is its structure.

Material Objects

The reader's attention is probably first awakened to the presence
of repetitions in *The Years* by recurrent references within the novel
to specific physical objects; objects which are also ideas in the
minds of the fictional characters. One obvious example of an object
which dominates the novel is the portrait of Rose Pargiter. First
introduced in a passage describing the family drawing-room at
Abercorn Terrace, the presence of the portrait makes itself felt
throughout the 1880 section in which Rose's death occurs: 'Over
the fireplace the protrait of a red-haired young woman in white
muslin holding a basket of flowers on her lap smiled down on
them' (p. 9). The portrait figures large in the minds of several of
Woolf's characters, though each attaches his or her own meaning
to it.[57] From Milly, the portrait draws tears (which Delia considers
insincere – p. 47) at the idea of her mother's approaching death
(p. 39). Delia, on the other hand, associates the picture with what
she sees as Mrs Pargiter's unwillingness to release her family from
the pressure under which her illness forces them to live (pp. 40,
47).[58] To Martin, the presence of the portrait in its familiar position
is a reassuring sign of stability after his mother's death (p. 160),
although the fact that a flower in the foreground has become
hidden beneath a layer of dirt serves to suggest the passing of
time (p. 171). For Maggie, the portrait has none of the personal
associations felt so strongly by Mrs Pargiter's immediate family, it
is simply that of 'a girl with red hair' (p. 179). To Peggy it is 'the
picture of her grandmother' (pp. 349, 352), and to North Peggy's
own face is like 'his grandmother's face in the picture' (p. 455).
Various characters in the novel, then, share the idea and memory
of Rose's picture, but differ in their response to it. The same
could be said of the 'spotted walrus brush' originally given to Mrs
Pargiter on her birthday by her son Martin (p. 35). After Rose's
death, Eleanor keeps this brush 'because it was part of other things
– her mother for example' (p. 96), but in the 1906 section we learn
that she has thrown the brush away, suggesting that the memory
of her mother has become less potent (p. 168).[59] In the final
chapter, the walrus brush stands in Eleanor's mind for those solid
objects which she sets at the opposite pole from her own abstract
feeling of happiness (p. 460). There is a marked contrast between
that which the brush symbolises for Eleanor, and its significance
for Crosby, the family servant. To Crosby, the brush represents

all that is of value in her own life, namely, her vicarious interest in the Pargiter family. It is as a symbol of the old life of Abercorn Terrace that she rescues it from the wastepaper basket, thereby fulfilling Eleanor's prediction that the 'solid object might survive them all. If she threw it away, it would still exist somewhere or other' (p. 96). Eleanor's willingness to be rid of the brush can be related to her gladness in finally putting the life of Abercorn Terrace behind her. Crosby's desire to keep it reflects her inability to escape from the past and live for the present and future. (Through the brush, then, Woolf implicitly criticises the social system of which Crosby is a victim, whilst avoiding intervening directly in her text to make this point.) Crosby's attitude to the rose-patterned family tea-kettle is similar. In the opening section of the novel the kettle's inefficiency is the focus for all the frustrations inherent in the Pargiter family life (p. 8). It is, like their father's teacup (p. 11), an object which the Pargiter children cannot possibly throw away without offending him, and as such it symbolises the oppressive nature of relations between Abel Pargiter and his children. The degree to which Eleanor is sacrificed to her family is suggested by the fact that in 1908 she is portrayed in exactly the same attitude as her sister twenty-eight years earlier, trying ineffectually to encourage the kettle to boil (p. 162). Rose Pargiter's memories of her childhood at Abercorn Terrace centre on this image of her sister, Milly, fraying the wick under the tea-kettle with a hairpin (p. 179).[60] (For Kitty Malone, the half-fallen tree in the college garden has the same negative associations with her childhood that the tea-kettle has for Rose – p. 451). To Crosby, on the other hand, the kettle represents the only period in her life which has any real meaning. It is for this reason that Eleanor is unable to joke with her about its inefficiency when the two women part, after the family house has been put up for sale (p. 232). The family dog is also inseparably linked with the Pargiters' history at Abercorn Terrace. It is present at key moments in the narrative; the night of Rose's death (pp. 40, 45, 48); the period of transition when Abel is still alive (p. 163); the day on which Eleanor leaves the house for the last time (p. 231).[61] The Pargiter children are happy to forget Rover, because of his associations with their childhood, whilst it is for these very associations that Crosby values him (p. 235).

The reappearance of material objects (or a particular character's memory of such objects), in the course of the narrative, contributes to our sense of time passing and attitudes changing in the novel. For example, the necklace which Eleanor buys at Mrs Lamley's shop for her father to give to Maggie (p. 129) is later specifically linked in Maggie's mind with the idea of her uncle (p. 179). Similarly, the Italian glass which Abel sees in Eugénie's front room at Browne Street (p. 125) is later recognised by Rose in Maggie and Sara's flat (pp. 177–8). The crimson chair which originally stood in the hall of their parental home (pp. 136, 141, 155,) also reappears in this new context. Subsequently Eleanor notices it at Maggie and René's house (p. 310), and North recognises it when he visits Sara on his return from Africa (p. 337). It is as much a symbol of the life of Browne Street as Rose's portrait is of the world of Abercorn Terrace.

Phrases, Images and Ideas

The majority of echoes in *The Years*, however, involve references not to specific material objects but to particular phrases, images or ideas. Perhaps the most dominant idea in the novel is that of pigeons cooing in the tree tops. It occurs on the opening page when Woolf describes how 'The pigeons in the squares shuffled in the tree-tops, letting fall a twig or two, and crooned over and over again the lullaby that was always interrupted' (p. 1).[62] Later, Kitty Malone translates the cooing of the pigeons in the garden below her bedroom window into the phrase 'Take two coos, Taffy' (p. 80), and the same phrase is heard by the group which gathers for a meeting in a London square in the 1910 chapter (p. 190). The cooing of the pigeons figures in Sara Pargiter's account of this meeting to her sister (p. 202). Eleanor notices the murmuring of the doves in the garden of Morris's mother-in-law's home in Dorset (p. 212), and Kitty remarks upon it on arriving at her house in the North of England (p. 297). In the penultimate passage of the novel, Eleanor draws the company's attention to the sound of the pigeons outside the very building in which the meeting has taken place in 1910: ' "Listen . . . " said Eleanor, raising her hand. Upstairs they were playing "God save the King" on the gramophone; but it was the pigeons she meant; they were crooning' (p. 467; Woolf's ellipsis). The national anthem has also appeared earlier in the novel in Sara's satirical comments about North (p. 308), but the pigeons' crooning is more important than this anthem because it links the characters in the novel at a more fundamental level. The anthem forms part of the social and linguistic structure developed by humankind in an attempt to assert its solidarity and community. But the sound made by the pigeons, like the cycle of the seasons on which Woolf focuses in the introductory passages to each chapter, reflects an essential pattern in the world itself.[63] To put this sound into words is not to impose an artificial form upon experience, but rather to draw attention to the order inherent in that experience.

Sometimes a phrase is repeated, perhaps in a slightly modulated form, within a short section of the novel. Abel Pargiter's encounter with Mira, for example, is summed up in the following image: 'He began fumbling, with the hand that had lost two fingers, rather lower down, where the neck joins the shoulders' (p. 6). The phrase, with its euphemistic tone (which is presumably Abel's own), recurs in a slightly different form two pages later. Similarly, the phrase with which Mrs Malone greets the news of Rose Pargiter's death, 'Rose is dead . . . Rose who was about her own age' (p. 87), automatically comes to the surface of her mind later in the evening when she returns to the subject, 'Rose was dead. Rose who was about her own age' (p. 88).[64] The repetition neatly captures the sense of fear at the idea of her own death which is inseparable in Mrs Malone's mind from the thought that Rose has died. During the 'Raid Scene' the phrase, the 'sparks went volleying up the chimney' recurs within the space of a few pages (pp. 317, 320), echoing a comment earlier in the narrative (p. 284). Kitty's description of the books in her husband's library which seem to exist 'by themselves, for themselves' (p. 298) is echoed later in her vision of the northern countryside which also exists 'by itself, for itself' (p. 300). The image through which Woolf captures Rose's nightmarish vision of the strange man in the nursery: 'An oval white shape hung in front of her dangling, as if it hung from a string' (p. 41), recurs in a slightly different form a few lines later. This repetition serves to suggest Rose's inability to clear her mind of the idea of the man whom she has encountered earlier in the day. Similarly, Sara Pargiter's irritable response to the dance music outside her bedroom window, 'It was impossible to read; impossible to sleep' (p. 141), is twice reiterated on the following page, suggesting the way in which one is kept awake on a summer's night by a fixed idea or obsession.[65]

When Eleanor remarks of the fire in the drawing room at Abercorn Terrace, 'And when it does catch . . . it'll be much too hot'

(p. 30), her comment is echoed by the narrator: 'it was beginning to burn, and when it did burn it would be much too hot' (p. 30). Through this technique of echoing a character's thought or remark in her narrative Woolf draws attention to the communal nature of all human discourse. Describing Kitty Lasswade's arrival at the meeting in 1910, the narrator remarks that 'There was something shining in her hair' (p. 190). Later Eleanor uses the same phrase in comparing her own dowdiness with Kitty's glamour (p. 192). Similarly, the passage at the beginning of the 1908 section, in which the narrator describes the wind blowing refuse against the area railings in London (p. 158), is echoed in Martin's thoughts on the following page (p. 159).[66]

Both Rose and Delia use the phrase 'sour-sweet smell' to describe the atmosphere of their mother's sick-room (pp. 16, 20). The phrase 'her eyes dazzled' is used to capture Delia's sensations not only as she looks through the window in the passage outside her mother's room (p. 20) but also on seeing her mother's coffin in its grave (p. 92).

A remark which Delia makes during the closing chapter of the novel: 'Don't wait to be introduced . . . Do just what you like – just what you like', is, we are told, echoed by her husband (p. 435). Sometimes characters consciously repeat what has been said by others, as, for example, when Sara imitates her mother's admiring reference to Sir Matthew Mayhew, 'A most distinguished man' (p. 151). In the 1910 section Sara repeats her sister's phrase, 'Drunken men following one' (p. 186), and when Maggie puts down a saucer of milk for the cat, with the words, 'There, poor puss' (p. 204), Sara deliberately copies her, 'There poor puss, there poor puss'. Similarly, sitting with Martin in a London restaurant, she mocks his sense of propriety by imitating his remark, 'Hush . . . Somebody's listening' (p. 247). Martin finds it 'impossible to talk. Too many people were listening' (pp. 249–50). Later in the same scene, he recalls Sara's remark good-humouredly when he says, 'and now, Sally, you can say whatever you like. Nobody's listening' (p. 254). When North, at Delia's party, struck by the discrepancy between youth and age, turns to Maggie and asks, 'Why – ? . . . when they're so lovely' (p. 409), Maggie, we are told, echoes his question, 'without a meaning in her echo, "why" ' (p. 409).

Instances of repetition in the novel are, though, by no means always so obvious. Often consecutive occurrences of a particular phrase or image are separated by a considerable interval. This applies, for example, to the idea of society as a 'caravan' which appears at several points in the text (pp. 1, 138, 184).[67] It is also true of the phrase which Abel Pargiter uses to deal with children, 'Grubby little ruffian(s)'. He first uses it of his own daughter Rose (p. 11), and later of her cousins Maggie and Sara (p. 135). Through this repetition Woolf suggests a degree of consistency in Abel Pargiter's character, thereby encouraging the reader to 'believe in' him.[68] The same effect is achieved when different characters use a particular image to describe the same person. For example, the comparison between Rose Pargiter and 'Uncle Pargiter of Pargiter's Horse' is made by Rose herself (p. 27), by Eleanor (p. 169), and by Martin (pp. 449, 453), and both Peggy and Nicholas also liken Rose to a 'military man' (pp. 386, 448). Eleanor considers Martin's short-lived career in the army quite inappropriate to his character. Rose, she feels, is the military member of the family, whereas Martin ought to have been an architect (p. 169). The fact that Martin himself independently expresses the wish that he had been an architect (p. 245) suggests that his character is, like that of his father and sister, to some degree consistent.[69] The idea of himself jumping over the bonfire on his children's birthdays, which comes to Abel Pargiter's mind when he visits Eugénie on Maggie's birthday (p. 32), is also for Delia representative of her father (p. 37). Both Delia and Martin associate with Colonel Pargiter the image of two white patches which appear on his face when he is upset (pp. 48, 251), and in both the 1891 and 1908 sections of the novel Eleanor remarks upon the fact that her father's age is betrayed by the fact that his face has become heavily veined (pp. 98, 161). Similarly, Crosby's character is summed up for various people by her 'prominent blue eyes' (pp. 38, 160, 179). Eleanor and Edward share the memory of Eleanor's irritation at Edward's characteristic manner of brushing up his hair in front of the mirror (pp. 45, 59). Various characters in the novel associate Edward with the nickname 'Nigs' which Eleanor has given him (pp. 45, 66, 440). Eleanor's own outstanding characteristic is her incompetence at simple arithmetic (pp. 19, 97, 359). She associates Morris with the white scar on his hand where he cut himself bathing (pp. 117, 217). Both Eleanor and Maggie notice that Martin adopts a particular tone of voice when he is thinking about himself (pp. 167, 264). The image of 'a horse that is going to bite' is used to describe the way in which Sara typically raises her lip when she is irritated (pp. 144, 345), and the idea of being curled up is also associated with her. Lying in her bedroom in Browne Street, Sara ignores her mother's advice that she 'Lie straight, lie still' (p. 151) and curls herself up 'with her back to the window' (p. 155). Similarly, in Hyde Park, she folds herself 'like a grasshopper with her back against the tree' (p. 263). She adopts a similar attitude, 'curled up opposite with her foot under her' when North dines with her, before going to Delia's party (p. 336), and at the party she curls up in a corner 'with her head against a table asleep apparently' (p. 466). The phrase 'brown-eyed cricketing boy' is one which Eleanor automatically associates with her nephew, North, even when he has become a middle-aged man (pp. 217, 330). Sara's phrase for her cousin Rose, 'Red hair; red Rose' (p. 177) is recalled in the chant in the 'Present Day' chapter (presumably sung by Sara), 'Red Rose, thorny Rose, brave Rose, tawny Rose' (p. 453). The comparison with 'the yolk of an egg' which Delia uses to describe the yellow patches in her mother's hair (p. 21) is later adopted by North when he looks at his aunt Milly (p. 405). This repetition (like the reiteration of the phrase, 'He was fond of children' in connection with both Abel and Martin), suggests a family likeness, thereby contributing to our sense of the physical relationship of the Pargiter family.

Throughout *The Years*, then, Woolf exploits the Dickensian technique of representing an individual through a simple external characteristic, which she first explored in *Night and Day*; a technique which one certainly does not associate automatically with the author of *To the Lighthouse* and 'Modern Fiction'.

The opening phrase of the novel 'It was an uncertain spring', reappears later in the phrases 'It was an uncertain day' (p. 89) and 'It was a brilliant spring' (p. 241). Similarly, the phrases 'leaves were falling' and 'rain was falling' re-echo throughout *The Years* (pp. 93, 122, 123, 137), as, indeed, does the phrase 'the heart of darkness'.[70] For Peggy, the expression represents the evil inherent in the world (p. 418), and her brother North uses it to describe his sense of isolation in the midst of London society (p. 444). He compares this feeling with that of being alone in a jungle (p. 444), thus recalling Martin's depiction of such an experience in his letter to Eleanor (p. 114).

The word 'unbuttoning' is associated both with the gestures of the exhibitionist outside Lamley's toyshop (p. 29), and also with Edward Pargiter's movements as he undresses in his room at

Oxford (p. 58). Here, the repetition may be coincidental, or it may be intended to suggest that both incidents involve a degree of sexual inadequacy. Whilst the man in London is more obviously pathetic, Edward Pargiter can also be seen to be confused by his own sexual instincts.

The question, 'Where am I?' is one which recurs throughout the novel. It is asked by Rose Pargiter as she wakes from a dream (p. 23), and later by Delia (p. 25), Eleanor (pp. 44, 460) and Kitty (p. 288). The phrase 'hammer, hammer, hammer', which first occurs in the 1880 section when Jo Robson is building a hen-coop in the back garden of the Robson family home (p. 70), resurfaces as the hammering of the dwarf and of Siegfried in the opera of the name (p. 197), and later as the banging of a drunken neighbour on the door of a house in Hyams Place (p. 204). It is also implicit in the 'three sharp taps' which Sara imagines Creon to make as he buries Antigone alive (p. 146). The *Antigone* play itself appears at several points in *The Years*.[71] Edward Pargiter is trying to read it in his rooms at Oxford in the opening section (p. 54). Sara half-reads the play as she lies awake in her room in the house in Browne Street (p. 145), and three years later she quotes from it during lunch with Rose and Maggie (p. 181). In the final chapter Eleanor tells her brother that she has just finished reading his translation of the play (p. 446).

Martin's phrase, 'Blast that kettle' (p. 10), which shocks his sister Milly in the opening chapter, is echoed in the 1908 section when he remarks to Eleanor, 'Damn that kettle' (p. 164). The phrase passes unnoticed by Eleanor, but Peggy is later startled to hear the remark, 'Damned bully' on her aunt's lips (p. 356). The remark which Maggie makes to her sister in the 1910 section – 'Don't be such an ass' (p. 177) – is echoed by Rose as she makes her way with Sara to a meeting (p. 187). Peggy adopts a similar phrase, 'Don't be an ass' in the 'Present Day' section, when Eleanor offers to pay the cab-fare to Delia's party (p. 371).

The phrase, 'I'm right and you're wrong' which captures for Eleanor the hostile atmosphere of the meeting in 1910 (p. 191), recurs when Kitty, questioning her own dislike of London society, asks herself, 'Who's right? . . . Who's wrong?' (p. 281). She turns the problem over in her mind during the train journey northwards: 'And which is right? . . . Which is wrong?' (p. 293). The phrase also sums up for North the atmosphere at his aunt's party: 'It was like hearing small boys at a private school, hearing these young men talk politics. "I'm right . . . you're wrong" ' (p. 436; Woolf's ellipsis). For Woolf herself, as we know from a letter written to her friend Margaret Llewelyn Davies, the phrase represents the negative aspects of strong political partisanship. She remarks in this letter: 'My difficulty always was the political attitude to human beings – that some were always right, others always wrong. I did hate that.'[72] in *The Years*, however, Woolf avoids expressing this opinion explicitly. Through repetition she is able to draw attention to the idea indirectly, without 'preaching' on it overtly. She treats various 'political' phrases in this way in the novel. For example, Kitty's remark at the 1910 meeting that, 'Force is always wrong' (p. 193) is repeated later in a comment which she makes to her cousin Edward (p. 453). Similarly, the phrase 'Justice and liberty' recurs throughout the novel. During the Hyde Park scene, Martin imitates the manner and accent of one of the speakers, 'Joostice and liberty' (p. 259). To North, the phrase, 'Justice! Liberty!' is typical of the empty rhetoric of political meetings, impressive when first heard, 'but next morning . . . there's not an idea, not a phrase that would feed a sparrow' (p. 437).[73] The idea of 'justice and liberty' is echoed when Eleanor remarks to her niece Peggy upon the important of 'Freedom and justice', concepts which for Peggy, as for Woolf, remain unsatisfactorily vague (p. 357).[74]

When Eleanor arrives at Maggie's house in 1917, she interrupts a discussion between René and Nicholas. The latter explains that they have been talking about Napoleon and the 'psychology of great men':

> 'I was saying we do not know ourselves, ordinary people; and if we do not know ourselves, how then can we make religions, laws, that . . . that – '
> 'That fit – that fit', she said . . .　　(p. 303)

Ironically, when, later in the novel, North encounters Nicholas, he is struck by what he considers the originality of the Pole's conversation: ' "If we do not know ourselves, how can we know other people" . . . They had been discussing dictators: Napoleon; the psychology of great men' (pp. 332–3).[75] When he relates the start of the conversation to Sara, however, she is able to complete it exactly. North remembers that they discussed 'Napoleon; the psychology of great men; if we don't know ourselves how can we know other people . . .' (Woolf's ellipsis), and Sara immediately supplies Nicholas's conclusion, 'how can we make laws, religions, that fit, that fit, when we don't know ourselves' (p. 339). Eleanor echoes this idea when she tries to describe Nicholas to herself at Delia's party, but failing to do so, concludes, 'If I can't describe my own life . . . how can I describe him' (p. 398). Eleanor's point (like the phrase, 'I'm right and you're wrong') brings to mind a corresponding passage in Woolf's non-fictional writing. In 'The Leaning Tower' Woolf discusses her own unsuccessful attempts to fathom the truth about her personality as a child, and she remarks that 'If you do not tell the truth about yourself you cannot tell it about other people'.[76] In her novel, however, Woolf avoids expressing this idea explicitly in her own voice, choosing instead to attribute it to her fictional characters, and to emphasise it through repetition. In so doing, she avoids the 'I'm right and you're wrong' approach in her own novel. Nicholas's point is sanctioned by his own personality as it is revealed to us in the response of other characters to him. Since he is admired by sympathetic figures like Eleanor and Sara, we, too, are prepared to take him seriously. But his views are never specifically commended to the reader by the narrator.

Nicholas's word, 'poppycock' (p. 309), is adopted by Sara in a letter which she writes to North in Africa (p. 346). North himself uses the word to express his attitude to war, political revolution and violent partisanship (pp. 405, 442). The phrase which Maggie uses to describe her sister curled up in a chair, 'like some great ape, crouching there in a little cave of mud and dung' (p. 203), is later echoed in Sara's description of the cellar at her sister's house during an air-raid as, 'this cave of mud and dung (p. 316). When Abel Pargiter visits his brother's family in Browne Street, we are told that, in his own eyes at least, 'He was very fond of children' (p. 129). Later, Woolf remarks of Martin that 'he liked children', 'He was fond of children' (pp. 261, 264). As Martin walks into the City from his house in Ebury Street, he sees 'flights of hats stuck on little rods' (p. 242). Similarly, in the 'Present Day' section, Peggy and Eleanor, driving to Delia's party, see people looking at 'flights of hats on little rods' in the shop windows (p. 359). A remark which Rose makes to her brother Martin in the 'Present Day' section, 'D'you think you can get a rise out of me at this time o' day?' (p. 386), recurs later in the same chapter as the comment, 'You can't get a rise out of me at this time of day, my good fellow'

(p. 454). This repetition reflects their ritualised behaviour towards one another, the 'old-brother-and-sister' turn' which Peggy despises (p. 387).

The phrase which Peggy uses to describe Eleanor when she becomes excited, 'She was flushed, the veins stood out on her forehead' (p. 417) reappears in the narrator's description of Peggy herself when she attempts to put her own vision of a new world into words, 'the veins on her forehead stood out' (pp. 421–2). The verbal parallel serves to suggest that Peggy's political enthusiasm has more in common with her aunt's than she herself would like to believe. North's understanding of his sister's speech is that it is 'about another world, a new world' (p. 456). The phrase recalls the ideal of a 'New World' to which Eleanor and her friends drink in the 'Raid Scene' (p. 315). When, however, Eleanor describes her own vision of being 'happy in this world – happy with living people' (p. 418), during her sister's party, Peggy mimics the phrase incredulously. Later Eleanor reasserts this idea when she attributes her own feeling of happiness to the fact that she is 'alive; in this room, with living people' (p. 460).

Two parallel phrases are used to describe Eleanor's reaction to incidents which she finds momentarily shocking, because they are accepted social taboos. When Sara explains Nicholas's homosexuality to her she is repulsed for a moment, but immediately realises that 'it touched nothing of importance' (p. 321). Again, she feels an unpleasant sensation when Peggy likens a picture of a nurse to an advertisement for sanitary towels. She soon recognises, though, that 'what was solid in her body it did not touch' (p. 362).

The image of violets occurs at several points in the narrative. In the 1880 section, Rose throws a bunch of violets on to her mother's coffin as it is carried out of the house (p. 89). In 1910, Sara and Rose buy violets from a street-seller (p. 187), and in the 1914 chapter Martin gives some money to a beggar selling violets to atone for his angry treatment of a waiter in a chop-house (p. 253). The use of repetition here encourages the reader to transfer the sense of pathos from one incident to another. The beggar woman, for example, seems the more pathetic because through her violets she is connected with the motherless child, Rose.

The description in the opening passage of 'Diners-out, trotting over the Bridge in hansom cabs' who 'looked for a moment at the charming vista' across Hyde Park (p. 2), is recalled later in the novel. Eugénie remarks upon the view across the park as she travels to a party with her husband and daughter (pp. 139–40), and Martin's cab takes the same route when he drives to Kitty's party (p. 267). He joins 'the long line of cabs that was streaming towards the Marble Arch' (p. 267). The phrase recalls the description of how Sir Digby and Lady Pargiter's cab had joined 'the long line of cabs, taking people in evening dress to plays, to dinner-parties, that was streaming towards the Marble Arch' (p. 140). In the 1910 section we are told that Kitty's own car has to join 'the long line of cars' making its way towards Covent Garden (p. 194). The fact that Digby and Eugénie's carriage has been replaced by Kitty's car illustrates, without comment, the kind of changes which have been taking place almost imperceptibly over the years.

The description of Eugénie wearing a flower in the front of her dress (p. 140) comes to mind in the scene towards the end of the novel when Eleanor looks at a young girl 'fastening a flower that had come undone in the front of her frock' (p. 409). Similarly, the gesture with which Eugénie puts the camellia which Abel gives her between her lips (p. 127) is echoed when she rescues Maggie's flower from the bedroom floor in the 1907 section (p. 150) and again when Kitty puts a flower which she has picked to her lips as she walks round her husband's estate (p. 300). Similarly, the dignified movement with which Eugénie flings out her hand (p. 131) is consciously imitated by Eleanor (p. 164), so that we recognise it as a distinct trait of Eugénie's character. There is a hint of this movement in the violent gesture with which Eleanor tears a newspaper in half in anger at its contents (p. 356).

The phrase 'eight-fifteen means eight-thirty' (p. 141), which Eugénie uses to calm her husband's anxiety that they will be late for a party, is echoed later when Martin remarks to himself in similar circumstances that 'eight-thirty means eight-forty-five' (p. 267). When Digby reproaches his wife for her absent-mindedness over the new lock for the kitchen door, Eugénie replies, 'I will tie a knot in my handkerchief' (p. 156). The metaphor recurs during Eleanor's conversation with Peggy about Runcorn's boy (p. 355; see also p. 438), and is also echoed in Nicholas's comment that people live 'screwed up into one hard little, tight little – knot' (p. 319). It is brought to mind, too, by the phrase which North uses to describe his sense of inadequacy at his aunt's party: 'But it was difficult to speak to a man whom he did not know, and say: "What's this knot in the middle of my forehead? Untie it" ' (p. 447). In a similar way, the blue shade which Woolf describes in Kitty's compartment of the night train (p. 292) reappears later as a metaphor in Peggy's mind.[77] Thinking of the suffering in the world, she wishes 'that there were blinds like those in railway carriages that came down over the light and hooded the mind' (p. 419). The episode, recalled by North, in which Eleanor shows him her new shower (p. 331) recurs later as a metaphor in his mind. As he discusses Africa with Edward, he asks himself: 'Why can't he flow? Why can't he pull the string of the shower bath' (p. 441).[78] Similarly, the scene in which the child, Rose, gives her nurse the slip (pp. 25–30) reappears as the metaphor which Kitty uses to capture the excitement both of visiting the Robsons in 1880 and of escaping from her party in the 1914 section of the novel (pp. 75, 291).

The song which Martin sings to himself as he walks away from the house in Browne Street (p. 159) comes back to him after he leaves his own house in Ebury Street six years later (pp. 242, 243), and again, later on the same day whilst he is with his cousin Sara (p. 252). He becomes self-conscious at the thought that Sara has overheard him singing to himself. The idea that people talk to themselves, but are embarrassed at being seen to do so, is often repeated in the novel. In the 1891 chapter, Eleanor catches herself talking aloud in an omnibus (p. 108). Later, as she reads a letter from her brother Martin, she repeats a phrase from it – 'They died away' – out loud. Rose, too, standing in an alcove overlooking the Thames, suddenly exclaims to herself, 'Damned humbugs', so that a passing clerk looks at her with surprise (p. 174).[79] Sara is standing talking to herself on the steps of St Paul's Cathedral when her cousin Martin catches sight of her (p. 245). Later, when Sara lags behind him to tie her shoelace, Martin finds that he is talking to himself (p. 255). Sara's remark that 'they all do it' seems to be justified when, shortly after, two ladies pass them, each talking to herself (pp. 256, 258), and later, Martin again catches Sara thinking out loud (p. 260). Crosby, living alone in her room in Richmond, carries on an angry conversation with herself as she crosses the Green on the way to the shops (p. 325). Through repeated references in the novel to individuals who talk to themselves, Woolf draws attention to the fact that one can only recognise one's own experience when it is expressed in terms of a common language.[80] Even when one is thinking to oneself, one must invent an imaginary listener with whom to communicate.

The Years, then, asserts the social nature of both language and experience.

The question of the relationship between the individual and society surfaces at specific moments in the novel. The problem, 'Was solitude good; was society bad' (p. 333) is one which confronts North, in particular, on his return to England from Africa. It is recalled in the lines from Marvell which he quotes to Sara: 'Society is all but rude – / To this delicious solitude' (p. 365), and is reiterated in his thoughts at Delia's party: 'Never have I felt so lonely. . . . The old platitude about solitude in a crowd was true' (p. 435). North recollects a remark made by someone earlier in the day that 'solitude . . . is the worst torture . . . that human beings can inflict' (p. 458; see also p. 333). Certainly the life which Crosby leads after her retirement seems to support this idea. North's own loneliness stems largely from the fact that he has no common experience to share with the people he meets. He is an outsider, unable to understand the private jokes being made all around him:

> He overheard scraps of talk. That's Oxford, that's Harrow, he continued, recognising the tricks of speech that were caught at school and college. It seemed to him that they were still cutting little private jokes about Jones minor winning the long jump; and old foxy, or whatever the headmaster's name was. (pp. 435–6)

The concept of private jokes, and particularly family jokes, is one which recurs throughout the novel. The joke is, of course, one obvious 'trick of speech' whereby a collection of individuals creates a sense of community. Jokes are important not so much because of their content, as because they enable particular groups within society to establish a sense of solidarity. Delia, seeing her mother chuckling to herself as she lies in bed, imagines that she is remembering 'some long-past family joke' (p. 25). The phrase, 'Eleanor's broody. It's her Grove day' (p. 31), is a family joke which Rose and Martin recall in the 1908 chapter (p. 169). Mrs Malone has her own wry little joke which she repeats to college visitors staying in the guest room at St Katherine's: 'the bed where Queen Elizabeth did *not* sleep' (p. 62). When Kitty visits the Robson family, she finds herself, like North, excluded by her incomprehension of 'some family joke' which she cannot follow 'about mending boots and hen-coops' (p. 75). Eleanor and her father share a joke about Sanders Curry's gullibility in buying sham oak (p. 112), as Eleanor recalls when she drives with Peggy past the house where she, Morris and Abel Pargiter had formerly dined with the judge (p. 358). Later, at Delia's party, Edward tells his sister about a self-made railway magnate he knows who is fond of buying old masters. Eleanor's response, 'shams, I should think' (p. 445), echoes her father's comment about Sanders Curry's old oak, 'All shams I suspect' (p. 112).

Eleanor, sitting with her brother in the drawing-room at Abercorn Terrace, is struck by the impossibility of ever discussing anything important with him, echoing Ralph Denham's feelings about his family: 'That was the worst of growing up, she thought; they couldn't share things as they used to share them' (p. 35). Remembering jokes is one way in which the adults in the novel try to communicate with one another. It is largely through memories that the brothers and sisters, Eleanor and Morris, Rose and Martin, Peggy and North, overcome their sense of disparity. Peggy despises Rose and Martin because their adult relationship depends upon recalling the past. Once they have gone through the 'old-brother-and-sister turn' of such recollections, they can only 'go back and repeat the same thing over again' (p. 387). Peggy and her brother, however, actually communicate in exactly the same way. Peggy finds it extremely difficult to express her own feelings about the world to her brother. She is overcome by the sense of 'the nearness of human beings and their distance, so that if one meant to help one hurt' (p. 428).[81] Only by remembering the past are the two able to gloss over the emotional distance between them: 'They had to fall back on childish slang, on childish memories, to cover their distance, their hostility' (p. 426). One such memory is of the night when, Peggy says, 'I let myself out of the window by a rope' (p. 426), and it reminds the reader of the period when Eleanor, staying with her brother's family in Dorset, hears a board creak outside her bedroom and thinks: 'Peggy, was it, escaping, to join her brother? She felt sure there was some scheme on foot' (p. 228).

Peggy's unsuccessful attempt to put her feelings into words at Delia's party finds its parallel in Nicholas's abortive efforts to make a speech, both at the party (p. 448), and also during the 'Raid Scene' when he is interrupted by René (p. 316). The language of Peggy's speech bears, she feels, very little relation to the ideas she wishes to express. None the less, her feeling is eventually communicated to her brother. He understands that 'It was what she meant that was true . . . her feeling, not her words' (p. 456). The exact substance of Peggy's speech is no more important than that of the various family jokes in the novel. What matters is her 'attempt to communicate'.[82] This idea is supported by the incident involving the caretaker's two children. When Martin asks the children to speak, they remain silent (p. 463). When they finally decide to communicate with the adults in the room, it is to sing a song which remains unintelligible to the entire assembled company (p. 463). Eleanor is struck by the 'contrast between their faces and their voices' (p. 465). Searching for a word to describe their performance, she alights on the adjective 'beautiful' (p. 465). Although Maggie outwardly agrees with Eleanor's choice of adjective, Eleanor is by no means convinced that she and her cousin mean exactly the same thing when they use the word (p. 465). Thus Eleanor's ability to speak clearly puts her at no great advantage over the children whose words remain inaudible. In both cases – though in differing degrees – the meaning must be taken on trust.

This idea that it is impossible to communicate the whole of one's experience to another person is, of course, extremely important to Woolf. Notwithstanding her recognition of the vagueness of language, and the scope implicit in it for misunderstanding, however, she emphasises the importance of at least attempting to communicate with one another. Although Nicholas does not make a speech, Kitty is anxious that he should tell her privately what he had intended to say in public (p. 459). The value of such private conversations is suggested at several points in the novel. When Maggie and Martin talk together in Hyde Park, whilst Sara and the baby sleep beside them, 'the presence of the two sleepers' seems, we are told, 'to enclose them in a circle of privacy' (p. 264). Eleanor and Nicholas have a comparable sense of 'talking, privately, together' (p. 319), after the air-raid in the 1917 chapter, so that Eleanor is startled when Maggie suddenly joins in their conversation. Maggie and North, too, feel that they are 'alone together, in private' (p. 408), when Eleanor falls asleep beside them at her sister's party.[83] The phrase 'alone together' captures what is important in the intimacy of conversation between two people, namely, the opportunity which it presents for confession and self-revelation which is at once public, yet private. It is this opportunity which Morris seizes when he finds his sister alone in the family sitting-room at Abercorn Terrace (p. 34). Eleanor, too, hopes that her brother will be on his own, when she comes down to dinner in the house in Dorset (p. 213), and North is irritated when, on arriving at Sara's flat, he hears her speaking on the telephone, and concludes that she has company, whereas he 'had hoped to find her alone' (p. 335). Similarly, Abel Pargiter is disappointed in his hope of remaining alone with Eugénie, so that they can discuss his affair with Mira (p. 136). Like Martin, at the end of Kitty's party, he senses that his hostess has her own life to lead, and wants him to go (p. 286). Rose, too, is thwarted in her hope that Maggie alone will accompany her to a political meeting (p. 187). It is Sara who accepts her invitation, whereas 'It was Maggie she wanted to come'. Kitty, likewise, deplores the fact that the brief conversation which she holds with Eleanor as they drive together through London is brought to an abrupt close when they arrive at the station (p. 194).[84]

The contrast between youth and age suggested by the novel's title and structure is specifically noted by different characters in *The Years*.[85] Kitty feels a moment's pity for the young girl, Ann Hillier, at her dinner party, when she compares her with the older generation represented by Aunt Warburton (p. 280). North expresses a similar pity for the girl at his aunt's party who is so soon to lose her loveliness (p. 409). Martin, looking at Maggie's baby asleep in Hyde Park, is struck by the thought that it will have to suffer in the same way that he himself has suffered (p. 265). The children in the park remind him of his first glimpse of Sally, 'asleep in her perambulator in the hall in Browne Street' (p. 261). The 'perambulator in the hall' which Eleanor glimpses as she arrives at her cousin Maggie's house (p. 302) is now used by the next generation.

As a young girl, watching from her bedroom window in the house in Browne Street, Sara seems to see a young man in the garden of the house opposite stoop and pick up something which is gleaming in the grass (p. 144). She imagines him saying to the lady beside him, 'Behold, Miss Smith, what I have found on the grass – a fragment of my heart; of my broken heart.' When her sister returns from her party, later in the evening, Sara asks, 'Did anybody give you a piece of glass . . . saying to you, Miss Pargiter . . . [Woolf's ellipsis] my broken heart?' (p. 148). In the 1910 section, when Sara is threatened with the loneliness consequent upon her sister's marriage, she comes to associate this phrase with René's proposal to Maggie (p. 201).

The idea of lamps being lit which is linked with Rose's experience on the way back from Lamley's toyshop ('The lamplighter was poking his stick up into the little trap-door' – p. 27) reappears in connection with certain other incidents in the novel. Like the recurrent image of violets, the repetition serves to connect these different episodes in the mind of the reader. Eleanor, visiting her sister Delia's flat, associates the lamplight with the sinister aspects of London life:

The streets they were driving through were horribly poor; and not only poor, she thought, but vicious. Here was the vice, the obscenity, the reality of London. It was lurid in the mixed evening light. Lamps were being lit.   (p. 121)

When Maggie and Sara watch from their window a drunken man being turned out of a public house, the scene is, similarly, 'lit up by the glare of the lamp over the public house door' (p. 203).

As Rose Pargiter makes her way to Lamley's toyshop, she imagines herself 'riding by night on a desperate mission to a besieged garrison' (p. 27). North uses the same metaphor to describe his sensation as he follows René to Delia's party: 'he felt . . . as if he were riding to the relief of a besieged garrison across a desert' (p. 376). The source of this feeling is René's emphatic remark about going to the party, 'We must – we must' (p. 376), which is itself echoed later in the novel, as the group delays before going into the building where the party is taking place: 'Come, we must' (p. 392).

The 1891 chapter of The Years includes an incident in which Abel Pargiter shouts at his cab driver because he is about to take a wrong turning (p. 124). This scene is reflected in the 'Present Day' chapter when the cab in which Eleanor and Peggy are travelling also takes a wrong turn (p. 363). Eleanor's calm indifference to the consequent delay is, however, in marked contrast with her father's anger in the earlier scene. The idea of a cab taking the long way round recurs when Delia describes how she deliberately instructs her driver to do this, in order that she may avoid passing her childhood home (p. 450). This passage in turn recalls Kitty's memory of her father, going the long way round to avoid the ugly red-brick villas in one of which Lucy Craddock lives (p. 67).

Kitty's dislike at being forced to show her father's visitors around the more presentable areas of Oxford (p. 62) is mirrored in Sara's memory of a visit to Edward. He had given her a copy of his *Antigone* 'one hot afternoon when they had been trailing through libraries and chapels' (p. 145).

In the 1880 section Kitty to some extent shares her mother's disapproval at the sight of the 'number of little pots and jars and a large powder-puff stained pink' which cover Mrs Howard Fripps's dressing-table (p. 63). But in 1914, Kitty's own dressing-table has become cluttered with 'silver pots, powder puffs, combs and brushes' (p. 287). Through this change in Kitty's outlook Woolf suggests the way in which attitudes in general have altered over three and a half decades. In the 'Present Day' section, for example, Eleanor is intrigued, rather than shocked, to observe that her niece Peggy paints her face (p. 371).

The 'famous Gainsborough' in Lord Lasswade's London house (p. 272) brings to mind 'the Gainsborough that was not quite certainly a Gainsborough' in the Master's Lodge at St Katharine's (p. 76). Martin remarks upon the contrast between this picture and the portrait of Kitty which he considers a 'horrid daub' (pp. 283, 284). (The references to Kitty's portrait recall the portrait of Rose Pargiter which dominates the opening chapter of the novel. Both paintings depict a young girl holding a basket of flowers.)[86] Woolf compares the gesture with which the women rise from Kitty's dinner table with the attitudes of the women in the Gainsborough (p. 275). Kitty likens the gentlemen arriving in the drawing-room to 'gulls settling on fish' (p. 281), thereby recalling the scene in Hyde Park, earlier in the day, in which Maggie and Martin had watched an old lady feeding fish to the gulls (p. 264). The activity which follows upon the arrival of Ann Hillier's mother is also compared with 'the flutter of white-winged gulls' (p. 285). The 'man in gold lace', who arrives at Kitty's party shortly after Martin, has a counterpart in the 'man in gold lace' next to whom Maggie sits at the party in 1891 (pp. 269, 148).

As Kitty settles down to sleep on the night train northward, after her party, she sees 'the tea-urn sliding past' and then: 'lights in factories and warehouses; lights in obscure back streets. Then there were asphalt paths; more lights in public gardens; and then bushes and a hedge in a field' (p. 291). These images refer back to the opening passage of the 1911 chapter, with its description of the numerous trains setting off from stations 'to bore their way through England':

> Now the guard standing with his hand raised dropped his flag and the tea-urn slid past. Off the trains swung through the public gardens with asphalt paths; past the factories; into open country. (p. 207)

As Kitty falls asleep on the train her thoughts become confused. She sees 'Margaret Marrable pinching the dress in her fingers, but she was leading a bull with a ring through its nose' (p. 293). The first image refers to the incident earlier in the evening in which Lady Margaret had felt 'the folds of golden satin' of a young woman's dress (p. 277). The second recalls the time when old Carter 'leading a bull with a ring through its nose' came upon Kitty and the farm hand Alf. It is a memory which she recalls when she meets Jo Robson in the 1880 section (p. 75), and again during the opera in 1910 (p. 198). The gesture with which Kitty kicks off her white satin shoes after her party (p. 288) also refers back to this opening chapter, where she makes a similar movement after dinner in the Master's Lodge (p. 64). We are again reminded of this scene when Patrick complains at his wife's party that his shoes are too tight, and Kitty advises him to 'Kick 'em off' (p. 434).

During Delia's party, Kitty remarks that as a girl she would 'have given anything to be a farmer' (p. 432). To North, her comment is incongruous with her status as widow to the Governor-General. To the reader, in contrast, it is Kitty's eminence and respectability in her old age which seem to be a betrayal of her youthful dreams and hopes. Kitty's early love of the countryside is, however, echoed in her enthusiasm for gardening (p. 425) and also in two separate incidents in which she expresses regret that flowers should be kept inside (p. 276, 430). At the end of the novel, Delia remarks upon Maggie's beautiful arrangement of some of these flowers (p. 469). Her comment brings to mind the scene earlier in the narrative in which Maggie arranges the flowers on the table in the sisters' flat, before Rose arrives for lunch (p. 175). There is a further echo of this scene when North, visiting Sara on his return from Africa, notices that her flat is bare of flowers (p. 335) – a small detail which serves to suggest the discrepancy between the warmth of the sisters' life together and the poverty of Sara's solitary existence. The two scenes are also linked through the description in both the 1910 and the 'Present Day' sections of glasses jingling on the table as traffic passes by in the street outside (pp. 180, 343). The opening and closing chapters of *The Years* are, similarly, connected through the invitation to his home for 'cubbing in September' which in 1880 Hugh Gibbs extends to Edward Pargiter (p. 55) and in the final chapter to North (p. 404).

The air-raid which interrupts the dinner party in 1917 recalls the way in which Rose's fainting fit disrupts the Pargiter family's meal in 1880 (p. 37). During the raid Eleanor counts the seconds between the booming of the guns, 'One, two, three, four' (p. 313). The same counting rhythm is used in the opening section of the novel, where Woolf describes how throughout London, 'virgins and spinsters . . . carefully measured out one, two, three, four spoonfuls of tea' (p. 2). Eleanor herself becomes representative of such 'virgins and spinsters' when, later in the novel, Woolf describes how, 'Stretching out towards the tea-caddy, she measured the tea. "One, two, three, four," she counted' (p. 163). Rose uses the same sequence as she tries to count sheep, 'One, two, three, four', in order to rid her mind of the idea of the strange man's face (p. 41). Similarly, Peggy counts the stars, 'one, two, three, four', in an attempt to put the egotistical young man with whom she has been talking at Delia's party out of her mind (p. 390).

In the course of a conversation with her niece, Peggy, Eleanor asks her: ' "D'you know the feeling when one's been on the point of saying something, and been interrupted; how it seems to stick *here*," she tapped her forehead, "so that it stops everything else" ' (p. 351). North shares this experience when, at Delia's party, he looks at his wine-glass and tries to remember what he had been thinking about before as he 'watched the bubbles rising in the yellow liquid' (p. 442): 'A block had formed in his forehead as if two thoughts had collided and had stopped the passage of the rest' (p. 446).

When Sara tries to describe the Pargiter family to her cousin Rose, she thinks of them as 'going on and on and on' (p. 182). The same phrase occurs to Martin as he listens to the old gentleman telling an anecdote about Ireland, at Kitty's dinner-party. 'Here we are', he thinks, 'going on and on and on' (p. 273). The words at the beginning of the gentleman's story refer back to the opening chapter of the novel: 'When I was in Ireland . . . in 1880' (p. 273).

The description of the old gentleman telling his after-dinner anecdote is one amongst numerous references to stories and story-telling in *The Years*, through which Woolf puts across obliquely her own view that in describing a particular experience one inevitably simplifies it and makes it conform to a familiar, or acceptable, narrative pattern. She felt that a similar process underlies one's response to other people. In reacting to people, one tends to reduce them to 'types' and discount their individuality, projecting one's own ideas of them on to them.[87]

Fictions

An obvious example of this tendency to simplify or parody other people in order to be able to classify, or pigeon-hole, them comes in the passage already quoted describing how the man on whose toe Eleanor treads in a bus 'sized her up; a well-known type; with a bag; philanthropic; well-nourished; a spinster; a virgin; like all the women of her class, cold; her passions had never been touched; yet not unattractive' (p. 108). As we have seen, Woolf herself uses the phrase 'virgins and spinsters' in the opening passage of the novel. When, in the 'Present Day' section, Peggy tries to make her aunt conform to such a phrase, she discovers that Eleanor's individuality belies such classification. Peggy cannot reduce her aunt's life to a story which can be told easily to her friend at the hospital, a collection of little facts about her 'to add to her portrait of a Victorian spinster' (p. 359).[88] She is forced to admit that this portrait has very little to do with her aunt's complex personality and history, and dismisses her own attempt to grasp Eleanor's character, with the thought that 'She's not like that – not like that at all' (p. 360). Through Peggy, then, Woolf puts across the idea which dominates *The Voyage Out* that the lives of apparently obscure women cannot be summed up and dismissed through simplistic caricature.

During Delia's party Peggy returns to the idea of the discrepancy between her own 'fact-collecting' about other people, and the complex and often enigmatic nature of individuals' personalities. As she watches her aunt Delia moving about the room, she asks herself: 'What do I know about her? That she's wearing a dress with gold spots; has wavy hair, that was red, is white; is hand-some; ravaged; with a past. But what past?' (p. 380).[89] It is the individual's past, which can never be completely remembered, let alone communicated to others, which remains hidden and mysterious. Eleanor repeatedly returns to the idea of the difference between her 'internal' view of herself, and the image which she presents to the outside world. For example, when, during her visit to Dorset, she expresses an interest in the white owl which flies past the house in the evening, she thinks to herself: 'But now I'm labelled . . . an old maid who washes and watches birds. That's what they think I am. But I'm not – I'm not in the least like that, she said' (p. 218). It is the fear of being cast in just such a general mould which prevents Eleanor from buying a house in the country. She feels that if she were to do so, 'I should turn into a grey-haired lady cutting flowers with a pair of scissors and tapping at cottage doors' (p. 209). Through this thought of Eleanor's, Woolf reiterates the idea which she dramatises in *The Voyage Out* that all human lives – including the hidden lives of elderly spinsters – are uniquely important and interesting.

Eleanor recognises that she herself has no very clear conception of her own character. Consequently, she is surprised by other people's willingness to circumscribe and define her life. When, at Delia's party, Sara tells her cousin that she and North have been discussing Eleanor's life, she remarks to herself: 'That was odd, it was the second time that evening that somebody had talked about her life. And I haven't got one, she thought' (p. 395). To Eleanor, her 'life of seventy odd years' is not 'something you could handle and produce', but a collection of disparate 'atoms'.[90] Once again, then, a particular character's thoughts in *The Years* echo remarks which Woolf herself makes elsewhere. Eleanor, like Neville in *The Waves*, considers that it is impossible to unravel her own life from the lives of her friends. Through Eleanor, Woolf dramatises her own theory that 'in some vague way we are the same person, and not separate people'.[91] It is because she recognises the complexity of her own personality that Eleanor is struck by the audacity of the obituaries which claim to tell the story of her uncle Digby's life.[92] After reading them, she can only feel that he was 'not like that in the least' (p. 165). Even Eleanor and her brother Martin, who have supposedly known their uncle well, cannot agree about his character. To Martin, Eugénie is attractive while Digby is simply 'a damned snob' (p. 164). Eleanor, on the other hand, is inclined to dismiss her aunt whilst responding more sympathetically to Digby.

Eleanor is struck by the contrast between their respective ideas of the same people. Thinking about her own childhood and 'Morris and herself, and old Pippy' (p. 317) she realises that were she to attempt to explain her past to other people, no one would understand what she meant. Through Eleanor, Woolf puts across her own belief that the individual must inevitably remain to some extent isolated, because one considers both one's own character and other people from a unique angle. Thus the artist's view of Rose Pargiter, as manifested in her portrait, remains quite unlike Eleanor's memory of her mother (p. 350). Similarly, the idea which Sara and Maggie have of Abercorn Terrace contrasts strongly with Rose's image of her own family. To Rose it seems that her cousins see the life of Abercorn Terrace as if it were a scene in a play: 'They talked as if they were speaking of people who were real, but not real in the way in which she felt herself to be real' (p. 180). Whilst Maggie and Sara can reduce Rose's life to a few simple memories, she herself considers it impossible to tell her own story: 'What is the use, she thought, of trying to tell people about one's past? What is one's past?' (p. 180). Although Rose feels that her own life, and that of her relatives, has been extremely interesting, she is unable to do more than generalise about it: 'What could be more ordinary? . . . A large family, living in a large house' (p. 181).[93] Eleanor, like Rose, recognises the inadequacy of the generalisations which one makes about the lives of other people. In an attempt to explain this point of view to her nephew, North, she remarks: 'old age they say is like this; but it isn't. It's different; quite different. So when I was a child; so when I was a girl; it's been a perpetual discovery, my life. A miracle' (p. 413).

Sara Pargiter is one amongst those visionary characters in Woolf's novels, like Lily Briscoe in *To the Lighthouse* and Rhoda in *The Waves*, who are unable to reduce the miracle of their own experience to the conventional narrative patterns adopted by society. The 'fictions' which Sara weaves (when she recounts her day to Maggie (p. 201), for example, or when she relates the events of her life to North (p. 366)) are far less stereotyped than the stories which the other characters tell. Sara – like Rachel Vinrace (*The Voyage Out*, p. 359) – wants to dispense with accepted phrases in order to express her own experience more completely. Whereas in *The Waves* it is the narrator who exploits metaphorical language in an attempt to capture the 'authenticity' of experience, in *The Years* it is Sara alone who makes this attempt. Sara's critical stance makes her unwilling to conform not only to linguistic, but also to social norms. Martin is embarrassed when, lunching with Sara in a London restaurant, she refuses to play the appropriate part. Only, finally, in deference to Martin himself does she adopt 'the manner of a lady lunching with a gentleman in a City restaurant' (p. 247). This episode has its counterpart in that restaurant scene in *The Waves* in which Bernard parodies the type of fictional narrative which we traditionally impose upon experience, relating his own story in deliberately conventional terms:

> The handsome man in the grey suit . . . now brushed the crumbs from his waistcoat and, with a characteristic gesture at once commanding and benign, made a sign to the waiter, who came instantly and returned a moment later with the bill discreetly folded upon a plate.[94]

In *The Years*, the narrator consciously adopts the voice of Bernard's mock-narrative. Many phrases in the later novel echo very closely the language of Bernard's parody. One such example is Woolf's description of how, after the meal in the chop-house with Sara, Martin suddenly 'beckoned to the waiter who came with alacrity and totted up the bill' (p. 250).

Just as Sara refuses to conform to accepted social attitudes, so too, she avoids describing people in customary fashion. When Martin asks her to tell him about Maggie's husband René, the description she gives him is not a fluent narrative, but a stringing together of isolated 'atoms': 'His mother was dead. . . . And he was afraid to tell his father that the horse was too big to ride . . . [Woolf's ellipses] and they sent him to England' (p. 257). Martin's curiosity as to why Maggie and René should have married one another remains unappeased because for Sara it is impossible to give a definitive account of another person's motives. Eleanor shares Sara's reticence over placing and defining other people. She is struck, for example, by the impossibility of analysing Nicholas's character. She can only think of him 'in the lump; she could not break off little fragments' (p. 397), and she asks herself: 'If I can't describe my own life . . . how can I describe him?' (p. 398). Just as Eleanor recognises the impossibility of reducing her own personality to a simple formula, so too she is unwilling to label other people. In the opening section, for example, we are told that: 'Eleanor did not like talking about "the poor" as if they were people in a book. She had a great admiration for Mrs Levy, who was dying of cancer' (p. 31). Being intimately involved with the people for whom she works, Eleanor cannot, like the rest of her family, see them merely as 'types' any more than she can see herself as 'an old maid' or 'a Victorian spinster'. In contrast, her brother Martin is content to assign his dinner companion at Kitty's party to a 'pigeon-hole'.[95] When she mentions the name of her aunt, he proceeds to classify her: 'Oh she's your aunt, is she? he said. He placed her. So *that* was her world' (p. 275). North, on the other hand, recognises the fact – one which is repeatedly asserted in *The Waves* – that individuals invent stories about other people to suit their own ends.[96] When North tells Sara that she has a smudge on her face, he notices that she leaves the room without looking in the mirror:

> From which we deduce the fact, he said to himself, that Miss Sara Pargiter has never attracted the love of men. Or had she? He did not know. These little snapshot pictures of people left much to be desired . . . (p. 341)

Later in the novel Peggy, listening to her uncle Patrick's stories about Ireland, sums them up in the idea of 'a faded snapshot of cricketers' (p. 380). In so doing, she alights upon what is general, rather than specific, in her uncle's history. North, returning to London society after years in Africa, is amazed at his friends' propensity to sum one another up.[97] He likens the superficial portraits which they paint of each other to the activities of a crawling fly (pp. 337, 341). When Sara describes him as 'My cousin from Africa' (p. 336), he remarks ironically to himself, 'That's my label'. The comment recalls Eleanor's reluctance to be labelled as an 'old maid'. Nevertheless, North recognises that reasonable social intercourse depends to a certain extent upon such 'ready-made' phrases (p. 332). He himself adopts the phrase 'money and politics' (p. 431) to protect himself from the exposure of being at a loss for words. His choice of phrase, however, has the effect of determining and circumscribing the way in which he sees the world.

It is the fact that the leading article in the newspaper 'rewrites' experience from a particular angle which makes it attractive to Mrs Malone. To Kitty, the article is merely boring in its 'pompous fluency' (p. 83), but her mother finds it comforting because it confirms her own attitudes and prejudices; in part, no doubt, because it has also formed them. To accept newspapers as vehicles of 'objective truth' is to fail to distinguish between a narrative which has been imposed upon experience, and the original event itself.

Abel Pargiter's stories are attractive to Delia not because they are truthful, but for the rather sentimental picture of life in India which they evoke (p. 37), and Peggy finds Eleanor's stories about her past reassuring precisely because they are unreal (pp. 351, 358). Eleanor, in contrast, is reluctant to tell such stories because, she feels, they bear only a slight relation to 'the truth'. Similarly, the story which Eugénie tells Maggie and Sara of how, in her youth, she 'danced out of the house onto the terrace and found a little note folded in [her] bouquet' (p. 153), which Sara finds so attractive, is not the 'true story'. The truth about her love-life is hinted at by Martin when he asks his sister Eleanor: 'Wasn't there some story . . . about a letter?' (p. 165).

Peggy attributes Eleanor's inability to order her thoughts and to keep to the point in conversation to her age. The elderly Eleanor's rambling speech (pp. 350, 353) is, however, consistent with her belief that any fluent narrative which one imposes upon experience must be a fiction. (We have seen that when Peggy herself attempts to express her view of life to the company at Delia's party, the 'speech' she makes has little to do with her original feeling – p. 421.) The story which Martin relates in his letter to Eleanor about his experience in India has a fluency which must be at odds with the complexity of the incident itself. Most of the characters in *The Years* interpret their own lives in terms of conventional stories. When Martin talks to his cousin Maggie about his love-affair (in an echo of Abel's visit to Eugénie), it is of 'his story; the story of the lady' that he speaks. Similarly, his account of his father's relationship with Mira takes the form of 'the story of the lady who kept a boarding house at Putney' (p. 265). The elderly gentleman at Kitty's party has, too – like Sir William Whatney (p. 216) – reduced his own experience to an easily communicable after-dinner anecdote: 'He spoke very simply; he was offering them a memory; he told his story perfectly; it held its meaning without spilling a single drop. And he had played a great part' (p. 273).[98] The old gentleman's story is a carefully ordered portrayal of himself which probably owes as much to imagination as the young Rose's projection of herself into the role of 'Uncle Pargiter of Pargiter's Horse'. Aunt Warburton is also careful of the effect of her life story upon her audience, and manipulates the events of her life accordingly: 'The old lady began making a selection from her memories; it was only a selection; an edition with asterisks; for it was a story that could hardly be told to a girl in white satin' (p. 280). North's accounts of his life-style in Africa in his letters to Sara are, similarly, consciously edited versions of his experience. He remembers later that 'There were some things he had not told her' (p. 344) and mocks the extravagance of those youthful 'purple passages' (p. 347).

The limitations of language are felt by North when, in the 'Present Day' section, he tries to describe Africa to his relatives (p. 391).[99] North admires his uncle Edward because the latter leaves his sentences unfinished (p. 438), thereby acknowledging the impossibility of expressing his whole meaning in words. Peggy, however, recognises the value of her own struggle to express her feelings about life, even though she fails, as she thinks, to do so: 'She had not said it, but she had tried to say it' (p. 422). (One is reminded of Lily's attempt to express her vision in *To the Lighthouse*.) Even Kitty Malone, who finds solitude incomparably more attractive than society, recognises the importance of the efforts which people make to communicate with one another. As she watches Aunt Warburton talking with a distinguished old man at her party, she feels that:

> there was something – was it human? civilised? she could not find the word she wanted – about the old couple, talking, as they had talked for the past fifty years. . . . They were all talking. They had all settled in to add another sentence to the story that was just ending, or in the middle, or about to begin . . . (p. 281; Woolf's ellipsis)

It is the act of talking which matters, rather than the words themselves. Peggy's 'speech', for example, seems to her to fall completely wide of its mark, and her meaning certainly remains initially unintelligible to her brother North. After a time, however, the sense behind her speech becomes plain to him in spite of the words: 'It was what she meant that was true, he corrected himself; her feeling, not her words. He felt her feeling now; it was not about him; it was about other people; about another world, a new world' (p. 456).

In *The Waves*, Woolf uses Bernard to put across her own belief that it is impossible to communicate all that we experience to others. The repeated references in *The Years* to fictions in the lives and thoughts of the novel's characters serve to draw attention obliquely to the same idea. The novel suggests that one's impressions of other people's lives are always and inevitably caricatures, thereby illustrating the argument put forward in *Three Guineas* that complete understanding between people can never be achieved, because each is bound by the limits of his or her unique personality and experience: 'mutual understanding could only be achieved by blood transfusion and memory transfusion'.[100] The emphasis within each novel is, however, slightly different. Whereas in *The Waves* Woolf focuses upon what she sees as the divorce between conventional language and the experience of the individual, the stress in *The Years* falls upon the fact that experience can, up to a point, be shared through a common language, and, indeed, that it is in articulating experience that it becomes 'real'. Language may be vague, and therefore open to a range of interpretations, but it is the product of a speech-community, and as such it is irrevocably bound up with the shared experiences of that community.

Woolf described her own intention for *The Years* in a diary entry for 25 April 1933:

> there are to be millions of ideas but no preaching – history, politics, feminism, art, literature – in short a summing up of all I know, feel, laugh at, despise, like, admire hate & so on.[101]

She rejected the original conception of *The Years* (as the 'essay-novel' *The Pargiters*) because in working on the novel she came to mistrust the overt authorial presence – the 'preaching' – of that work. In the published version of the novel, Woolf exploits the familiarity of the 'realist' genre in order to put across as persuasively as possible her own ideas about society. As in *The Voyage Out* and *Night and Day*, in *The Years* she uses repetitions and parallels to draw attention to ideas which are particularly important to her, and these repeated phrases, images and ideas are integrated into the novel in such a way as to appear 'natural'. Thus, although Woolf implicitly directs the reader's response to her narrative, we remain under the illusion while reading that we are responding freely and independently to her fictional characters. Moreover, because Woolf creates the impression that the repetitive patterns in *The Years* are 'natural', the reader is encouraged to share her belief in a corresponding structure and order beneath the whole of experience.

Woolf's modernist fiction, and particularly *The Waves*, reflects the contempt which she shares with dramatists like Brecht for the uncritical reader who accepts literary conventions unquestioningly. In *The Years*, on the other hand, Woolf deliberately adopted the 'realist' mode, thereby encouraging the reader to sympathise and identify unselfconsciously with her fictional characters. Implicit in this choice of narrative method for *The Years* is a deliberate political (and artistic) strategy. Woolf recognised the potential in the 'realist' novel for disseminating theoretical, and particularly feminist, ideas amongst a possibly hostile readership. The fact that *The Years* quickly became a best-seller in America, whilst *Three Guineas* remained relatively unpopular, attests to the shrewdness of Woolf's judgement.[102]

5
Conclusion

In conclusion, we should perhaps consider briefly, in the light of the foregoing discussion, certain criticisms levelled at Woolf by Elaine Showalter and Patricia Stubbs respectively in *A Literature of their Own* (1978) and *Women and Fiction* (1979).[1]

Showalter's argument rests on her belief that the carefully culti-vated impersonality of *A Room*, like that of Woolf's fiction, is a sign of weakness and timidity on the part of a writer who was all too aware of the price which women like Charlotte Brontë had paid for their outspokenness in literature.[2] *A Room* is, she suggests, 'an extremely impersonal and defensive book':

> Impersonality may seem like the wrong word for a book in which a narrative 'I' appears in every third sentence. But a closer look reveals that the 'I' is a persona whom the author calls 'Mary Beton', and that her views are carefully distanced and depersonalized, just as the pronoun 'one' in the title deperson-alizes, and even de-sexes, the subject. The whole book is cast in arch allegorical terms from the start . . . In fact the characters and places are all disguised or delicately parodied versions of Woolf's own experience.[3]

It seems, Showalter argues, 'like a rationalisation of her own fears that Woolf should have developed a literary theory that makes anger and protest flaws in art', and she suggests that Woolf's concept of 'androgyny' was in fact 'the myth that helped her evade confrontation with her own painful femaleness and enabled her to choke and repress her anger and ambition'.[4] As we have seen, however, it was Woolf's view that the theoretical ideas which are embodied in a work of fiction are the more likely to be taken on board by the (possibly sceptical) reader if he or she does not feel that they are being foisted upon them. Whilst the sympathetic reader may respond favourably to the revolutionary (in both aesthetic and political terms) in literature, a work which entertains, and with whose fictional characters one can easily identify, will have a much wider appeal and popularity.

Showalter's attack in fact fails to do justice to the sophistication of Woolf's art. That Woolf was quite capable of producing powerful and direct criticism of patriarchal society is illustrated by *Three Guineas*.[5] It was not, then, simply fear for her own reputation in polite society, as Showalter implies, which led her to avoid adopting an angry, bitter tone in her writing. Rather, she felt that the novel cannot be both 'the dumping ground for the personal emotions' and a compelling vehicle of political ideas.

Patricia Stubbs's criticisms of Woolf also centre on *A Room*. Stubbs argues that in her own novels Woolf fails to put into practice the narrative approach which she advocates so convincingly in that essay. The essay, as we have seen, draws attention to the fact that in the past women have been portrayed in literature exclusively in terms of their emotional lives and their relationships with men. Woolf urges modern novelists to counter this misplaced emphasis by focusing upon the whole of women's lives in their fiction. Stubbs, though, maintains that 'when it came to her own novels she failed to carry out the tranformation of women's image which she knew was necessary and which she herself seemed well-equipped to attempt':

> there is no coherent attempt to create new models, new images of women. The feminism is only ever a small part of the novels . . . Nor does she bring before us that 'accumulation of unrecorded life' (*A Room of One's Own*, p. 89) which she wanted to see break in on the novel's traditional indifference to women's everyday experience.[6]

Our discussion of Woolf's 'dramatic' novels would seem to undercut Stubbs's argument. An examination of Woolf's first novel, for example, reveals that in *The Voyage Out* Woolf produced a work of fiction which, although contained within an essentially 'realist' framework, none the less deliberately disappoints some of the reader's traditional expectations. What appears at first sight to be a conventional novel of courtship and marriage is in fact something wholly different and considerably more exciting. Although Rachel's relationship with Terence Hewet does, as Stubbs suggests, play a part in *The Voyage Out*, the novel is, at a deeper level, concerned with relations between the individual – and particularly the woman – and society. *The Voyage Out* is not simply another novel about falling in love, although it draws upon certain conventions associated with that type of fiction. Where it differs from *Night and Day* is in the degree to which it expands the boundaries of the 'realist' form.

In *The Years*, similarly, Woolf produced a novel which deals with the everyday lives of women within the community as a whole, and in which the question of these women's sexual and emotional relationships remains peripheral.[7] As in *The Voyage Out*, Woolf exploits the 'realist' form for tactical reasons. What makes *The Years* exciting, however, is the tension between its dependence on the 'realist' tradition in fiction, and the originality of the ideas contained within it.

Stubb's criticisms of Woolf are based on a belief that 'her artistic theories could not comfortably accommodate her feminism and that she apparently had to choose between them.'[8] She maintains, then, that in her fiction Woolf fails to reconcile aesthetic and political considerations. The foregoing chapters have shown, however, that in her 'dramatic' novels Woolf adopted the 'realist' mode as the one through which she felt her own feminist ideas could be put across most effectively. Indeed, one could argue that it was her interest in questions of aesthetics which led Woolf to recognise the potential implicit in the 'realist' genre for political persuasion.

It would be a mistake, then, to equate Woolf's concept of 'unconsciousness' in fiction with an absence of social commitment. The illusion of 'unconsciousness', 'impersonality' or 'anonymity' which Woolf creates in *The Voyage Out* and *The Years* (and to a degree in *Night and Day*) is the product not of political indifference but of political strategy. It is because Woolf believes that overt partisanship in the 'realist' novel destroys the illusion of 'naturalism' and thereby alienates the potential convert that she adopts an 'impersonal' approach in her fiction. The reader is encouraged to respond unconsciously to ideas which are embodied, or 'dramatised' in her narrative, ideas which he or she might be inclined to dismiss if they were presented in the form of overt authorial comment. Those critics who have – like the Marxist poets of the 1930s and some feminist writers of more recent years – attacked Woolf for the apparent lack of commitment in her novels, have failed to recognise the motives behind her choice of narrative approach. Ironically enough, Woolf herself would have welcomed the criticism that her 'dramatic' novels seem devoid of political partisanship, as an unconscious tribute to the effectiveness of their method.

Notes

Notes to Chapter One: Introduction

1. Throughout this study the terms 'dramatic' and 'realist' are used in opposition to the terms 'experimental' and 'modernist'. David Lodge focuses upon some of the problems inherent in the use of the term 'realist' when he remarks that, 'We have no term for the kind of modern fiction that is not modernist except "realistic" (sometimes qualified by "traditionally" or "conventionally" or "social"). It makes a confusing and unsatisfactory antithesis to "modernist" because the modernists often claimed to be representing "reality" and indeed to be getting closer to it than the realists' (David Lodge, *The Modes of Modern Writing* (London: Edward Arnold, 1977) p. 46).

2. Ibid., p. 177.

3. Elaine Showalter argues: 'Woolf belonged to a tradition other than modernism and . . . this tradition surfaces in her work precisely in those places where criticism has hitherto found obscurities, evasions, implausibilities, and imperfections' (Elaine Showalter, 'Feminist Criticism in the Wilderness', in *Writing and Sexual Difference*, ed. Elizabeth Abel (Brighton: Harvester, 1982) p. 33).

4. In this context, Stephen Spender remarks of the Imagist Poets:

   They wanted to release poetry from the burden of past conventions and traditional ways of thinking by concentrating upon reproducing the image which springs naked into the mind from the impact of modern life. Yet the most intelligent of them soon realized that poetry could not be completely modern and new in the way that the other arts could be, because it uses as its material words which are old and social, and which only to a limited extent can be used in new ways. The limitation is imposed by the fact that the meaning words have outside the poem has to be maintained – even if it is stretched – within the poem.

   He suggests that what differentiates Joyce from Gertrude Stein, for example, is that whilst Joyce produced a 'literary language', Stein invented a 'non-language' (see Stephen Spender, *The Struggle of the Modern* (London: Hamish Hamilton, 1963) pp. 190, 193).

5. Her strategy resembles that attributed to Marx and Engels by Terry Eagleton:

In a letter of 1885 to Minna Kantsky, who had sent Engels her inept and soggy recent novel, Engels wrote that he was by no means averse to fiction with a political 'tendency', but that it was wrong for an author to be *openly* partisan. The political tendency must emerge unobtrusively from the dramatized situations; only in this indirect way could revolutionary fiction work effectively on the bourgeois consciousness of its readers. . . . Independently of each other, they both criticized Lassalle's verse-drama *Franz von Sickingen* for its lack of a rich Shakespearian realism which would have prevented its characters from being mere mouthpieces of history; and they also accused Lassalle of having selected a protagonist untypical for his purposes. In *The Holy Family* Marx levels a similar criticism at Eugène Sue's best-selling novel *Les Mystères de Paris*, whose two-dimensional characters he sees as insufficiently representative. (Terry Eagleton, *Marxism and Literary Criticism* (London: Methuen, 1976) pp. 46–7)

6. Woolf's 'dramatic' novels, then, correspond to the 'thesis novel' described by Wolfgang Iser which 'allows its reader sufficient latitude to imagine that he is accepting voluntarily an attitude that has in fact been foisted upon him' (Wolfgang Iser, *The Act of Reading* (London: Johns Hopkins University Press, 1978) p. 194).
7. Steve Neale, 'Propaganda', *Screen*, vol. xviii, no. 3 (Autumn 1977) pp. 9–40.
8. Catherine Belsey, *Critical Practice* (London: Methuen, 1980) p. 72.
9. *Letters*, iv, p. 151. All references to the *Diary, Letters* and MSS of Virginia Woolf preserve her eccentric spelling and punctuation.
10. In so far as modernist writers recognise the role played by language in determining the way in which one 'sees the world', they anticipate the interest in the relationship between language and experience generated in more recent years by the work of Wittgenstein and Saussure.
11. Lawrence, too – though scornful towards aestheticism – deplored the public's demand for the familiar in art. In a letter to Edward Marsh of 19 November 1913 he remarked:

If your ear has got stiff and a bit mechanical, *don't* blame my poetry. That's why you like *Golden Journey to Samarkand* – it fits your habituated ear, and your feeling crouches subservient and a bit pathetic. 'It satisfies my ear,' you say. Well, I don't write for your ear. This is the constant war, I reckon, between new expression and the habituated mechanical transmitters and receivers of the human constitution. (Quoted in Spender's *Struggle of the Modern*, p. 104)

12. See, for example, Floris Delattre, 'La Durée Bergsonienne dans le roman de Virginia Woolf', *Revue Anglo-Américaine*, vol. ix, no. 2 (December 1931) pp. 97–108; Floris Delattre, *Le Roman psychologique de Virginia Woolf* (Paris: Librairie Philosophique, 1932) pp. 142–59.

However, George Poulet's study of Proust – *L'Espace Proustien*, trs. E. Coleman (London: Johns Hopkins University Press, 1977, 1st edn 1963) – effectively undermines the idea that *À la recherche du temps perdu* illustrates Bergson's concept of 'la durée'. Joyce Megay's more recent study, *Bergson et Proust* (Paris: Librairie Philosophique, 1976), supports Poulet's thesis.

13. Jonathan Culler, *Saussure* (Brighton: Harvester, 1976) p. 22.
14. Karin Stephen, *The Misuse of Mind: A Study of Bergson's Attack on Intellectualism* (London: Kegan Paul, Trench, Trubner, 1922) p. 42.
15. Ibid., pp. 23–4.
16. Roger Fry, 'An Essay in Aesthetics', *New Quarterly*, vol. II (1909), rptd in his *Vision and Design* (London: Chatto & Windus, 1920) p. 13.
17. Fry, *Vision and Design*, pp. 16–17.
18. Compare Wolfgang Iser's argument that, 'While the structure of everyday experience leads to pragmatic action, that of aesthetic experience serves to reveal the workings of this process' (Iser, *The Act of Reading*, pp. 61, 133).
19. Victor Shklovsky, 'Art as Technique', in *Russian Formalist Criticism: Four Essays*, ed. Lee Lemon and Marion Reis (Lincoln, Nebr.: University of Nebraska Press, 1965) p. 13.
20. Ibid., p. 22.
21. See, for example, *Diary*, III, pp. 123, 128, 139, 177, 185.
22. Marcel Proust, *Remembrance of Things Past*, trans. C. K. Scott Moncrieff and Terence Kilmartin (London: Chatto & Windus, 1981) I, p. 706.
23. *The Waves*, p. 174.
24. See, for example, *Diary*, III, pp. 233, 234, 235.
25. *To the Lighthouse*, p. 294.
26. Proust, *Remembrance of Things Past*, I, pp. 898–9. John Sturrock, in an article on Jakobson and Bakhtin, points to the flaws in this line of argument, as it is applied to literature by formalist critics:

> The Formalists had thought that the great aim of literature was to spring-clean the language and to rid it of its stale and debilitating associations. . . . The point of literature is to make things 'strange', and you cannot do that if the language of literature is so familiar that no one notices it. This, says Bakhtin, is a false materialism of the word. The fact that language is so 'dirty' when it comes into literature is our very reason for esteeming it. (John Sturrock, 'Jamboree', *London Review of Books*, vol. 8, no. 3 (20 February 1986) p. 13)

27. *To the Lighthouse*, p. 34.
28. Samuel Beckett, in his discussion of Proust, emphasises the French writer's preoccupation in *À la recherche du temps perdu* with the importance of undermining existing formal and linguistic paradigms:

> But when the object is perceived as particular and unique and not merely the member of a family, when it appears independent of

any general notion and detached from the sanity of a cause, isolated and inexplicable in the light of ignorance, then and only then may it be a source of enchantment. Unfortunately, Habit has laid its veto on this form of perception, its action being precisely to hide the essence – the Idea – of the object in the haze of conception – preconception. (Samuel Beckett, *Proust* (London: Chatto & Windus, 1931) p. 11)

29. Shklovsky illustrates this idea with the help of a passage from Tolstoy's diary. Tolstoy describes how he:

> was cleaning a room and, meandering about, approached the divan and couldn't remember whether I had dusted it. Since these movements were habitual and unconscious, I could not remember and felt that it was impossible to remember – so that if I had dusted it and forgot – that is, had acted unconsciously, then it was the same as if I had not. (Lemon and Reis (eds), *Russian Formalist Criticism*, p. 12)

30. Ibid., p. 57.
31. *Diary*, III, p. 209; *CE*, II, p. 92.
32. The fact that neither Richardson nor Sterne ever completed their novels can be related both to their achronological method and to their scepticism over the 'neatness' of the conventional form of, and ending to, the novel. Elaine Showalter remarks that Richardson's 'conception of the book as a continuous process was the myth that enabled her to publish at all; without such a sustaining illusion, Olive Schreiner, a novelist of very similar temperament, found herself endlessly writing and rewriting the same unfinished book' (Elaine Showalter, *A Literature of their Own* (London: Princeton University Press, 1978) p. 261).
33. Richardson's narrator, Miriam Henderson, describes her friend George Taylor's personality as 'feminine' (Dorothy Richardson, *Pilgrimage* (London: Dent, 1938) III, p. 372); and in *The Voyage Out* and *Night and Day* – as the following chapters will show – Woolf creates 'feminine' heroes. Both Elaine Showalter and Phyllis Rose emphasise the fact that to talk of a 'masculine', 'feminine' or 'androgynous' style – rather than content – in the art of Richardson or Woolf is simply to make use of a convenient metaphor (see Showalter, *A Literature of their Own*, p. 258; Phyllis Rose, *Woman of Letters: A Life of Virginia Woolf* (London: Routledge & Kegan Paul, 1978) p. 190).
34. Wilson is a fictionalised portrait of H. G. Wells.
35. Richardson, *Pilgrimage*, IV, p. 638. See also Dorothy Richardson, 'Data for Spanish Publisher', ed. Joseph Prescott, *London Magazine*, vol. VI, no. 6 (June 1959) p. 15.
36. 'Modern Fiction', in *CE*, II, p. 107.
37. Richardson, 'Data for Spanish Publisher', p. 19.

38. Like the deaths in *To the Lighthouse*, those of Mrs Henderson, Max, Eve and Eleanor Dear in *Pilgrimage* are all treated parenthetically.
39. Richardson, *Pilgrimage*, III, p. 377.
40. Ibid., pp. 285, 128.
41. Ibid., I, p. 384.
42. Ibid., III, p. 146. In *Revolving Lights* Miriam reiterates this criticism of the neglect of 'life itself' in traditional novels:

> Generally the surroundings were described separately, the background on which presently the characters began to fuss. But they were never sufficiently shown as they were to the people when there was no fussing; what the floods of sunshine and beauty indoors and out meant to these people as single individuals, whether they were aware of it or not. (Richardson, *Pilgrimage*, III, p. 243)

43. Ibid., II, p. 383.
44. Ibid., III, p. 123; Richardson's ellipsis.
45. Ibid., IV, pp. 243–4.
46. Ibid., III, p. 218; see also IV, p. 164. David Lodge notes that at the time when Woolf was working on *Mrs Dalloway* she

> had an interesting correspondence about aesthetics with the painter Jacques Raverat . . . He suggested that writing, as an artistic medium, was limited by being 'essentially linear', unable therefore to render the complex multiplicity of a mental event, which he compared to a pebble cast into a pond, 'splashes in the outer air in every direction. [sic] and under the surface waves that follow one another into forgotten corners.' Virginia Woolf replied that it was precisely her aim to go beyond 'the formal railway line of the sentence' and to disregard the 'falsity of the past (by which I mean Bennett, Galsworthy and so on) . . . people don't and never did think or feel in that way; but all over the place in your way.' (Lodge, *The Modes of Modern Writing*, p. 184)

47. Richardson, *Pilgrimage*, II, p. 256; Richardson's ellipsis.
48. Ibid., I, p. 121; *Diary*, I, p. 13.
49. Woolf expressed doubts about the narrative method of *Pilgrimage* in her review of *The Tunnel* in *The Times Literary Supplement* of 13 February 1919, p. 81. She believed that, as David Lodge remarks: 'The modernist enterprise . . . had its dangers and its problems. The logical terminus of their fictional realism was the plotless "slice of life" or the plotless "stream of consciousness", and plotlessness could easily become shapelessness, or randomness' (Lodge, *The Modes of Modern Writing*, p. 138).
50. *The Waves*, p. 191.
51. Ibid., p. 103. The treatment of Lily Briscoe in *To the Lighthouse* illustrates Woolf's belief that such crises are a necessary and salutary part of the life of the artist.

52. *CE*, ii, pp. 80–1.
53. Henry James, Preface to *The Portrait of a Lady*, rptd in Henry James, *The Art of the Novel*, ed. Richard P. Blackmur (New York: Charles Scribner's Sons, 1934) p. 46.
54. *CE*, ii, p. 82.
55. *The Waves*, p. 131.
56. The internal structure of *The Waves* depends largely upon the juxta-position of the 'interludes' with the 'episodes' which deal more obviously with the world of humanity. There is a metaphoric relationship between these apparently contrasted sections, which means that they are felt to be not only juxtaposed with one another but also superimposed upon one another. (Woolf aimed at a similar effect in *To the Lighthouse*, as she remarks in her diary – see *Diary*, iii, p. 106.) As in Elstir's painting of Carquethuit harbour, we are encouraged to perceive properties in the human world which by convention we associate with the natural world, and vice versa (see Proust, *Remembrance of Things Past*, i, pp. 893, 894).
57. Shklovsky, in 'Literature and the Film', criticises those who try to make art specific: 'People who try to "solve" paintings as if they were cross-word puzzles want to take the form off the painting in order to see it better' (quoted in Victor Erlich's *Russian Formalism*, 4th edn (New Haven, Conn.: Yale University Press, 1980; 1st edn 1955) p. 187).
58. *The Waves*, p. 177.
59. Bernard, like Proust's narrator, attacks the assumption that life can be, as it were, reproduced in art. Marcel argues that nothing could be farther from actual experience than the procession of a series of visual images across the screen of a cinematograph.
60. *A Room*, p. 166.
61. *Three Guineas*, pp. 12, 265.
62. Her *oeuvre* cannot, then, be subsumed by either side in the long-standing debate over the relative merits of a formalist or a socio-political approach in, or to, art.
63. Woolf's 'dramatic' novels differ, then, from those overtly partisan works which sprang up, as Elaine Showalter notes, in direct response to the suffrage campaign, and whose tone was often 'bitter', 'partisan' and 'militant' (see Showalter, *A Literature of their Own*, p. 221).
64. T. S. Eliot, 'Tradition and the Individual Talent', in *The Sacred Wood* (London: Methuen, 1920) p. 48. In a letter to Eliot of 3 September 1924, Woolf warmly praises this collection of essays (*Letters*, iii, p. 129).
65. 'The Leaning Tower', in *CE*, ii, p. 166. Compare a remark in her diary for 22 August 1922:

> It is a mistake to think that literature can be produced from the raw. One must get out of life – yes, thats why I disliked so much the irruption of Sydney [that is, his visit] – one must become externalised; very, very concentrated, all at one point, not having

to draw upon the scattered parts of one's character, living in the brain. Sydney comes & I'm Virginia; when I write I'm merely a sensibility. (*Diary*, II, p. 193)

See, too, her comment in a letter to Ethel Smyth of 29 October 1933:

Psychologically speaking . . . I believe unconsciousness, and complete anonymity to be the only conditions . . . in which I can write. Not to be aware of oneself. And all these people insist that one must be aware of oneself. Thats why I wont see my friends. (*Letters*, V, p. 239)

In a similar vein Eliot argues that

the bad poet is usually unconscious where he ought to be conscious, and conscious where he ought to be unconscious. Both errors tend to make him 'personal'. Poetry is not a turning loose of emotion, but an escape from emotion; it is not the expression of personality, but an escape from personality. (Eliot, *The Sacred Wood*, pp. 52–3)

Elaine Showalter argues that although women novelists in the 1930s rejected many aspects of the modernist enterprise, Woolf's concept of 'the artist as passive consciousness' influenced writers like Rosamund Lehmann (Showalter, *A Literature of their Own*, pp. 298–9).

66. Spender, *The Struggle of the Modern*, p. 27.
67. *Diary*, V, p. 229; Woolf's ellipsis. It is hard to see how Woolf would reconcile this comment on Wordsworth with his more overtly political poems.
68. 'The Leaning Tower', in *CE*, II, p. 172. For Spender's account of Woolf's reaction to the poetry of the 1930s see his autobiography, *World Within World* (London: Hamish Hamilton, 1951) pp. 158–9.
69. *CE*, II, p. 172.
70. Ibid., p. 221.
71. *Letters*, V, p. 408.
72. Ibid., VI, p. 171.
73. Ibid., V, p. 83. This is not the *Letter to a Young Poet* which was published by the Hogarth Press in July 1932 and was also, nominally at least, addressed to John Lehmann.
74. Ibid., VI, p. 348.
75. *Diary*, V, pp. 267, 298.
76. 'The Leaning Tower', in *CE*, II, p. 175.
77. *Letters*, II, p. 403. Woolf remarks in her diary for 3 November 1918, after a conversation with Janet Case:

but I felt . . . the depressing effect of talking to some one who seems to want all literature to go into the pulpit; who makes it all infinitely worthy & safe & respectable. I was led into trying to define my own particular search – not after morality, or beauty or reality – no; but after literature itself.   (*Diary*, i, pp. 213–4)

See also *Letters*, ii, pp. 119, 529.

78. *Three Guineas*. Quoted by Jane Marcus in ' "No more horses": Virginia Woolf on Art and Propaganda', *Women's Studies*, vol. iv, nos 2/3 (1977) p. 265.

79. The exception is, perhaps, *Orlando*, a work which suffers because its intensely personal elements and private jokes remain oblique to the uninitiated reader.

80. *Diary*, iii, p. 49; *Letters*, iii, p. 370.

81. In her diary for 28 November 1928 Woolf remarked: 'I used to think of him [her father] & mother daily; but writing The Lighthouse, laid them in my mind. And now he comes back sometimes, but differently' (*Diary*, iii, p. 208). She was annoyed, however, by a passage in Herbert Fisher's autobiography in which he equated the fictional protagonists of *To the Lighthouse* with Julia and Leslie Stephen (see *Letters*, vi, p. 464).

82. *Diary*, ii, p. 248.

83. Ibid., iii, p. 236.

84. *Diary*, v, p. 141.

85. In her novels, Woolf attributes her own point of view on this subject to fictional characters like Mrs Dalloway and Mrs Ramsay (see *Mrs Dalloway*, p. 139; *To the Lighthouse*, p. 19).

86. *Letters*, iv, p. 333. In her essay on 'Women and Fiction' she describes herself as one who prefers 'the butterfly to the gadfly – that is to say, the artist to the reformer' (*CE*, ii, p. 147).

87. *Letters*, i, p. 442.

88. The same reasoning possibly explains why she remained comparatively uninvolved at a practical level in the militant branch of the suffragist movement. Jane Marcus points out that 'She had seen the suffragettes under Emmeline Pankhurst and her daughter Christabel turned into warmongers overnight' (Marcus, ' "No more horses" ', p. 270). Her political commitment found more private expression through, for example, her teaching at the workers' institute, Morley College, from 1905 to 1907, and later through her involvement with the Richmond Branch of the Women's Co-operative Guild and as Secretary of the Rodmell Labour Party (see Quentin Bell, *Virginia Woolf: A Biography* (London: The Hogarth Press, 1972) i, p. 105; ii, pp. 36n, 186).

89. *Letters*, iv, pp. 315–16.

90. *Diary*, iv, p. 126.

91. *A Room*, p. 167. Compare Eliot's view that 'Without doubt, the effort of the philosopher proper, the man who is trying to deal with ideas in themselves, and the effort of the poet, who may be trying to *realize* ideas, cannot be carried on at the same time' ('Dante', in Eliot, *The Sacred Wood*, p. 147). Eliot criticises Blake, Goethe, Ibsen and Shaw on these grounds (ibid., pp. 59, 62, 141).

92. *Diary*, iv, p. 126.

93. *Letters*, v, p. 122; iv, p. 329.
94. Ibid., v, p. 167.
95. Henry James, *Notes on Novelists: With Some Other Notes* (London: Dent, 1914) p. 299. I am indebted, in the discussion of James which follows, to Vivien Jones's *James the Critic* (London: Macmillan, 1984).
96. Henry James's review of *The Gayworthys* by Adeline D. Whitney, in his *Notes and Reviews*, ed. Pierre de Chaignon la Rose (Cambridge, Mass.: Dunster House Press, 1921) p. 92.
97. Henry James, *Partial Portraits* (London: Macmillan, 1888) pp. 137–8. Vivien Jones points out that 'James always made a clear distinction between the specific ideas which George Sand embodied didactically in her novels and the "general truthfulness" which involved a receptiveness to the power of ideas but was much more a matter of tone and characterisation' (Jones, *James the Critic*, p. 71).
98. James, *The Art of the Novel*, p. 45; James, *Partial Portraits*, p. 406.
99. Leon Edel and Gordon Ray (eds), *Henry James and H. G. Wells: A Record of their Friendship, their Debate on the Art of Fiction, and their Quarrel* (London: Hart-Davis, 1958) p. 264. The quarrel between James the 'aesthete' and Wells the 'moralist' has affinities with that between Woolf and Arnold Bennett.
100. *Diary*, v, p. 259; 'Modern Fiction', in *CE*, ii, p. 105. T. S. Eliot puts forward a similar argument in the Introduction to *The Sacred Wood*, pp. xi–xii.
101. *CE*, ii, p. 117; 'The Rights of Youth', in *CW*, p. 91. Patricia Stubbs argues that Wells is:

> a writer who shows on every page that he is primarily concerned with the state of society. But like many of the feminist novelists working in the 'nineties, he never found a way of incorporating his politics successfully into his fiction, though he experimented tirelessly with the novel form in his efforts to do so, producing a flamboyant amalgam of fiction, prophesy, science-fiction and utopian daydreaming . . . he worked too *quickly*, he tended to handle his themes crudely, and he all too often concentrated myopically on a particular idea, clarifying his political position at the expense of the complexities of human experience. (Patricia Stubbs, *Women and Fiction: Feminism and the Novel, 1880–1920* (Brighton: Harvester, 1979) p. 179)

Stubbs none the less praises Wells because with Shaw and even Galsworthy, he

> tried to show how society was structured and how people actually lived. They made mistakes, but they never retreated from the pressures of life behind an aesthetic smoke-screen like Mrs Woolf. (Ibid., p. 180)

Stubb's criticism of Woolf fails, however – as the argument of this book will suggest – to do justice to the degree of political and social commitment implicit in Woolf's choice of narrative method.

102. *Diary*, IV, p. 6.
103. Joan Bennett argues that Woolf's own novels successfully reflect this point of view:

> The moral, social, economic and religious problems which play so large a part in the novels of the nineteenth century are important in her books too, but we are made aware of them only as they colour the world for the people she presents and form part of what life feels like to them.   (Joan Bennett, *Virginia Woolf: Her Art as a Novelist*, 2nd edn (Cambridge: Cambridge University Press, 1964) p. 10)

104. *Diary*, IV, pp. 276, 222. Similarly, Woolf criticised a novel manuscript by W. J. H. Sprott because, she said, 'it seems as if your theme interested you, and not the people' (*Letters*, III, p. 173).
105. *Diary*, IV, p. 281.
106. 'The Novels of E. M. Forster', in *CE*, I, p. 349.
107. Ibid., pp. 350, 351.
108. 'The Novels of George Meredith', ibid., pp. 229, 230. Goldsmith, Trollope, Samuel Butler, J. D. Beresford, Compton Mackenzie and Gissing are just some of the other novelists whom Woolf attacks for failing to create the illusion of independence in their fictional characters. Of the heroine of Compton Mackenzie's *Sylvia and Michael*, for example, Woolf remarks rather amusingly that she:

> says many smart things about war and religion and nationality . . . but in the process of saying them she fades out of existence . . . and leaves us wondering why so clever a journalist should think it necessary to get himself up as a young woman.   ('Sylvia and Michael', in *CW*, p. 86)

Woolf attacked Joyce for his egotism, responding to *Ulysses*, for example, with the remark:

> I'm reminded all the time of some callow board school boy, say like Henry Lamb, full of wits & powers, but so self-conscious & egotistical that he loses his head, becomes extravagant, mannered, uproarious, ill at ease, makes kindly people sorry for him, & stern ones merely annoyed.   (*Diary*, II, p. 199)

It is difficult to see what prompted these criticisms, since in all but his earliest novel, *Stephen Hero*, Joyce is careful to eliminate any overt authorial presence from his narratives. Woolf was, however, consistently unreliable in her assessments of Joyce (see, for example, *Diary*, II, 195–6; *Letters*, II, pp. 167, 533, 551, 566, 598).
109. 'George Moore', in *CE*, I, 338–9.

110. 'Craftmanship', ibid., II, p. 248; 'On Re-Reading Novels', ibid., p. 127.
111. The narrator in Richardson's *Pilgrimage* echoes Woolf's criticisms of the author who emphasises his or her own presence within the novel, whether through overt didacticism – as in Holmes's *Elsie Venner* (Richardson, *Pilgrimage*, II, p. 427) – or through the overall tone of the book. In *Revolving Lights*, for example, Miriam criticises the novelist Hypo Wilson because he 'comes forward' in his writing to tell the reader what to feel (ibid., III, p. 251). She questions Wilson's belief that the writer should describe the people in his novels, maintaining that to do so is to draw attention away from the fictional characters towards the author as manipulator of these characters. It is, she suggests, 'just that stopping, by the author, to describe people, that spoils so many novels' (ibid., IV pp. 613–14). Miriam praises Henry James because in a novel like *The Ambassadors* he manages to create the illusion of his absence; he conveys information 'without coming forward to announce it' (ibid., III, p. 409).
112. Quoted in Enid Starkie's *From Gautier to Eliot* (London: Hutchinson, 1960) p. 64.
113. *CE*, II, p. 92.
114. *Diary*, II, p. 136.
115. *Letters*, V, pp. 190, 194–5, 249.
116. Ibid., p. 249.
117. Ibid., p. 195. In a similar vein she remarked to G. L. Dickinson of *A Room*:

> I'm so glad you thought it good tempered – my blood is apt to boil on this one subject as yours does about natives, or war; and I didnt want it to. I wanted to encourage the young women – they seem to get fearfully depressed – and also to induce discussion. (*Letters*, IV, p. 106)

In his review of *A Room* – 'An Olive Branch' – Desmond MacCarthy praised the essay for its balanced tone:

> This is . . . the most charming argumentative opuscule, brochure, tract, pamphlet, or whatever you like to call it, I have ever read on a quarrelsome subject. It is feminist propaganda, yet it resembles an almond-tree in blossom. (*The Sunday Times*, 26 January 1930, p. 8)

118. The letter in question, which Woolf orginally intended to send to the *New Statesman*, is now published in *CE*, II, p. 196, under the title 'Middlebrow'. Attacks on the 'middlebrow' are also to be found in Woolf's manuscript sketches, *Three Characters* and 'There He Is Again, the Man I Hate' – see *MHP*, MH/B9(i) and MH/B10(c).
119. Katharine Rogers, *The Troublesome Helpmate: A History of Misogyny in Literature* (London: University of Washington Press, 1966).
120. She draws a similar distinction between the writing of different men.

Some men, she feels, have become self-conscious and sex-conscious as a result of the suffrage campaign, and feel obliged, in consequence, to dwell upon their virility (see *A Room*, p. 152).

121. Elaine Showalter argues that Olive Schreiner's *From Man to Man* (London: Fisher Unwin, 1926) anticipates the language, as well as the symbolism, of a *A Room* (see Showalter's *A Literature of their Own*, p. 202).

122. Quoted in *The Pargiters*, p. xli.

123. *Diary*, III, pp. 242, 262. Jane Marcus suggests that:

> Although Woolf's nearest literary ancestor is Swift . . . she might prefer to be compared to Swift's spiritual heir of the opposite side, the witty Sydney Smith. . . . Smith's causes were the emancipation of slaves and of Catholics, but he preached them with humor, wit, and style and with a lack of that egotistic patronizing tone, that smug holier-than-thou Puritanism, which Virginia Woolf felt characterized reformers of her own and Victorian times.

Marcus goes on to speak of 'Smith's gay, elegant eighteenth-century detachment, so effective in propaganda' (Marcus, ' "No more horses" ', p. 275).

124. *A Room*, p. 8.

125. *Diary*, IV, p. 77. Jane Marcus notes that:

> The preacher's tone was wrong, she felt, not only for fiction but for pamphlets – *Three Guineas* gestated for six years as *On Being Despised*, a draft inspired by personal insults, salt in her wounds, from Yeats, Huxley, E. M. Forster, and others. But all of the personal lamentation and the preaching were removed to make the essay grow into *Three Guineas* as we have it. (Marcus, ' "No more horses" ', pp. 275–6)

126. Olive Schreiner, *Woman and Labour* (London: Fisher Unwin, 1911) p. 280.

127. *Diary*, IV, p. 361. The brilliance of both pamphlets remains unparalleled in feminist writing. Even a perfectly competent book such as Mary Ellmann's *Thinking about Women* (New York: Harcourt, Brace, 1968) repeats much that Woolf has already expressed more humorously, more entertainingly, and therefore more persuasively, in *A Room* and *Three Guineas*.

128. In the course of *Three Guineas* Woolf opposes the use of the word 'feminist' on the grounds that it encourages sex-consciousness (see *Three Guineas*, pp. 184–5).

129. 'American Fiction', in *CE*, II, p. 113. Elaine Showalter attacks this argument on the grounds that

> few readers will agree that the great flaw in American literature is its national consciousness, its insistence on exploring what is local and special in American culture, or its use of the language

which that culture has generated. The sort of perfect artist who can forget where he comes from is a figure more pathetic than heroic. Similarly, the notion that women should transcend any awkwardly unorthodox desire to write about being women comes from timidity and not strength. (Showalter, *A Literature of their Own*, p. 290)

Showalter's criticisms of Woolf will be considered in my Conclusion.

130. 'Women and Fiction', in *CE*, II, p. 145. Dale Spender argues that Woolf's criticism is affected by her sex-consciousness. Even in a work like *A Room* which is ostensibly addressed to women, Woolf's reticent, conciliatory tone suggests that her narrative approach was dictated, in part at least, by her need to win approval from the male establishment (see Dale Spender, *Man Made Language* (London: Routledge & Kegan Paul, 1980) pp. 201ff.) It might be more true to say that it was her reluctance to alienate an audience of potential converts to feminism which dictated Woolf's choice of narrative method in *A Room* and *Three Guineas*.
131. *Three Guineas*, pp. 95ff.
132. *Letters*, I, p. 465.
133. 'Women Novelists', in *CW*, p. 25. Henry James, similarly, deplored the fact that 'throughout the field of English art and letters, the influence of the "young person" and her sensitive cheek is perceived to prevail' (see Henry James, 'The Grosvenor Gallery and the Royal Academy', in *Nation*, 31 May 1877, p. 321). See also Jones's *James the Critic*, p. 110.
134. Showalter, *A Literature of their Own*, pp. 81–2. Phyllis Rose goes so far as to link Woolf's mental illness to her 'feeling that in being a writer she was doing something her family and society did not fundamentally support' (Rose, *Woman of Letters*, p. 169).
135. 'Women and Fiction', in *CE*, II, p. 144.
136. Ibid., p. 148.
137. Elaine Showalter notes that Charlotte Brontë admonished the critic of the *Economist*:

'To you I am neither man nor woman. I come before you as an author only. It is the sole standard by which you have a right to judge me – the sole ground on which I accept your judgment.' Anne Brontë prefaced the second edition of *Wildfell Hall* with a defiant declaration of equal literary rights: 'I am satisfied that if the book is a good one, it is so whatever the sex of the author may be.' George Eliot stopped reading reviews of her books when criticism became personal; all were vetted by Lewes. However, one sees signs of self-censorship both in her shift after 1860 to less autobiographical fiction, and in her careful elimination of possible double entendres in proof. (Showalter, *A Literature of their Own*, p. 96)

138. 'Women and Fiction', in *CE*, II, p. 144. Woolf argues that George

Eliot is not only sex-conscious, but also class-conscious. When in *The Mill on the Floss*, she sets her characters in middle-class drawing-rooms, she cannot avoid indulging in clumsy satire. Her tone reveals 'the vindictiveness of a grudge which we feel to be personal in its origin' ('George Eliot', in *CE*, I, 203).

139. *A Room*, p. 101. Patricia Stubbs argues that many late nineteenth-century women's novels are marred by the fact that the author uses her fiction as a vehicle for overt moral argument:

> Obscurity is where we must go to find most of the topical but transient feminist novels of the 'nineties. There were novels on wives, spinsters and virgins, on marriage, sex and motherhood, on career girls and suffragettes. . . . But most of them were treatises first, novels second.

She considers Sarah Grand's *The Heavenly Twins* 'a better novel than [Grant Allen's] *The Woman Who Did*' because 'it is less diagrammatic and the figures in it are more, though little more, than Allen's one-dimensional spokespeople for or against emancipation' (Stubbs, *Women and Fiction*, pp. 117, 119).

140. 'Women Novelists', in *CW*, p. 25. (To adopt a male pseudonym is, of course, by no means to escape from sex-consciousness, nor is it a guarantee that one will write from a 'masculine' point of view.) Showalter notes that

> In 1855 George Eliot asked her friend Charles Bray not to tell anyone that she had written the essay on the evangelist Cumming for the *Westminster:* 'The article appears to have produced a strong impression, and that impression would be a little counteracted if the author were known to be a *woman.'* . . . To their contemporaries [Showalter argues] nineteenth-century women writers were women first, artists second. A woman novelist, unless she disguised herself with a male pseudonym, had to expect critics to focus on her femininity and rank her with the other women writers of her day, no matter how diverse their subjects or styles. The knowledge that their individual achievement would be subsumed under a relatively unfavorable group stereotype acted as a constant irritant to feminine novelists. George Eliot protested against being compared to Dinah Mulock; Charlotte Brontë tried to delay the publication of *Villette* so that it would not be reviewed along with Mrs Gaskell's *Ruth*. Brontë particularly wanted to prevent the male literary establishment from making women writers into competitors and rivals for the same small space. (Showalter, *A Literature of their Own*, pp. 60, 73)

141. 'Women and Fiction', in *CE*, II, p. 144.
142. *A Room*, p. 46. Elaine Showalter connects the episode in *A Room* in which Woolf discovers this work with the moment in Dorothy Richardson's *Pilgrimage* when Miriam reads an insulting entry on

'Woman' in an encyclopedia (Showalter, *A Literature of their Own*, p. 250).

143. '*Jane Eyre* and *Wuthering Heights*', in *CE*, ɪ, p. 189.

144. 'Phases of Fiction', in *CE*, ɪɪ, p. 96.

145. *A Room*, p. 101. Henry James linked Austen's 'light felicity' and her 'extraordinary grace' with 'her unconsciousness'. See Sandra Gilbert and Susan Gubar's *The Madwoman in the Attic: The Woman Writer and the Nineteenth-Century Literary Imagination* (London: Yale University Press, 1979) p. 110.

146. 'Jane Austen Practising', in the *New Statesman*, 15 July 1922; rptd in *Women and Writing*, ed. Michèle Barrett (London: The Women's Press, 1979) p. 107.

147. 'Phases of Fiction', in *CE*, ɪɪ, p. 76.

148. 'Jane Austen', ibid., ɪ, p. 149.

149. *A Room*, pp. 102, 86. It is on these grounds that Barbara Currier Bell and Carol Ohmann praise Woolf's own biographical and critical essays (see their 'Virginia Woolf's Criticism: a Polemical Preface', in *Feminist Literary Criticism*, ed. Josephine Donovan (Lexington, Ky: University of Kentucky Press, 1975) pp. 55, 58).

150. 'Personalities', in *CE*, ɪɪ, p. 275. For an interesting discussion of the manner in which Shakespeare effaces himself from his art, see John Bayley, *The Uses of Division: Unity and Disharmony in Literature* (London: Chatto & Windus, 1976) p. 15. Sandra Gilbert and Susan Gubar point out that Austen 'did not admire the prototypical Madame de Genlis; she was "disgusted" with her brand of didacticism and with the evangelic fervor of novelists who considered themselves primarily moralists'. They suggest that:

> With its insistent evocation of two generic frameworks, the *Bildungsroman* and the burlesque, *Northanger Abbey* (1818) supplies one reason for Austen's fascination with coding, concealing, or just plain not saying what she means, because this apparently amusing and inoffensive novel finally expresses an indictment of patriarchy that could hardly be considered proper or even permissible in Austen's day. Indeed, when this early work was published posthumously – because its author could not find a publisher who would print it during her lifetime – it was the harsh portrayal of the patriarch that most disturbed reviewers. (Gilbert and Gubar, *Madwoman in the Attic*, pp. 116, 128)

In adopting an 'impersonal' approach in a work such as *Northanger Abbey*, Jane Austen was motivated, they suggest – like Woolf in her 'dramatic' novels – not only by artistic, but also by political, considerations.

151. '*Twelfth Night* at the Old Vic', in *CE*, ɪ, p. 28.

152. In a letter to Hugh Walpole of 12 September 1932 Woolf remarks: 'One of the things I want to write about one day is the Shakespearean talk in Scott: the dialogues: surely that is the last appearance in

England of the blank verse of Falstaff and so on!' (*Letters*, v, p. 104). See also *Letters*, *V*, p. 335.

153. 'Sir Walter Scott', in *CE*, i, pp. 141, 142, 143. Recalling a discussion of *Ulysses* with T. S. Eliot, Woolf noted in her diary:

> indeed, he [Eliot] said, this new method of giving the psychology proves to my mind that it doesn't work. It doesn't tell as much as some casual glance from outside often tells. I said I found Pendennis more illuminating in this way. (*Diary*, ii, p. 203)

Herbert Marder rightly remarks that Woolf's own novel, *The Years*,

> demonstrates that every statement about the outer life is also a statement about the inner life. . . . My relation to other people shapes my inner being, and conversely, my inner being determines my capacity for meaningful social relations. (Herbert Marder, *Feminism and Art* (London: University of Chicago Press, 1968) p. 173)

154. David Lodge argues that 'It is in dialogue above all, that the novelist has most opportunity, if he so wishes, to suggest continuity between his fictional world and the real world, and to allow his own activity as "verbal maker" to recede from sight' (David Lodge, *Language of Fiction: Essays in Criticism and Verbal Analysis of the English Novel*, 2nd edn (London: Routledge & Kegan Paul, 1984; 1st edn 1966), p. 47). Similarly, Lilian Furst and Peter Skrine note in their book on Naturalism that the German novelists, Holz and Schlaf, 'posited that the Naturalistic narrative should be mainly in dialogue in order to attain the highest degree of objectivity. Speech, including the phonetic notation of personal peculiarities, is used as a means of characters-ation' (Lilian Furst and Peter Skrine, *Naturalism* (London: Methuen, 1971) p. 48).

155. Preface to Henry James, *The Awkward Age* (London: Heinemann, 1899); rptd. in James, *The Art of the Novel*, pp. 110–11.

156. James, *The Art of the Novel*, p. 115.

157. Compare the method of Ivy Compton-Burnett's novels, works written almost entirely in dialogue, but in which the author, like James, allows herself to tell the reader a few essential facts about her characters.

158. For example: 'evidently', 'clearly', 'doubtless', 'no doubt', 'it seemed', 'it appeared', 'it looked as if', 'perhaps', 'perceptibly', 'distinctly', 'unmistakably', 'almost', and so on.

Notes to Chapter Two: *The Voyage Out*

1. The young men's argument about where the Portsmouth Road becomes macadamised (*The Voyage Out*, pp. 417–18) is based on a

quarrel which started between Thoby and Adrian Stephen in a hotel in Greece, while Vanessa lay ill in bed upstairs (see Bell's *Virginia Woolf*, i, p. 109). (Hereafter, all references to *The Voyage Out* appear parenthetically within the text.) In a letter to Violet Dickinson of 27 November 1910, Woolf asks: 'Do you think it would be indecent to put Aunt Minna upon the stage, and Aunt Fisher, and the Quaker? Such riches as we have in our relations it seems a pity to neglect' (*Letters*, i, p. 440). The autobiographical elements are, however, dramatised in the novel, becoming aspects of the lives of Woolf's fictional characters. As John Bayley remarks, the hero and heroine of *The Voyage Out* 'have, as it were, forgotten that they are Clive Bell and the author' (John Bayley, 'Diminishment of Consciousness: a Paradox in the Art of Virginia Woolf', *Virginia Woolf: A Centenary Perspective*, ed. Eric Warner (London: Macmillan, 1984) p. 69).

2. Kate Millett praises Meredith's *The Egoist* (London: Kegan, Paul, 1879) for the same reason:

> The surprising parallels to Meredith's own life are unmistakable. Clara Middleton is his own first wife, Mary Nicolls. Her irresponsible epicurean parent is Thomas Love Peacock, Meredith's former father-in-law. Willoughby jilted is Meredith deserted after some seven years of bitter cohabitation, when Mary left him for Henry Wallis the painter. What is astonishing is that the book is not the revenge one would inevitably expect, but is instead a careful analysis of incompatability. (Kate Millett, *Sexual Politics* (London: Hart-Davis, 1971) p. 135)

3. Phyllis Rose notes that

> There were some ten drafts of *The Voyage Out* (as compared to Woolf's usual three for later novels), and as she wrote and rewrote the book over the years Woolf changed the portrait of Rachel, eliminating some gratuitous self-description. In an earlier version Rachel is even closer to Virginia Stephen as the world saw her in the early twenties.

Rose argues, however, that at times, even in the published version of the novel, Woolf 'falls into gratuitous autobiography' – a view which will be questioned in the course of this chapter (Rose, *Woman of Letters*, pp. 52, 50).

4. In a letter of February 1909, Clive Bell criticised Woolf's approach in an early draft of *Melymbrosia* [*The Voyage Out*] on the grounds that it was too didactic,

> not to say priggish. Our views about men & women are doubtless quite different, and the difference does'nt [sic] matter much; but to draw such sharp & marked contrasts between the subtle, sensitive, tactful, gracious, delicately perceptive, and perspicacious women, & the obtuse, vulgar, blind, florid, rude, tactless,

emphatic, indelicate, vain, tyrannical, stupid men, is not only rather absurd, but rather bad art, I think. (Quoted in Bell's *Virginia Woolf*, I, p. 209)

In a pungent rejoinder, Woolf writes:

> Your objection, that my prejudice against men makes me didactic 'not to say priggish', has not quite the same force with me; I dont remember what I said that suggests the remark; I daresay it came out without my knowledge, but I will bear it in mind. I never meant to preach, and agree that like God, one shouldn't. Possibly, for psychological reasons which seem to me very interesting, a man, in the present state of the world, is not a very good judge of his sex; and a 'creation' may seem to him 'didactic'. (*Letters*, I, p. 383)

5. *CE*, I, p. 252. That feminist ideas are more powerful when they are fictionalised was recognised by Caroline Norton (the model for Meredith's Diana of the Crossways) who remarked in her account of her struggle to gain custody of her children in the mid-nineteenth century:

> I REALLY lost my young children – craved for them, struggled for them, was barred from them – and came too late to see one that had died . . . except in his coffin. I REALLY have gone through much that, if it were invented, would move you; but being of your everyday world, you are willing it should sweep past like a heap of dead leaves on the stream of time and take its place with other things that have gone drifting down. (Ray Strachey, *The Cause* (London: Bell, 1928) pp. 39–40)

6. One might be inclined to question the motives which induced Woolf – like Austen and Charlotte Brontë (in traditional readings of these authors, at least) – to assign the most authoritative position in her novel to a man. In doing so, however, she was, of course, adopting one more device for disguising the autobiographical element in her novel.

7. In this respect, *The Voyage Out* resembles Sewell's novels in which, as Elaine Showalter notes, 'the heroines are frequently spinsters or widows – intentionally so, because she wishes to de-emphasize the importance of marriage' (Showalter, *A Literature of their Own*, p. 146).

8. Strachey, *The Cause*, pp. 283–4.

9. *Night and Day*, p. 77.

10. Simone de Beauvoir, *The Second Sex*, trans. H. M. Parshley (Harmondsworth: Penguin Books, 1983; 1st edn 1949) p. 70.

11. Mary Wollstonecraft, *A Vindication of the Rights of Woman* (London: Johnson, 1792) p. 47.

12. Carolyn Heilbrun, *Towards Androgyny* (London: Gollancz, 1979) p. xiv.

13. Mary Poovey, *The Proper Lady and the Woman Writer: Ideology as Style in the Works of Mary Wollstonecraft, Mary Shelley, and Jane Austen* (London: University of Chicago Press, 1984) p. 6.

14. Barbara Taylor, *Eve and the New Jerusalem: Socialism and Feminism in the Nineteenth Century* (London: Virago, 1983) p. 30.

15. Poovey, *The Proper Lady*, p. 15.

16. Taylor, *Eve and the New Jerusalem*, p. 25.

17. Showalter, *A Literature of Their Own*, p. 210.

18. As Florence Nightingale puts it: 'The family uses people, *not* for what they are, nor for what they are intended to be, but for what it wants them for – its own uses' (excerpt from her unpublished book *Suggestions for Thought to Searchers after Religious Truth*, written in 1852 and published under the title 'Cassandra' in Strachey's *The Cause*, p. 404).

19. The parallels between *The Old Wives' Tale* and *The Voyage Out* outlined below should lead us to reconsider the accepted view – fostered by study of essays by Woolf herself like 'Modern Fiction' and 'Mr Bennett and Mrs Brown' – that Woolf's novels have nothing in common with those of the 'Edwardians'.

20. Arnold Bennett, *The Old Wives' Tale* (London: Chapman & Hall, 1908) p. 36. (Hereafter all references to this novel appear parenthetically within the text.)

21. D. H. Lawrence, *The Rainbow* (London: Methuen, 1915) pp. 336–7.

22. A man might – as Woolf recognised – exploit the ideal of 'womanliness' in order to dominate not only his daughters but also his wife. Mr Shelby, in *Uncle Tom's Cabin*, for example, responds to his wife's argument that she will earn some money to buy Tom's liberty – and thereby become an independent moral agent – with the comment that to do so would be to degrade herself (Harriet Beecher Stowe, *Uncle Tom's Cabin* (Harmondsworth: Penguin Books, 1981; 1st edn 1852) p. 373).

23. Quoted in Strachey's *The Cause*, p. 139.

24. One is reminded of Hewet's imaginary description of the Hirst household in *The Voyage Out* (which in turn echoes the argument of *A Room*): ' "Can't you imagine the family conclaves, and the sister told to run out and feed the rabbits because St John must have the school-room to himself – 'St John's working,' 'St John wants his tea brought to him.' Don't you know the kind of thing?" ' (p. 253). Sylvia Townsend Warner uses the same image in *Lolly Willowes* to represent the suppression of women. Mrs Willowes remarks to her sons: 'Now play nicely with Laura. She has fed your rabbits every day while you have been at school' (Sylvia Townsend Warner, *Lolly Willowes: or the Loving Huntsman* (London: Chatto & Windus, 1926) p. 14). Both these examples recall the incident in *The Mill on the Floss* in which Maggie lets her brother Tom's rabbits die while he is away at school (George Eliot's *The Mill on the Floss* (Edinburgh: Blackwood, 1860) I, pp. 57ff).

25. J. S. Mill, *The Subjection of Women* (London: Longmans, Green, Reader and Dyer, 1869) p. 523; quoted in Millett's *Sexual Politics*, p. 103.

26. Barbara Taylor quotes an anonymous letter written to an Owenite newspaper in 1839, in which 'A Friend to Truth' writes: 'There are, I believe, many women who, like me, deplore the irrational education they are compelled to receive, and who, when they have got rid of their school-mistress, and can withdraw from a round of insipid and frivolous pursuits, strenuously cultivate their own minds, and dare to think for themselves' (Taylor, *Eve and the New Jerusalem*, p. 64). The discrepancy between girls' and boys' education is illustrated, Elaine Showalter points out, in studies made by Richard Altick and Raymond Williams. She comments that: 'Women writers were deprived of education because of their sex, not because of their class. For the middle-class Victorian girl, the departure of a brother for school was a painful awakening to her inferior status; the scene echoes in English fiction from George Eliot's *The Mill on the Floss* (1860) to Sarah Grand's *The Beth Book* (1897)' (Showalter, *A Literature of their Own*, p. 41).

27. Clive Bell remarked of the picnic scene in *The Voyage Out*: 'Honestly, I think it challenges comparison with Box Hill & holds its own, & something more' (quoted in Bell's *Virginia Woolf* i, p. 210). The influence of Forster – and particularly of *A Room with a View* – is also very much in evidence in this novel, as it is in *Night and Day*.

28. 'I have to delve from books, painfully and all alone, what you get every evening sitting over your fire and smoking your pipe with Strachey etc. No wonder my knowledge is scant. Theres nothing like talk as an educator I'm sure' (*Letters*, i, p. 77).

29. In this respect Willougby Vinrace resembles Mr Wilcox in E. M. Forster's *Howards End*. His attitude also brings to mind Kurtz's treatment of his absent fiancée in Conrad's 'Heart of Darkness' – a novella, incidentally, whose influence is felt throughout *The Voyage Out* (Joseph Conrad, 'Heart of Darkness', in *Youth: A Narrative, and Two Other Stories* (Edinburgh, Blackwood, 1902) pp. 49–182).

30. Compare Huxley's comments on Burlap's feelings for his dead wife in *Point Counter Point*: 'These agonies which Burlap, by a process of intense concentration on the idea of his loss and grief, had succeeded in churning up within himself were in no way proportionate or even related to his feelings for the living Susan' (Aldous Huxley, *Point Counter Point* (London: Chatto & Windus, 1928) p. 231).

31. Clive Bell remarked that 'the Dalloways enjoy the advantage of being more like the people whom the world knows. They are very amusing, and more than life-like' (Bell, *Virginia Woolf*, i, p. 209).

32. Carolyn Heilbrun draws attention to Simone de Beauvoir's argument that men have found in women more complicity than the oppressor usually finds in the oppressed (Heilbrun, *Towards Androgyny*, p. xi). In a more recent book, Heilbrun notes that 'public opinion polls show that a higher proportion of women than men oppose passage of the Equal Rights Amendment' (Carolyn Heilbrun, *Reinventing Womanhood* (London: Victor Gollancz, 1979) p. 88).

33. Woolf's own mother, Julia Stephen, signed Mrs Humphry Ward's anti-suffrage petition. Elaine Showalter points out, however, that

Beatrice Webb, who also signed the 'Appeal Against Female Suffrage' later recanted, and, she suggests, 'her explanation of her earlier motives probably speaks for other women as well: "At the root of my anti-feminism lay the fact that I had never myself suffered the disabilities assumed to arise from my sex" ' (Showalter, *A Literature of their Own*, p. 217).

34. Caroline Willowes in Sylvia Townsend Warner's novel *Lolly Willowes*, Lady Wathin in Meredith's *Diana of the Crossways* – a novel which Rachel reads at the villa – or Mrs Gould in Conrad's *Nostromo* all illustrate this idea.

35. Forster, *Howards End*, pp. 219, 227.

36. This willingness to vilify their own sex in order to gain acceptance within the establishment is a characteristic of many nineteenth-and early twentieth-century women. We find it, for example, in Q. D. Leavis's spiteful and emotive review of Woolf's *Three Guineas* in *Scrutiny*, vol. VII, no. 2 (September 1938) pp. 203–14. In this review, Leavis adopts a 'masculine' voice, at once hostile to her own sex and conciliatory towards the male establishment of Oxbridge.

37. 'Lettice [Clarissa] is almost Kitty verbatim; what would happen if she guessed?' (*Letters*, I, p. 349).

38. Ibid., p. 103.

39. Indeed, she refuses to dismiss any character in *The Voyage Out* completely. Part of Woolf's skill in the novel stems from her ability to avoid the kind of personal criticism in her fictional narrative which we find in her diaries and letters, and whose effect would be to alienate the reader.

40. Clarissa is one of those women whom Florence Nightingale describes in 'Cassandra' as being completely dedicated to sustaining the *status quo*:

> That man and woman have an equality of duties and rights is accepted by woman even less than by man. Behind *his* destiny woman must annihilate herself, must be his only complement. A woman dedicates herself to the vocation of her husband, she fills up and performs the subordinate parts in it. (Strachey, *The Cause*, p. 407)

41. Ray Strachey comments in her account of the history of the women's movement that:

> Oxford, when it admitted women to the examinations [in 1884], excluded theology, medicine and law (the three chief directions in which University studies might lead directly to professional appointments), but in 1895 an exception was made in favour of Miss Cornelia Sorabji, who was preparing for legal work in India. It thus became clear that the exclusion was based not so much on any inherent impropriety as upon the desire to reduce competition; but it continued all the same. (Ibid., p. 263)

42. Ann Douglas, Introduction to Stowe, *Uncle Tom's Cabin*, p. 17.
43. Taylor, *Eve and the New Jerusalem*, pp. 126–7, 153.
44. Quentin Bell's account of Woolf's involvement in the 'Dreadnought Hoax' – like *Three Guineas* – illustrates the degree to which Helen's views on this subject coincide with those of her author (Bell, *Virginia Woolf*, I, pp. 157–61).
45. See, for example, her remarks in a letter to Margaret Llewelyn Davies of 23 January 1916: 'I become steadily more feminist, owing to the Times, which I read at breakfast and wonder how this preposterous masculine fiction [the war] keeps going a day longer – without some vigorous young woman pulling us together and marching through it – Do you see any sense in it?' (*Letters*, II, p. 76). Like Helen Ambrose, Woolf 'cant believe in wars and politics' (ibid., I, p. 325).
46. Terence's remarks recall the objections to history voiced by Austen's Catherine Morland and Anne Elliott: 'The quarrels of popes and kings, with wars or pestilences, in every page; the men all so good for nothing, and hardly any women at all – it is very tiresome' (Jane Austen, *'Northanger Abbey' and 'Persuasion'* (London: Murray, 1818) I, pp. 255–6). Sandra Gilbert and Susan Gubar draw attention to Austen's

> only attempt at history, a parody of Goldsmith's *History of England*, written in her youth and signed as the work of 'a partial, prejudiced, and ignorant Historian'. What is conveyed in this early joke is precisely Catherine's sense of the irrationality, cruelty, and irrelevance of history, as well as the partisan spleen of most so-called objective historians. Until she can place herself, and two friends, in the company of Mary Queen of Scots, historical events seem as absurdly distant from Austen's common concerns as they do to Charlotte Brontë in *Shirley*, George Eliot in *Middlemarch*, or Virginia Woolf in *The Years*, writers who self-consciously display the ways in which history and historical narration only indirectly affect women because they deal with public events never experienced at first hand in the privatized lives of women. . . . like Woolf, Austen asserts that women see male-dominated history from the disillusioned and disaffected perspective of the outsider. (Gilbert and Gubar, *The Madwoman in the Attic*, pp. 132–3, 134)

47. Rachel's image of the old woman in Leeds (p. 71) brings to mind a remark in Woolf's diary: 'its all bombast, this war. One old lady pinning on her cap has more reality' (*Diary*, v, p. 285).
48. As the novel progresses, Terence takes over from Helen the role of educator-guide to Rachel (and the reader). Terence becomes Woolf's spokesman, casting a faintly ironic light on Helen, and thus becoming, in her place, the most authoritative character in the novel.
49. In this respect the Dalloways resemble the Bradshaws 'begetting one son in Harley Street by Lady Bradshaw' (*Mrs Dalloway*, p. 195) or Soames Forsyte in Galsworthy's novel.

50. *Letters*, I, p. 385. See also ibid., pp. 300, 319–20, 386; *Letters*, II, p. 195.

51. Similarly, in the published version of *The Years* Woolf avoids adopting an angry tone by attributing her own impatience with narrow-minded University men to her fictional character, Kitty Malone.

52. That Helen's situation is a typical one is suggested by a remark in a letter from Woolf to Ethel Smyth of 15 April 1931: 'I have also been listening to two love lorn young men: they caterwaul – with an egotism that, if I were a feminist, would throw great light on the history of the sexes – such complete self-absorption: such entire belief that a woman has nothing to do but listen' (*Letters*, IV, p. 312).

53. In her article 'Professions for Women' she describes the typical Victorian wife or daughter, 'The Angel in the House':

    She was intensely sympathetic. She was immensely charming. She was utterly unselfish. She excelled in the difficult arts of family life. She sacrificed herself daily. If there was chicken, she took the leg; if there was a draught she sat in it – in short she was so constituted that she never had a mind or a wish of her own, but preferred to sympathize always with the minds and wishes of others.   ('Professions for Women', in *CE*, II, p. 284)

    Woolf's argument is illustrated through the female characters in *The Voyage Out* and their relationships with men.

54. Compare a remark in Woolf's diary for 20 March 1926: 'Dining with Clive last night to meet Lord Ivor Spencer Churchill . . . I was greatly impressed by masculine cleverness, & their ability to toss balls swiftly & surely to & fro: no butter fingers' (*Diary*, III, pp. 67–8).

55. In this respect both Helen and Mrs Ramsay resemble Woolf's own mother, of whom Leslie Stephen remarked:

    I used sometimes I must confess (as indeed I confessed to her) to profess a rather exaggerated self-depreciation in order to extort some of her delicious compliments. They were delicious, for even if I could not accept her critical judgement as correct, I could feel that it was distorted mainly by her tender love. Although she could perceive that I was 'fishing for a compliment' she could not find it in her heart to refuse me. Again and again she would tell me that it was unworthy of me to complain of my want of popular success – which, as you have seen, was not my serious complaint, though I sometimes put it in that way. She assured me that she was a better judge of writing, of my own writing at least, than I was.   (*Sir Leslie Stephen's Mausoleum Book*, ed. Alan Bell (Oxford: Oxford University Press, 1977) p. 93)

56. That Ridley's attitude is one which Woolf was to encounter is illustrated by a passage from her diary in which she remarks: 'I record Mary [Hutchinson]'s telling me last night how she loved cigars; but

Jack refuses to let her smoke them – against his idea of what his wife should do – silly affectation – or to let her dress in a dress cut low at the back. . . . Its indecent – yet will praise Diana for wearing the same' (*Diary*, IV, p. 75).

57. In a similar way, and for similar reasons, Mrs Hilbery in *Night and Day* objects when her daughter makes what she considers a cynical remark (*Night and Day*, p. 98).

58. For a specific example, compare Quentin Bell's account of the manner in which Leslie Stephen issued books to his daughter Virginia from his library (Bell, *Virginia Woolf*, I, p. 51) with the scene in which Rachel visits Ridley Ambrose in his study (*The Voyage Out*, pp. 202–3).

59. Elaine Showalter notes that G. H. Lewes and Gerald Massey both argued that the happily married woman is unlikely to be a genius. Women, on the other hands, had 'a different sense of the advantages and disadvantages of maternity than that expressed by Lewes. Whereas he, and other male writers, saw only a conflict of interests, they saw the possibility of a balanced life in which the domestic role enriched the art, and the art kept the domestic role spontaneous and meaningful' (Showalter, *A Literature of their Own*, pp. 69, 76, 85).

60. Margaret Kirkham, however, questions the reading of *Emma* which sees Knightley as a 'reliable' narrator, and 'the belief that *Emma* is a novel of education in which all the learning is done by the heroine, all the instruction provided by the hero' (see Margaret Kirkham, *Jane Austen: Feminism and Fiction* (Brighton: Harvester, 1983) p. 133). In contrast, Sandra Gilbert and Susan Gubar feel that the male protagonists in Austen's novels are 'older and wiser', 'the representatives of authority' (see Gilbert and Gubar, *The Madwoman in the Attic*, p. 154).

61. In this respect he resembles Ralph Touchett who is one amongst many male characters in nineteenth-century novels who, through illness or disability, are able to identify with the woman's position of relative helplessness in a male-dominated society.

62. See, for example, *Letters*, VI, p. 20; *Three Guineas*, pp. 63, 193.

63. In *A Room*, Woolf remarks that 'Women have served all these centuries as looking-glasses possessing the magic and delicious power of reflecting the figure of a man at twice its natural size' (*A Room*, p. 53).

64. One must, then, question Hermione Lee's argument that

childless, fussy Mrs Elliot, absent-minded Mrs Thornbury, bovine Susan Warrington and her tyrannical old aunt, and the would-be liberated flirt, Evelyn M., are callous caricatures. There is little warmth even in the treatment of the kind academic spinster, Miss Allan, or of the jolly eccentric Mrs Flushing. The tone for the presentation of the minor characters is feebly satirical. (Hermione Lee, *The Novels of Virginia Woolf* (London: Methuen, 1977) p. 38)

Indeed, it is difficult to see how we could know that Miss Allan *is* kind or Mrs Flushing jolly unless it is through Woolf's sympathetic treatment of them. Jean Guiget's description of the hotel visitors as 'a set of grotesque and ungainly puppets' is equally inappropriate (Jean Guiget, *Virginia Woolf and her Works*, trans. Jean Stewart (London: Hogarth Press, 1965) p. 202). To describe the novel's minor characters in these terms is to make the mistake of accepting Rachel's response to them as authoritative.

65. That Terence is the spokesman here for Woolf's own views is clear if one thinks of the inspiration behind the originally unpublished 'Journal of Mistress Joan Martyn', or the 'Memoirs of a Novelist' (*CSF*, pp. 33–62, 63–73), the projected 'Lives of the Obscure' 'which is to tell the whole history of England in one obscure life after another' (*Diary*, III, p. 37), or the introductory letter to Margaret Llewelyn Davies's *Life as We Have Known It: By Co-operative Working Women* (London: The Hogarth Press, 1931) pp. xv–xxxix). In this introduction Woolf remarks of the writings collected in Davies's volume: 'These pages are only fragments. These voices are beginning only now to emerge from silence into half articulate speech. These lives are still half hidden in profound obscurity. To express even what is expressed here has been a work of labour and difficulty. The writing has been done in kitchens, at odds and ends of leisure, in the midst of distractions and obstacles' (ibid., p. xxxix).

66. This is not, however, to agree with Herbert Marder's view that:

> Terence Hewet seems at times to be little more than a mouthpiece. The young aspiring novelist is especially interested, we are told, in the prosaic day-to-day lives of women, the portion of experience that has never yet been recorded. This is a subject that fascinated Virginia Woolf, but she was not altogether convincing when she attributed the same interest to a young man. (Marder, *Feminism and Art*, p. 68)

There seems no obvious reason why a young man should not be interested in such things. It is instructive to compare Woolf's treatment of Terence with the method of Sylvia Townsend Warner's novel *Lolly Willowes*. Warner introduces the fantastic figure of 'the Devil' into her narrative as an audience for a number of monologues on the subject of woman's subservient position in society (Warner, *Lolly Willowes*, pp. 234–6). Her narrative is considerably less persuasive than Woolf's because she makes no obvious attempt to conceal the fact that she has a palpable design upon her readers. (Whereas Terence Hewet's long speech to Rachel on the theme of the status of women seems 'natural' in the context of the novel as a whole, Laura Willowes's extremely similar speech does not.) The same argument applies to Rebecca West's novel *The Judge* which – like Lawrence's *Sons and Lovers* – deals with the way in which a woman who is neglected by her husband may form an over-possessive relationship with her son. The melodramatic events which conclude West's novel have the effect of the drawing attention to the author's didactic purpose. Olive Schreiner's novels also throw an interesting light upon the question of didacticism and fiction. The least persuasive parts of her novels are probably those in which she obviously betrays a narrow didactic purpose. One thinks, for example, of Part Two, Chapter Four, of *The Story of an African Farm* in which, in what is essentially a monologue, Lyndall expounds her ideas on feminism to Waldo (see Olive Schreiner, *The Story of an African Farm* (London: Chapman and Hall, 1883) II, pp. 25–68). More generally, the novel's events become 'unrealistic' and melodramatic when Schreiner is using them specifically to illustrate a feminist point. Thus Lyndall's 'elopement' and subsequent death in exile is the weakest part of the book. The section in *From Man to Man* dealing with Bertie's departure for England with a Jew and their subsequent life together in Bloomsbury is, similarly, lacking in conviction (see Schreiner, *From Man to Man*, pp. 348–410).

67. *A Room*, p. 124.

68. When she came to write *The Years*, Woolf rejected the idea of juxtaposing theoretical statements in her own voice and fictional scenes illustrative of those statements within a single work of art. In *The Voyage Out* she avoids this problem by putting her own ideas into the mouth of one of her fictional characters.

69. See 'Walter Raleigh', in *CE*, I, pp. 314–18. In a letter to Vita Sackville-West of 17 February 1926 she asks: 'why are all professors of English Literature ashamed of English Literature? Walter Raleigh calls Shakespeare "Billy Shaxs" – Blake, "Bill" – a good poem "a bit of all right." This shocks me' (*Letters*, III, p. 242). Compare ibid., III, p. 252. Woolf's light-hearted portrayal of Hughling Elliot in *The Voyage Out* – like her depiction of Oxford dons in *The Years* – is far more persuasive than a personal attack upon academics of the kind to be found in her essay on Walter Raleigh would be.

70. Barbara Taylor notes:

> From the late eighteenth century onward the number of unmarried women in Britain had increased rapidly, while at the same time the economic prospects of such women steadily deteriorated. Eliza Macauleys proliferated, eking out a precarious existence on the margins of professional or literary society. Such women were pitied for their man-less state, but as one woman sharply pointed out, the reason 'so many unmarried women are unhappy is *not* because they are old maids, but in consequence of *poverty* and the difficulty they encounter in maintaining a decent position in society'. (Taylor, *Eve and the New Jerusalem*, p. 72)

71. Compare Mr Widdowson in Gissing's *The Odd Women* who, 'Like most men of his kind . . . viewed religion as a precious and powerful instrument for directing the female conscience' (George Gissing, *The Odd Women* (London: Lawrence & Bullen, 1893) II, p. 39).

72. 'Modern Fiction', in *CE*, II, p. 107.

73. Through Mr Bax, Woolf dramatises the anti-ecclesiastical argument

which she was later to put forward in *Three Guineas*, and which, in that essay, centres around the Archbishop's Commission on the Ministry of Women.

74. Susan, like many of the characters in *The Voyage Out*, seems to be based on one of the people whom Woolf met at the Grand Hotel in Perugia in 1908, a girl whose deepest plot was, according to Woolf, 'to be mistress of a good man's home, and bear him children' (*MHP*, MH/A7).

75. Barbara Taylor notes that

middle-class domestic life . . . had hardened into the familiar 'Victorian' pattern even before Victoria ascended the throne. For women, this meant a narrowing of their occupational possibilities to marriage and motherhood, and a corresponding idealisation of the dependent domestic role as woman's life mission. Yet in the same years when femininity was being thus family-defined, it was becoming much more difficult for middle-class women to establish their own families. By the 1830s a combination of male preference for late marriage and a high ratio of women to men in the population had created large numbers of middle-class spinsters – 'surplus women', in the language of the day. Since single women of this background faced an almost total lack of employment opportunities, most were either forced into unhappy dependence on some male relative, or left to face destitution and marginality. (Taylor, *Eve and the New Jerusalem*, pp. 192–3)

76. Compare Woolf's remark in a letter to Vanessa Bell of August 1911:

I suppose though there is a kind of unity in marriage (barring children) which one doesn't get from liaisons. I'm thinking a good deal, at intervals, about marriage. My quarrel with it is that the pace is so slow, when you are two people. (*Letters*, I, p. 475)

Woolf reiterates this idea in a subsequent letter: 'the extreme safeness and sobriety of young couples does apall me, but then so do the random melancholy old maids' (ibid., p. 492).

77. Some critics interpret Terence's description of himself as a great lover as a pretence on his part. See, for example, Louise DeSalvo's *Virginia Woolf's First Voyage: A Novel in the Making* (London: Macmillan, 1980) p. 46, and Mitchell Leaska, *The Novels of Virginia Woolf: From Beginning to End* (London: Weidenfeld & Nicolson, 1977) p. 22.

78. *CE*, II, p. 144. She reiterates this argument in *A Room*, pp. 105–6.

79. Ray Strachey describes the prostitute's position in society:

It was actually because of their sex that they were outcasts, not because of their behaviour. The men who did as they did, and who shared their vice and degradation, were not dealt with in the same manner, nor held in the same disgust. The double moral standard allowed to men what it forbade to women; and it was from this root that the worst of the evil grew. (Strachey, *The Cause*, pp. 189–90)

80. Olive Schreiner's novel *From Man to Man* illustrates this idea, the central theme of the novel being expressed in the heroine Rebekah's remark:

> Who is the prostitute – the wretched woman whom the policeman drags along the street, or the man, often of wealth and learning and power, whose selfish lust and gold alone keep alive the institution whose bitter fruit she is? When you have crushed and destroyed the woman prostitute, what have you done more than cut out the tiny rotten place on the surface of an apple, while you leave gnawing away in the dark at the core the worm that produced it? (Schreiner, *From Man to Man*, p. 198)

Rebekah's relationship with her husband Frank and, more particularly, her sister Bertie's relationship with John-Ferdinand, illustrate – like Hardy's *Tess* – the degree to which a woman can be the victim of society's double-standard.

81. In *The Old Wives' Tale*, Bennett, like Woolf, sets out to undermine the accepted idea that prostitutes are criminals rather than victims. But he spoils his point by over-emphasising it, rather than allowing the incident in which Mme Foucault and Mme Laurence rescue Sophia to speak for itself. In consequence, he deprives us of the sense that we have discovered a meaning in the narrative for ourselves. We feel that the figures of Aimée and Mme Laurence, and the episode in which they are involved, have been created, not out of interest in the women themselves, but in order to illustrate a theoretical point.

82. Josephine Butler's campaign against the Contagious Diseases Acts met with wide publicity in the late 1860s. The Acts, Patricia Stubbs explains, 'allowed the forcible examination of prostitutes suspected of having venereal disease and the detention of those found to be infected. It was yet another statutory enactment of the double standard and gave wide powers to the police' (Stubbs, *Women and Fiction*, p. 13). The campaign inspired a great many works on the subject.

83. E. M. Forster dramatises the double moral standard in *Howards End*. In the course of this novel, Margaret Wilcox finds herself called upon to forgive her husband for having had a mistress. Mr Wilcox himself, however, is unable to forgive Margaret's sister for becoming pregnant by a married man. Forster weakens the effect of his novel, though, by inserting passages of didactic commentary in his own voice into the text, which destroy our 'belief' in his fictional characters. The way in which women are sexually exploited by men such as Mr Wilcox is far more persuasively illustrated in a novel like Ivan Turgenev's *On the Eve* (trans. C. E. Turner (London: Hodder & Stoughton, 1871)) or Rosamond Lehmann's *The Weather in the Streets* (London: Collins, 1936) in which the reader is drawn to identify

completely, and therefore to sympathise, with the heroine. For a discussion of didacticism in *Howards End* see Bayley's *The Uses of Division*, pp. 27–35.

84. *Letters*, II, p. 82.
85. David Daiches comments:

> The Victorian novelist tended on the whole to produce a narrative art whose patterns were determined by a public sense of values. Virginia Woolf, on the other hand, sensitive to the decay of public values in her time, preferred the more exacting task of patterning events in terms of her personal vision, which meant that she had on her hands the additional technical job of discovering devices for convincing the reader, at least during his period of reading, of the significance and reality of this vision. (David Daiches, *Virginia Woolf*, 2nd edn (Norfolk. Conn.: New Directions, 1963; 1st edn 1942) p. 154)

86. Lily Briscoe serves a similar purpose in *To the Lighthouse*.
87. One is reminded of Miriam Henderson's objection in *Pilgrimage* to the way in which most people read a novel to find out 'what happens in the end' (Richardson, *Pilgrimage*, I, p. 384).
88. Woolf expressed a similar view when writing *The Years*: 'Its not the writing but the architecting that strains' (*Diary*, IV, p. 306). See also *Letters*, IV, p. 354.
89. See *Letters*, IV, p. 397. Compare *Diary*, III, pp. 104, 218; *Letters*, IV, p. 381.
90. Commenting upon her 'vision of a fin rising on a wide blank sea' which was, she believed, the germ from which *The Waves* grew, Woolf remarked: 'No biographer could possibly guess this important fact about my life in the late summer of 1926: yet biographers pretend they know people' (*Diary*, III, p. 153). Compare her remarks on biography/history in *Letters*, I, p. 354; IV, p. 83; *Diary*, II, pp. 65, 92.
91. This problem was particularly vivid to the young Virginia Woolf who, at the time of writing *The Voyage Out*, had already witnessed the death of her mother, father, step-sister and brother. Given that in writing the novel – as with *The Waves* (see *Diary*, IV, p. 10) – she was, in a sense, coming to terms with the death of her brother Thoby, her 'objective', impersonal tone is the more remarkable. She has no wish to use the novel as a 'dumping-ground' for personal experience, but aims, rather, to assimilate that experience into a work of fiction.
92. *Diary*, III, p. 339. Hillis Miller rightly argues:

> Though Woolf deals with extreme spiritual situations, her work would hardly give support, to a scheme of literary history which sees twentieth-century literature as more negative, more 'nihilistic' or more 'ambiguous' than nineteenth-century literature. . . . the possibility that the realm of death, in real life as in fiction, really exists, is more seriously entertained by Woolf than it is, for

example, by Eliot, by Thackeray, or by Hardy. The possibility that repetition in narrative is the representation of a transcendent spiritual realm of reconciliation and preservation, a realm of the perpetual resurrection from the dead, is more straightforwardly proposed by Virginia Woolf than by most of her predecessors in English fiction. (J. Hillis Miller, *Fiction and Repetition: Seven English Novels* (Oxford: Blackwell, 1982) pp. 201–2)

93. David Lodge argues that

whereas the classic nineteenth-century novel accounted for all its characters (however implausibly) in terms of the plot, thus conveying the sense of society as something that was, however corrupt, ultimately intelligible and therefore redeemable, most of Virginia Woolf's characters drift in and out of focus in a curiously random way, and the plot that might unite them into a single pattern never transpires. (Lodge, *The Modes of Modern Writing*, p. 181)

The characters in Woolf's novels are, however, united not at the level of plot but of form. One thinks, for example, of the relationship between Clarissa Dalloway and Septimus Warren Smith in *Mrs Dalloway*, two characters who, although they never meet, are bound together through the structure, or pattern, of the novel.

94. *Letters*, IV, p. 397. Hillis Miller detects a similar idea behind *Mrs Dalloway*, and also in Conrad's *Lord Jim*:

the novel represents human life as happening to fall into repetitive patterns, whether in the life of a single person, as Jim repeats variants of the same action over and over, or from person to person, as Brierly's jump repeats Jim's jump. The question the novel asks and cannot unequivocally answer is 'Why is this?' To say it is because Conrad designed his novel in recurring patterns is to trivialize the question and to give a misplaced answer to it. (Hillis Miller, *Fiction and Repetition*, pp. 181–2, 36)

95. Stephen, *Mausoleum Book*, p. 60.
96. Hillis Miller argues:

A novel is interpreted in part through the noticing of . . . recurrences. [These recurrences work in various way] to generate meaning or to inhibit the too easy determination of a meaning based on the linear sequence of a story. The reader's identification of recurrences may be deliberate or spontaneous, self-conscious or unreflective. In a novel what is said two or more times may not be true, but the reader is fairly safe in assuming that it is significant. (Hillis Miller, *Fiction and Repetition*, p. 2)

97. In an early draft of the novel, Helen thinks to herself that, 'All the

disasters in her experience seemed to have come from civilised people forgetting how easily they may die' (quoted by DeSalvo in *Virginia Woolf's First Voyage*, p. 43).

98. Thus, whereas in *The Waves* Bernard laments the fact that his anguish at Percival's death is so short-lived (*The Waves*, p. 110), in *The Voyage Out* Woolf emphasises the positive aspects of our ability to forget suffering.

99. That Woolf aimed at a similar effect in *Mrs Dalloway* is suggested by a comment on that novel in the holograph notebook of *Jacob's Room:* 'All must bear finally on the party at the end; which expresses life in every variety . . . while S[eptimus]. dies' (quoted in Phyllis Rose's *Woman of Letters*, p. 135).

100. *Letters*, i, p. 358.

101. Both David Daiches (*Virginia Woolf*, p. 14) and Hermione Lee (*Virginia Woolf*, p. 50) argue that Rachel's death is not sufficiently anticipated in the novel. But Alice van Buren Kelley is right to argue that in *The Voyage Out*, 'Once the visionary aspect of death is revealed with Rachel's actual dying, all earlier hints of tragedy take on a deeper significance' (Alice van Buren Kelley, *The Novels of Virginia Woolf: Fact and Vision* (London: University of Chicago Press, 1973) p. 12).

102. Compare Woolf's comment in her diary for 27 November 1925: 'That there is no substance in ones friendships, that they fade like – . . . Nothing like a coin is struck & left for ever in one's possession. People die; Madge dies, & one cannot beat up a solitary tear' (*Diary*, iii, p. 48). See, too, a remark for 17 January 1928: 'Lady Strachey slowly fading, but it may take years. Over all this broods for me some uneasy sense, of change, & mortality, & how partings are deaths' (*Diary*, iii, p. 174). Compare ibid., p. 188.

103. Her idea anticipates Eleanor's thought about the walrus-brush in *The Years:* 'That solid object might survive them all. If she threw it away it would still exist somewhere or other' (*The Years*, p. 96).

104. Here we have a further example of the way in which Woolf translates personal experience into fiction in the novel. There is an obvious link between these two friends of Mrs Paley – like Prue and Andrew in *To the Lighthouse* – and Woolf's own half-sister and brother.

105. Eric Warner makes this point when he remarks that 'Rather than let Rachel fall into the end of banal routine and sacrificed spirit, [Woolf] kills the girl off with an unnamed tropical fever'. In contrast, in *The Waves*, the 'contagion of the world's slow stain' feared in *The Voyage Out* is realised (see Eric Warner, 'Some Aspects of Romanticism in the Work of Virginia Woolf' (D.Phil. thesis, Oxford University, 1980) pp. 119, 373). A remark which Alice van Buren Kelley makes about Woolf's second novel links it with *The Voyage Out*: '*Night and Day* ends before the lovers can experience those blows to vision that life in the real world invariably inflicts upon those who look for unity' (Kelley, *Virginia Woolf*, p. 62).

106. In a letter to Roger Fry of 27 May 1927 Woolf remarked of her use of symbolism in the later novel:

I meant *nothing* by The Lighthouse. One has to have a central line down the middle of the book to hold the design together. I saw that all sorts of feelings would accrue to this, but I refused to think them out, and trusted that people would make it the deposit for their own emotions – which they have done, one thinking it means one thing another another. I can't manage Symbolism except in this vague, generalised way. Whether its right or wrong I don't know, but directly I'm told what a thing means, it becomes hateful to me.   (*Letter*, III, p. 385)

107. Clarissa – in *Mrs Dalloway* – remarks upon 'the terror; the over-whelming incapacity, one's parents giving it into one's hands, this life, to be lived to the end, to be walked with serenely' (*Mrs Dalloway*, p. 203).
108. *Letters*, I, p. 358.
109. Compare the excursion to Fiesole in Chapter Six of Forster's *A Room with a View* (pp. 89–105).
110. The novel implicitly endorses Keat's idea of life as a 'vale of soul-making', a view which Woolf makes more explicit in a letter to Edward Sackville-West of 22 September 1926: 'I like people to be unhappy because I like them to have souls' (*Letters*, III, p. 294). *The Voyage Out* could be said to offer a more subtle, less obviously schematised, version of the response to the 'problem of evil' which we find in Huxley's *Brave New World*.
111. In a similar way remarks about Jacob's future in *Jacob's Room* take on a pathos with his death at the end of that novel.
112. Implicit in Woolf's portrait of Rodriguez is her own dislike of, and scepticism about, doctors. In a letter to Violet Dickinson of 25 August 1907 she asks: 'why do you see doctors? They are a profoundly untrustworthy race; either they lie, or they mistake' (*Letters*, I, p. 306). In *The Voyage Out*, however she avoids the angry tone which we find in the portrayal of Dr Holmes and Sir William Bradshaw in *Mrs Dalloway*. To indulge in such bitterness in a work of fiction is to draw attention away from the 'world of the novel' and its characters to the person of the author. (Hillis Miller is, though, right to point out that even in the passage on 'Proportion' and 'Conversion' in *Mrs Dalloway*, 'the narrator catches herself up and attributes some of her own judgment of Sir William Bradshaw to Rezia' (Hillis Miller, *Fiction and Repetition*, pp. 179–80).
113. In a letter to Vita Sackville-West of 7 September 1930, written while Woolf herself was ill, she remarks rather gracelessly of Vita's mother, Lady Sackville: 'Now if the sunstroke descended on her head and left you £5,000 a year the richer I should think all the better of God. Why choose me and Potto, who have nothing to leave? It often strikes me that Heaven is a blundering affair – clumsy past belief' (*Letters*, IV, p. 210).

Notes to Chapter Three: *Night and Day*

1. Phyllis Rose puts it forward as a criticism of *Night and Day* that in this novel the characters 'overthrow the accepted social order (that engagements are not broken, that the abandoned woman does not help her ex-fiancé to find a new bride, that great poets' granddaughters do not marry law clerks) so discreetly and placidly that one hardly knows anything of moment has happened' (Rose, *Woman of Letters*, p. 96). Her remark in fact implicitly pays tribute to the success of Woolf's oblique method in the novel.

2. In a similar manner, Henry James dramatises the two sides of the feminist question in *The Bostonians* (London: Macmillan, 1886) with a good deal of humour at the expense of feminists and anti-feminists alike. Oliver Chancellor and Basil Ransom are allowed to reveal the absurdities and inconsistencies of their respective positions in the same way as, for example, Mrs Seal and William Rodney, without any explicit comment on the part of the author. The form of Tennyson's poem, *The Princess*, similarly allowed him to put forward and satirise various points of view in the feminist debate. As Paul Turner remarks: 'the narrative method . . . justified internal contradictions, lowered the emotional temperature, and presented the poem as a forum for all shades of opinion' (Paul Turner, *Tennyson* (London: Routledge & Kegan Paul, 1976) p. 103).

3. *A Room*, p. 157.

4. Herbert Marder argues that:

   Katharine and Ralph, Virginia Woolf implies, are both essentially androgynous; each one combines the opposite within his own personality. . . . the function of their marriage, both as symbol and as reality, is to enable them to complete each other, to help each other perfect their androgyneity. (Marder, *Feminism and Art*, p. 128)

5. *Night and Day*, p. 536. (Hereafter all references to this novel appear parenthetically within the text.)

6. *Letters*, II, p. 414.

7. Ibid., p. 394.

8. Elizabeth Gaskell, *The Life of Charlotte Brontë* (London: Smith, Elder, 1857) II, pp. 49–50. Elaine Showalter notes that in the early twentieth century certain women,

   Stella Benson was one – insisted vehemently 'on being a writer first and a wife second; a man would insist and I insist. A hundred years hence it will seem absurd that a woman would have to say this, just as it would seem absurd now if we should hear that Mr William Blake's wife wanted him to take up breeding pigs to help her and he obstinately preferred writing poetry.' (Showalter, *A Literature of their Own*, pp. 244–5)

9. Compare George Bernard Shaw's remarks about Gertrude Lindsay and Sidney Trefusis in *An Unsocial Socialist* (London: Swan, Sonnenschein, Lowry, 1887) p. 242; 'She, who had lived in the marriage market since she had left school, looked upon love-making as the most serious business of life. To him it was only a pleasant sort of trifling, enhanced by a dash of sadness in the reflection that it meant so little.'

10. Henrik Ibsen, *A Doll's House*, trans. W. Archer (London: Fisher Unwin, 1889) pp. 96, 100.

11. In this respect he brings to mind St John Rivers in Charlotte Brontë's *Jane Eyre* or Sir Willoughby Patterne in Meredith's *The Egoist*.

12. George Bernard Shaw, *The Quintessence of Ibsenism* (London: Scott, 1891) p. 32.

13. Ray Strachey discusses this case at some length in her history of the women's movement, *The Cause*, pp. 175ff.

14. *Three Guineas*, p. 118.

15. Ibid., pp. 238–46. Woolf finds Hardy's Henchard, in *The Mayor of Casterbridge*, guilty of a similar 'jealous paternal passion' (see 'The Novels of Thomas Hardy', in *CE*, I, p. 261). Everard Willowes (in Sylvia Townsend Warner's *Lolly Willowes*, p. 27) is susceptible to this type of jealousy over his daughter Laura.

16. The relationship between Mr Hilbery and Katharine – like that between Rachel and Willoughby Vinrace – is clearly inspired in part by relations between Leslie Stephen and his daughters. Phyllis Rose notes that when Woolf's elder sister, Stella, agreed to marry Jack Hills: 'The marriage of Stella and Jack, which seemed so good and so natural, was taken as a personal blow by Leslie Stephen. Virginia was to say later that if only her father could have said "I am jealous" rather than "You are selfish," the whole family atmosphere would have been lightened' (Rose, *Woman of Letters*, p. 13).

17. That Woolf found specific aspects of the suffrage movement unattractive is suggested by various remarks in her letters. Writing to Violet Dickinson to describe her own involvement in the suffrage movement, she commented in a letter of 27 February 1910: 'The office, with its ardent but educated young women, and brotherly clerks, is just like a Wells novel' (*Letters*, I, p. 422), and in a subsequent letter of 14 November of the same year she remarked: 'My time has been wasted a good deal upon Suffrage' (ibid., p. 438).

18. Strachey, *The Cause*, p. 272.

19. In her diary, for example, she remarks:

It seems to me more & more clear that the only honest people are the artists, & that these social reformers & philanthropists get so out of hand, & harbour so many discreditable desires under the disguise of loving their kind, that in the end there's more to find fault with in them than in us. (*Diary*, I, p. 293)

Compare Mary Datchet's thought that 'no work can equal in importance, or be so exciting as, the work of making other people do what you want them to do' (*Night and Day*, p. 174).

20. Similarly, Woolf avoids criticising Miss Kilman directly in *Mrs Dalloway*. It is primarily Clarissa the society woman, rather than Woolf the narrator, who attacks the Christian philanthropist in that novel.

21. In this respect she resembles Miss Birdseye and Olive Chancellor in James's *The Bostonians*.

22. 'Four Figures', in *CE*, III, p. 195. Miss Kilman (in *Mrs Dalloway*) is an obvious example of a 'lover of mankind' who hates individuals, as, indeed, are the two main characters in the short story 'The Man Who Loved His Kind' and the philanthropist Miss Pryme in the story of that name (*CSF*, pp. 189–94, 229–30).

23. Contemporary feminists such as Elaine Showalter have responded with varying degrees of impatience to Woolf's advocation of a liberal tolerance in political matters. But Woolf not only felt that a novel will be more persuasive if it is not obviously militantly partisan, she was also very sensitive to the dangers implicit in unquestioning commitment to specific ideals. Through Mary, Woolf shows that it is possible to be politically committed without being narrow-minded and bigoted. Mrs Seal and Mr Clacton, on the other hand, illustrate the argument of *Three Guineas* that the dividing-line between victim and victimiser, oppressor and oppressed, can be a fine one.

24. *Three Guineas*, pp. 185, 258.

25. In a letter to Katherine Cox of 18 March 1913, Woolf remarks:

> But my dear Ka, I see at a glance that nothing – except perhaps novel writing – can compare with the excitement of controlling the masses. The letters you'd get! The jobs you'd be sent on – and then people would always be telling you things, and if you could move them you would feel like a God. I see now where Margaret [Llewelyn Davies] and even Mary MacCarthur get their Imperial tread. The mistake I've made is in mixing up what they do with philanthropy. (*Letters*, II, p. 19)

Compare ibid., I, p. 441; VI, p. 94; *Diary*, I, p. 293.

26. One could argue that just as Mary brings Ralph, through humour, towards her own way of thinking, so too Woolf uses comedy in her novel to persuade the reader of the validity of her feminist position. In contrast, the alienating effect of overt propaganda, in life or literature, is illustrated in the complete failure of Mrs Seal's attempt to 'convert' Katharine.

27. That she shares her author's point of view is suggested by a remark in Woolf's diary: 'never pretend that the things you haven't got are not worth having . . . Never pretend that children, for instance, can be replaced by other things' (*Diary*, II, p. 221).

28. *A Room*, p. 156. Woolf's concept of 'androgyny' has traditionally been seen as a call for the union of the 'masculine' and the 'feminine'. Toril Moi questions this interpretation, however, arguing that in her ideal of 'androgyny' Woolf was in fact positing not the flight from fixed

gender identities – as Elaine Showalter and Nancy Topping Bazin, for example, would maintain – but the breaking down of what is a purely metaphysical distinction between the 'masculine' and the 'feminine'. 'She has understood', Moi contends, 'that the goal of the feminist struggle must precisely be to deconstruct the death-dealing binary opposites of masculinity and femininity' (Toril Moi, *Sexual/Textual Politics: Feminist Literary Theory* (London: Methuen, 1985) p. 13). Sandra Gilbert argues that 'Carpenter's notions of the "man-womanliness" of such artists as Shelley, Shakespeare, and Michelangelo clearly influenced Woolf (probably through Forster but perhaps more directly), for they are exactly analogous to the ideas she defines in *A Room of One's Own*' (Sandra Gilbert, 'Costumes of the Mind: Transvestism as Metaphor in Modern Literature', in Abel (ed.), *Writing and Sexual Difference*, p. 217).

29. The contrast between 'helping' and 'hurting' is one to which I will return later in this chapter.
30. This passage brings to mind the fact that St John Hirst measures Rachel Vinrace's value in terms of her capacity to appreciate Gibbon (see *The Voyage Out*, p. 180).
31. *Letters*, II, p. 474.
32. Compare Leslie Stephen's remark about his wife Julia: 'Her instincts were far more to be trusted than my ratiocinations' (Stephen, *Mausoleum Book*, p. 95).
33. Some contemporary feminist critics have attacked Woolf because in creating figures such as Mrs Hilbery and Mrs Ramsay she seems to be perpetuating traditional sexual stereotypes. Woolf's admiration for such women is, however, always qualified in her novels by her recognition of the stumbling block which they constitute to the cause of women's emancipation.
34. *The Years*, p. 13.
35. Compare Lily's response to Charles Tansley during the dinner in *To the Lighthouse* (p. 142), and Peggy's reaction to the egotistical writer at Delia's party in *The Years* (p. 389). Margaret Schlegel in E. M. Forster's *Howards End*, similarly, has 'an almost morbid horror of "drawing people out", of "making things go"' (Forster, *Howards End*, p. 35).
36. Describing the claustrophic atmosphere of the Victorian family home, Florence Nightingale remarks that: 'Marriage is the only chance (and it is but a chance) offered to women for escape from this death; and how eagerly and how ignorantly it is embraced!' (Strachey, *The Cause*, p. 405). Bernard Shaw illustrates this idea in his treatment of Gertrude Lindsay in *An Unsocial Socialist*, p. 156.
37. *Three Guineas*, p. 140.
38. Compare the relationship between Mary, Gwendolen and Alice Cartaret and their father in May Sinclair's *The Three Sisters*:

> After all (as they had frequently reminded themselves), without them he could never have lived comfortably on his income. They did the work and saved him the expenses of a second servant, a

housekeeper, an under-gardener, an organist and two curates. (May Sinclair, *The Three Sisters* (London: Macmillan, 1914) p. 92)

39. It is for this reason that Brontë's Jane Eyre wishes to continue as governess to Adèle after her marriage to Mr Rochester (Brontë, *Jane Eyre* (London: Smith, Elder, 1847) II, p. 243). Caroline Helstone, in *Shirley*, suffers from the fact that there is no financial pressure upon her to find employment outside her father's house. Yet, Brontë remarks, 'Many that want food and clothing have cheerier lives and brighter prospects than she had; many, harassed by poverty, are in a strait less afflictive' (Charlotte Brontë, *Shirley* (London: Smith, Elder, 1849) II, p. 50). Marigold, in Rosamond Lehmann's *The Weather in the Streets* voices the woman's desire for a profession: 'But I just feel anything would be better than this frittering futile. . . . [Lehmann's ellipsis] I'd like to have to work – have my day filled up from start to finish and come home too weary not to be peaceful' (Lehmann, *The Weather in the Streets*, p. 114).

40. In the same way Eleanor, in *The Years*, cannot fulfil her desire to go to India until both her parents have died. The pressure which Ralph's family exerts upon him because of their relative poverty parallels that which Katharine's parents put upon her because she is a woman. The privacy of Ralph's room is won at the price of an emotional struggle akin to Mary's battle with her father (*The Years*, pp. 20, 55).

41. In May Sinclair's *The Three Sisters*, Alice Cartaret marries Jim Greatorex – an individual renowned for his drunkenness and for his relationship with the family servant – to escape from the claustrophobia of life with her father at the Vicarage, which is steadily driving her insane. Although Alice's marriage is described in the novel as a happy one, the whole incident serves to draw attention to the way in which a woman may be driven to the most unsuitable of marriages as the only obvious means of escape from the oppressively dreary life of the paternal home. It is just such a temptation which Henry Crawford offers to Fanny Price in Jane Austen's *Mansfield Park* (London: Egerton, 1814).

42. E. M. Forster's Margaret Schlegel anticipates the argument of Woolf's *A Room* when she remarks that 'independent thoughts are in nine cases out of ten the result of independent means' (Forster, *Howards End*, p. 124).

43. Florence Nightingale remarks upon how difficult it is for a woman to combine serious scientific study with the management of a household: 'Women often try one branch of intellect after another in their youth, *e.g.* mathematics. But that, least of all is compatible with the life of "society". It is impossible to follow up anything seriously' (Strachey, *The Cause*, p. 400).

44. 'Phyllis and Rosamond', in *CSF*, p. 18.

45. Ibid., pp. 26–7.

46. Ibid., p. 28.

47. The double love-plot, reminiscent of a romantic comedy such as Shakespeare's *Much Ado*, consists of a series of encounters between

the four protagonists – originally Mary, Ralph, Katharine and William, though Mary is subsequently replaced by Cassandra – in clearly visualised settings.

48. Woolf remarks in a letter to Ethel Smyth of 2 November 1930 that 'nothing describes character like a letter' (*Letters*, iv, p. 245).

49. *Diary*, i, p. 310.

50. Bernard Blackstone argues that in *Night and Day*,

> The moments of vision which are found here and there in the book don't seem to fit: they are not assimilated into the texture of the whole, they stand out as purple passages. In a way, it is a retrogression from *The Voyage Out*. (Bernard Blackstone, *Virginia Woolf: A Commentary* (London: The Hogarth Press, 1949) p. 47)

51. See, for example, the opening to Chapter 15.

52. *Diary*, iii, p. 37.

53. Ibid., i, p. 205.

54. On more than one occasion, Katharine's parents are described sitting hunched up in their armchairs (*Night and Day*, pp. 96, 499). Mr Hilbery has the habit of fingering the green stone which he wears on his watch chain (pp. 96, 442). Mrs Seal, similarly, is typified by the two crucifixes which continually entangle themselves upon her breast (pp. 78, 279). Rodney, like Mrs Crosby in *The Years*, is remarkable for his prominent eyes (pp. 48, 141, 179). On several occasions Ralph's attention is caught by the sight of a tall figure whom he afterwards recognises as Katharine (pp. 242, 348).

55. In fact, throughout the novel Woolf's treatment of Cassandra is rather weak; it could be argued that she is brought into existence merely as a solution to the complexities of the love-plot, and that Woolf had little interest in her as a credible character. Indeed, she remarked in a letter to Lytton Strachey of 28 October 1919: 'Then was Rodney's change of heart sufficiently prepared for to be credible? It came into my head on the spur of the moment that he was in love with Cassandra, and afterwards it seemed a little violent' (*Letters*, ii, p. 394).

56. *CE*, ii, p. 59.

57. I cant believe [She commented to Ottoline Morrell] that any human being can get through Night and Day which I wrote chiefly in bed, half an hour at a time. But it taught me a great deal, or so I hoped, like a minute Academy drawing: what to leave out: by putting it all in. (*Letters*, vi, p. 216)

Compare a letter to Ethel Smyth of 16 October 1930 about the composition of *Night and Day*:

> And I made myself copy from plaster casts [one thinks, for example, of Meredith's *The Egoist*], partly to tranquillise, partly to learn anatomy. Bad as the book is, it composed my mind, and I think

taught me certain elements of composition which I should not have had the patience to learn had I been in full flush of health always.   (Ibid., IV, p. 231)

58. The scene in which Katharine comes to Mary for help and confesses, 'I am desperate' (p. 473) echoes the episode earlier in the novel in which Ralph, describing his feelings for Katharine to Mary, exclaims, 'I'm in torment' (p. 413). There is a similar verbal echo in the phrase 'She loves me!' which Ralph uses of Mary, and William of Katharine (pp. 241, 341). The phrase heralds each man's realisation that his own love is not as strong as he had previously imagined. Another phrase which echoes amongst the lovers – 'I am in love with you' – is first used by Mary as she looks at the Elgin Marbles and thinks of Ralph (p. 80). Ralph, sitting in his room after Katharine has left it, exclaims to himself, 'But I'm in love with you' (p. 409). Later when he remarks sarcastically to Katharine, 'Very well. I'm not in love with you' she replies: 'But I think you *are* in love with me' (p. 449). Her remark anticipates Mrs Hilbery's exclamation, in response to Katharine's tender description of Ralph, 'But, Katharine, you *are* in love' (p. 510).
59. See, for example: *Night and Day*, pp. 26, 71, 222, 223, 224, 247–80, 251, 271, 286, 317, 384, 403, 431, 432, 440, 488, 493, 523.
60. *Diary*, I, p. 269.
61. See, for example, *Night and Day*, pp. 33, 35, 40, 97, 157, 222, 295, 369.
62. A work like *Flush* belittles the concept of the 'great man' whose life is worth recording in a two-volume biography, as does the unpublished sketch on the life of Saxon Sydney-Turner entitled *One of [our] the great men* (*MHP*, MH/A13(c)).
63. Mr Hilbery's position as editor of a Review has its humour, too, since he spends a good deal of his time accumulating little-known facts about the lives of the Romantic poets (*Night and Day*, pp. 108, 109). Woolf implicitly mocks this type of scholastic pedantry when she describes the response which several professors make to Mrs Hilbery's suggestion that Shakespeare's sonnets are, in fact, written by Anne Hathaway (p. 322).

Notes to Chapter Four: *The Years*

1. A large number of scenes and passages in *The Years* echo *Night and Day*. In particular, the episode in which Kitty Malone visits the Robsons for tea corresponds very closely to that in which Katharine visits the Denham family at Highgate.
2. The early drafts of the 1880 section of *The Years* were collected and edited by Mitchell Leaska and published under the title *The Pargiters* in 1978.
3. Olive Schreiner makes the same point through Rebekah in *From Man to Man:*

What has humanity not lost by the suppression and subjection of the weaker sex by the muscularly stronger sex alone? We have a Shakespeare; but what of the possible Shakespeares we might have had, who passed their life from youth upward brewing currant wine and making pastries for fat country squires to eat, with no glimpse of the freedom of life and action, necessary even to poach on deer in the green forests, stifled out without one line written, simply because, being of the weaker sex, life gave no room for action and grasp on life?   (Schreiner, *From Man to Man*, p. 219)

4. *A Room*, p. 71.
5. Ibid., pp. 71–2.
6. Ibid., p. 79.
7. Gilbert and Gubar draw attention to

the runaways who abound in Austen's novels, young women whose imaginations are tainted by romantic notions which fuel their excessive materialism or sexuality, and who would do anything with anyone in order to escape their families: Eliza Brandon, Julia and Maria Bertram, Lydia Bennet, Lucy Steele, and Georgianna Darcy.

They remark of the girls in Austen's novels that 'Although their mothers' example proves how debilitating marriage can be, they seek husbands in order to escape from home' (Gilbert and Gubar, *The Madwoman in the Attic*, pp. 122, 125).
8. *A Room*, pp. 81–2.
9. Mary Poovey points out that:

Needing to be needed, needing to express her 'spirit of activity', yet lacking any vehicle for expression more meaningful than accumulating capital or 'projecting' charity, Mrs Norris is a typical victim of the discrepancy between romantic expectations and social possibilities. Her irritating officiousness focuses this discrepancy, for it is really a woman's imaginative energy misdirected by her dependence and social uselessness. To the extent that Mrs Norris becomes an artist manquée, she does so because she has been deprived of an appropriate profession by the strictures society has placed on the very imagination it has aroused. (Poovey, *The Proper Lady*, p. 216)

Barbara Taylor argues that by the late eighteenth century:

the expansion of personal wealth had encouraged *nouveau-riche* men to view their homes, and the women within them, as display cases for their affluence. Women who had once made an essential contribution to family economies became idle, decorative accessories to their husbands, expected to do nothing but supervise

servants and fill male leisure hours with gentle chatter and sexual
pleasure . . . Thus robbed of all serious social or economic func-
tions, such women deteriorated . . . into 'mere parasites' who
lacked any sense of themselves as rational, self-determining
beings.   (Taylor, *Eve and the New Jerusalem*, p. 4)

10. In a passage which echoes very closely the argument of *A Room*,
Richardson's narrator argues that Shakespeare's female characters
are lacking in reality because they are portrayed from a male point
of view:

How much more real was the relation between Portia and Nerissa
than between either of the sadly jesting women and their complac-
ently jesting lovers. . . . Shakespeare did not know the meaning
of the words and actions of Nerissa and Portia when they were
alone together, the beauty they knew and felt and saw, holy
beauty everywhere.   (Richardson, *Pilgrimage*, II, pp. 187–8)

Richardson's objection to *Anna Karenina* as 'untrue' rests on the same
premise, namely, that it is the 'story of a woman told by a man with
a man's ideas about people' (ibid., III, p. 59).

11. Patricia Stubbs notices the way in which women themselves become
affected by this tradition:

In *A Drama in Muslin* . . . Moore took up some of the issues which
were very closely related to middle-class feminism – the imbalance
in numbers between single women and single men, and the frus-
trating, humiliating life imposed on spinsters. . . . The sordid in-
fighting among women rapidly approaching spinsterhood is one
of the most effective, if depressing, things in the novel. But a more
original and more important observation made by Moore in the
book is the way women regulate and evaluate the way they spend
their time according to whether or not a man is present. For in
this novel women simply do not feel they exist unless they are in
some way relating to men.   (Stubbs, *Women and Fiction*, p. 94)

12. The narrative implicitly illustrates Florence Nightingale's argument
that 'young women at home have so little to occupy and to interest
them – they have so little reason for *not* quitting their home, that a
young and independent man cannot look at a girl without giving
rise to "expectations" if not on her own part, on that of her family'
(Strachey, *The Cause*, p. 411).

13. We have, perhaps, to turn to Austen's portrayal of Miss Bates in
Emma for a more obviously sympathetic treatment of woman as
society's victim.

14. Compare the Cartaret girls' jealousy over Dr Rowcliffe in May
Sinclair's *The Three Sisters*.

15. *The Pargiters*, p. 33.

16. Ibid., p. 35.

17. Gilbert and Gubar argue that:

> The parodic portrait in [Austen's] 'Jack and Alice' of the compe-
> tition between drunken Alice Johnson and the accomplished
> tailor's daughter, Lucy, for the incomparable Charles Adams . . .
> is . . . not so different from the rivalry Emma Woodhouse feels
> toward Harriet Smith or Jane Fairfax over Mr Knightley. . . .
> Because such females would rather marry a man they dislike than
> teach school or enter the governess 'slave-trade,' they fight
> ferociously for the few eligible men who do seem attractive. The
> rivalries between Miss Bingley and Miss Bennet, between Miss
> Dashwood and Miss Steele, between the Musgrove sisters for
> Captain Wentworth are only the most obvious examples of fierce
> female competition where female anger is deflected from powerful
> male to powerless female targets.   (Gilbert and Gubar, *Madwoman
> in the Attic*, p. 126)

18. Indeed, given that she was writing – as both Marilyn Butler and
    Margaret Kirkham point out – in the context of the social conserva-
    tism which followed upon the French Revolution, and at a time
    when, largely through the posthumous reputation of Mary Woll-
    stonecraft, feminism and Jacobinism were closely connected in the
    public mind, it would have been most impolitic of her to do so, even
    had she so desired (see Marilyn Butler, *Jane Austen and the War of
    Ideas* (Oxford: Oxford University Press, 1975) passim; and Kirkham,
    Jane Austen, Feminism and Fiction, pp. 53ff.).
19. *The Pargiters*, p. 29.
20. Ibid., p. 24.
21. Elaine Showalter notes that:

> Caricatures like Dickens' Mrs Jellyby (in *Bleak House*, 1853) had
> spread the stereotype of the frowsy career woman. . . . In the
> early part of the century, attacks on the barren spinster novelist
> were part of the common fund of humor. Harriet Martineau was
> an irresistible target for lampoons like Thomas Moore's 'Blue Love
> Song'.   (Showalter, *A Literature of their Own*, pp. 66, 70–1)

22. *To the Lighthouse*, p. 120.
23. If one compares the published 1917 section of *The Years* with the
    galley proofs relating to that section (as Grace Radin does in her
    article, ' "Two enormous chunks": Episodes Excluded During the
    Final Revision of *The Years*', *Bulletin of the New York Public Library*,
    LXXX (1976–7) pp. 221–51), one finds that in the later version Woolf's
    references to Nicholas's homosexuality are much less explicit than
    in the earlier draft.
24. *The Pargiters*, pp. 151–2; Woolf's ellipses.
25. *Diary*, IV, p. 300.
26. Discussing Ethel Smyth's book, *Female Pipings in Eden*, for example,
    Woolf remarks: 'I think the personal details immensely diminish

the power of the rest. . . . I hate any writer to talk about himself;
anonymity I adore' (Letters, v, p. 191).

27. See, for example, Diary, IV, pp. 168, 261, 266, 282, 321, 347, 353;
Letters, v, p. 445.
28. Diary, IV, p. 133.
29. Letters, v, p. 335.
30. Diary, IV, p. 266.
31. Ibid., p. 347.
32. See The Notebooks of Henry James, ed. F. O. Matthiessen and Kenneth
B. Murdock (Oxford: Oxford University Press, 1947).
33. Vivien Jones argues that James's 'achievement and example unmistakably [inform] Woolf's discussions of the art of fiction, as one who
has demonstrated the possibility of a liberating use of "pattern" '
(Jones, James the Critic, p. 194).
34. David Lodge remarks that: 'the realist author can, by selection (or
deletion) and repetition within a field of contiguities, construct a
metonymic metaphor, or symbol, without disturbing the illusion of
reality' (Lodge, The Modes of Modern Writing, p. 107). Similarly, Hillis
Miller comments of Thackeray's Henry Esmond: 'One of the greatest
"pleasures of the text" in Henry Esmond, is the subtle and unosten-
tatious way in which motifs, once introduced – the colour red, Diana,
the moon, etc. – recur, cunningly woven into passages which
remain, from Henry's point of view, seemingly no more than
accurate descriptions of what there was to be seen' (Hillis Miller,
Fiction and Repetition, p. 74).
35. Diary, IV, p. 282. Similarly, in writing Mrs Dalloway, she remarked:
'But how does one make people talk about everything in the whole
of life, so that one's hair stands on end, in a drawing room? How
can one weight and sharpen dialogue till each sentence tears its way
like a harpoon and grapples with the shingles at the bottom of
the reader's soul?' (Letters, III, p. 36). Hermione Lee's comment on
Between the Acts: 'everyday speech is significant, even if it dwells on
insignificant topics, because it is silted up with the detritus of the
past' (Lee, The Novels of Virginia Woolf, p. 209), applies equally to The
Years. Woolf's approach in The Years links her with T. S. Eliot. In
his 'Selected Essays', Eliot remarks that:

> It is not merely in the use of imagery of common life, not merely
> in the use of the imagery of the sordid life of a great metropolis, but
> in the elevation of such imagery to the first intensity – presenting it
> as it is, and yet making it represent something much more than
> itself – that Baudelaire has created a mode of release and
> expression for other men. (quoted in Starkie's From Gautier to
> Eliot, p. 166)

36. The Years, p. 108. (Hereafter all references to this edition appear
parenthetically within the text.)
37. James Joyce, Ulysses (Paris: Shakespeare, 1922) pp. 84–111. Despite

Woolf's hostility to Joyce's writing, this was a scene which she found particularly impressive (see 'Modern Fiction', in *CE*, II, p. 107).

38. See Lyndall Gordon, *Virginia Woolf: A Writer's Life* (Oxford: Oxford University Press, 1984) p. 27.

39. Similarly, Phyllis Rose notes, in a discussion of *The Voyage Out*, that:

> Mrs Vinrace's death . . . is mentioned again and again in one earlier version, but all it serves to tell us is how important Julia Stephen's death was to Virginia – it is not worked into the novel in anything more than a tantalizing way. The over-insistence on it disappears in the revisions, although the fact that Rachel's mother has died remains.   (Rose, *Woman of Letters*, p. 53)

40. *Letters*, VI, p. 20; *Three Guineas*, pp. 63, 193.
41. *The Pargiters*, p. 123.
42. See *MHP*, MH/B4(d).
43. Compare *Three Guineas*, pp. 195–8.
44. *MHP*, MH/B4(d).
45. Ibid., MH/A13(e).
46. *The Waves*, p. 103.
47. See R. A. Waldron, *Sense and Sense Development* (London: André Deutsch, 1967) p. 50.
48. This use of the 'indirect free style' makes *The Years* perhaps the most Flaubertian of Woolf's novels.
49. *Letters*, VI, p. 116.
50. Compare Miriam Henderson's thought: 'How can people talk about coincidence? How not be struck by the inside pattern of life? It is so obvious that everything is arranged. Whether by God or some deep wisdom in oneself does not matter' (Richardson, *Pilgrimage*, III, p. 282). Like Woolf, Richardson makes use of repetition in her novel to suggest an underlying pattern in experience.
51. Forster was mistaken, then, when he remarked in his Rede lecture (1941) that in *The Years*, as in *Night and Day*, Woolf 'deserts poetry, and again she fails' (E. M. Forster, *Virginia Woolf* (Cambridge: Cambridge University Press, 1942) p. 14).
52. Jean Guiget remarks rather unconvincingly in the course of a discussion of *The Years*:

> In the opinion of the sensible, clear-headed Kitty, who has chosen Lord Lasswade's fortune rather than Edward's love, 'The years changed things; destroyed things; heaped things up – worries and bothers; here they were again'. This, formulated as prosaically as possible, is what the novel is trying to show, what the constantly changing, constantly renewed sea of *The Waves* has already told us with its infinitely more mysterious, more moving voice, and surely with far more truth diffused through its poetic imprecision.   (Guiget, *Virginia Woolf*, p. 310)

53. *Diary*, IV, pp. 353–4.

54. Herbert Marder notes that in *The Years:* 'Solid objects like the spotted walrus, scenes like that of the dawning day, hint a transcendent meaning without making the reader aware that they are being manipulated for his benefit' (Marder, *Feminism and Art*, p. 154).

55. Many people say that it is hopelessly sad – but I didnt mean that. I did want somehow to make out if only for my own satisfaction a reason for things. . . . I did mean that in some vague way we are the same person, and not separate people. The six characters were supposed to be one. . . . I wanted to give the sense of continuity, instead of which most people say, no you've given the sense of flowing and passing away and that nothing matters. Yet I feel things matter quite immensely. What the significance is, heaven knows I cant guess; but there is significance – that I feel overwhelmingly. Perhaps for me, with my limitations, – I mean of reasoning power and so on – all I can do is to make an artistic whole; and leave it at that.   (*Letters* IV, p. 397)

56. Hillis Miller notes the superimposition in each passage of Thackeray's *Henry Esmond* of all the other similar passages, and comments:

This occurs through the repetition in each of the same motifs. As each of these passages follows the last, they gradually accumulate into a resonating line of similar configurations, each echoing all the others and drawing its meaning from that echoing . . . The meaning of this echoing is its affirmation that Henry's life hangs together. His life has meaning because the same elements recur in it and give it a total design justifying the drawing of a line connecting each part to all the others.   (Hillis Miller, *Fiction and Repetition*, p. 89)

For an article which argues that the repetition in *The Years* fails to unify the novel see Victoria Middleton's '*The Years:* "A Deliberate Failure" ', *Bulletin of the New York Public Library*, vol. LXXX (1976–7) pp. 158–71.

57. Similarly, the phrases 'Erridge and the microscope' and 'Miss Pym's cats' refer to particular incidents in the childhood of the Pargiters and have a different significance for each of them (*The Years*, pp. 16, 42, 169, 171, 248, 386, 387).

58. The Stephen girls felt the same kind of pressure during the months when their father was dying of cancer (see Noel Annan, *Leslie Stephen: The Godless Victorian* (London: Weidenfeld & Nicolson, 1984) p. 125).

59. This is one example of the method whereby Woolf achieves the sense of 'a changing temporal atmosphere . . . the old fabric insensibly changing without death or violence into the future' in the novel (see *Letters*, VI, p. 116).

60. In one of the two longer sections which Woolf cut from her novel at the galley proof stage, she contrasts Eleanor's independent life-

style in her London flat with her former position of servitude in the Pargiter family house. This contrast is summed up through Eleanor's thought that 'she had only to light the gas ring and the kettle would be boiling in five minutes' (see Grace Radin, ' "Two Enormous Chunks" ', p. 232).

61. When, in old age, the family dog suffers from eczema (*The Years*, p. 235), it brings to mind Mira's dog at the beginning of the novel (p. 6). Similarly, the chalk marks which Rose sees on the pavement outside Sara and Maggie's flat (p. 185) recall the chalk marks which Abel sees on the pavement outside Mira's house (p. 5).

62. The phrase 'over again' itself recurs in the course of the novel. See, for example, ibid., pp. 143, 387, 434.

63. Compare the interludes in *The Waves*.

64. Woolf remarks in her diary: 'Viola Tree died last night, of pleurisy: 2 years younger than I am' (*Diary*, v, p. 187), and later she comments: 'Then Joyce is dead – Joyce about a fortnight younger than I am' (ibid., pp. 352–3).

65. The remark is echoed in several phrases in the 1914 section of the novel: 'It was impossible to talk' (*The Years*, pp. 249, 253); 'Conversation was impossible' (p. 252); 'But it was impossible' (p. 253).

66. This episode, like the scene in which Sara describes her life in London to North (ibid., pp. 366–7), is reminiscent of Eliot's evocations of the life of the metropolis.

67. At one time, Woolf considered calling the novel *The Caravan* (see *Diary*, IV, p. 274).

68. Abel's phrase is echoed in Lady Warburton's description of Kitty's son as a 'little red-haired ruffian' (*The Years*, p. 278).

69. The phrase which Martin uses to describe his sensation on looking up at St Paul's Cathedral: 'All the weights in his body seemed to shift' (ibid., p. 244), is echoed when Woolf describes Maggie's feeling as she watches René and North talking together about Africa (p. 375).

70. It also occurs in *Between the Acts* (p. 256) and *Night and Day* (p. 538).

71. Antigone had a special significance for Woolf as a feminist symbol, appearing, for example in *The Voyage Out* (p. 46) and *Three Guineas* (p. 250). Jane Marcus suggests that in *Three Guineas* Woolf argues

> that *Antigone* could be made 'into anti-Fascist propaganda,' that Creon, tyrant and patriarch, resembles Hitler and Mussolini – even though Sophocles in the end is such a great artist that he makes us sympathise 'even with Creon himself.' The plot and the 'buried alive' theme of *Antigone* form the mythology and structure of *The Years* and as *novelist* Woolf makes her reader sympathise with her English Creons. It is only as a 'pamphleteer' that she chooses between good and evil. (Marcus, ' "No more horses" ', p. 266)

72. *Letters*, IV, p. 191.

73. The image which North uses here brings to mind the words of another of the speakers in Hyde Park who 'held a little book in her

hand and she was saying something about sparrows' (*The Years*, p. 259).

74. That Peggy is expressing Woolf's own point of view here is revealed by a remark in her diary for 13 April 1918: 'sometimes I try to worry out what some of the phrases we're ruled by mean. I doubt whether most people even do that. Liberty, for instance' (*Diary*, I, p. 138).

75. Woolf's ellipsis.

76. *CE*, II, p. 177.

77. It is also recalled in the blue-painted lights of war-time London (*The Years*, pp. 324, 338).

78. In this scene Woolf uses North to put across obliquely her own dislike of the academic who is 'a priest, a mystery monger', a 'guardian of beautiful words' (ibid., p. 441).

79. The episode recalls the opening scene of *The Voyage Out*.

80. Woolf herself makes this point in the *Letter to a Young Poet* when she criticises the poet who tries to invent a 'private language'. She argues that 'the more sincere he is in keeping to the precise outline of the roses and cabbages of his private universe, the more he puzzles us who have agreed in a lazy spirit of compromise to see roses and cabbages as they are seen, more or less, by the twenty-six passengers on the outside of an omnibus' (*CE*, II, p. 189).

81. The concluding phrase recalls an important theme in *Night and Day*.

82. The phrase comes from *Mrs Dalloway*, p. 202.

83. As she sleeps, she makes a clicking noise at the back of her throat like that which Sara makes whilst asleep in Hyde Park (*The Years*, p. 264).

84. Kitty's offer of a lift in her car is repeated later, at the end of the 'Present Day' chapter (ibid., p. 467).

85. In this respect *The Years* resembles *The Forsyte Saga*, although Woolf's treatment of the idea is considerably more subtle than Galsworthy's.

86. Hillis Miller identifies a similar 'portrait motif' in Thackeray's *Henry Esmond* (see Hillis Miller, *Fiction and Repetition*, p. 85).

87. Neville makes this point in *The Waves* when he remarks: 'I am merely "Neville" to you, who see the narrow limits of my life and the line it cannot pass. But to myself I am immeasurable: a net whose fibres pass imperceptibly beneath the world' (*The Waves*, p. 152).

88. This scene between Eleanor and her niece, Peggy, has certain affinities with the episode in *The Old Wives' Tale* in which Lily and Dick visit Constance Baines (Bennett, *The Old Wives' Tale*, pp. 496–503), although Peggy, unlike Bennett's characters, is aware of the way in which she is tempted to caricature her elderly relative.

89. Similarly, Bernard in *The Waves* remarks: 'Who and what are these unknown people? . . . I could make a dozen stories of what he said, of what she said – I can see a dozen pictures. But what are stories? Toys I twist, bubbles I blow, one ring passing through another. And sometimes I begin to doubt if there are stories. What is my story? What is Rhoda's? What is Neville's?' (*The Waves*, p. 103).

90. The idea is, of course, central to 'Modern Fiction' (*CE*, II, p. 106),

but also finds expression in a manuscript fragment in which Woolf remarks:

> The biographer cannot e[x]tract the atom. He gives us the husk. Therefore as things are, the best method would be to separate the two kinds of truth. Let the biographer print fully, completely, accurately, the known facts without comment; Then let him write the life as fiction. (*MHP*, MH/B5)

Compare Brecht's argument that: 'the continuity of the ego is a myth. A man is an atom that perpetually breaks up and forms anew' ('Conversation with Bert Brecht', in *Brecht on Theatre*, ed. John Willett (London: Methuen, 1964) p. 15).

91. *Letters*, IV, p. 397.
92. Similarly, Woolf, in a sketch of the life of Sir Henry Taylor entitled *A Scene from the Past*, questions the value of the traditional 'life' of the 'great man' to be found, for example, in the *Dictionary of National Biography* – see *MHP*, MH/B10(e).
93. The irony here, of course, is that Woolf herself does take up the challenge of making the story of 'a large family, living in a large house' interesting. At one time she contemplated calling the novel *Ordinary People* (*Diary*, IV, p. 271).
94. *The Waves*, p. 103.
95. The phrase 'pigeon-holes' comes from *The Waves*, p. 189.
96. In *To the Lighthouse*, Lily Briscoe acknowledges this to be the case when she remarks to herself of Charles Tansley that 'He did for her instead of a whipping-boy' (*To the Lighthouse*, p. 303).
97. North's situation recalls that of Leonard Woolf, who returned to London in 1911 after working for the civil service in Ceylon for seven years.
98. The idea of 'playing a part' recalls Delia's belief that her own father dramatises his situation following his wife's death (*The Years*, p. 49).
99. Eleanor experiences the same difficulties when she attempts to describe Spain to her sister-in-law, Celia (ibid., pp. 211–12).
100. *Three Guineas*, p. 14.
101. *Diary*, IV, p. 152.
102. Ibid. V, pp. 90, 91, 269.

Notes to Chapter Five: Conclusion

1. For an attack on these criticisms of Woolf see the introduction to Toril Moi's *Sexual/Textual Politics*.
2. Phyllis Rose notes that 'the curiously drained quality of *The Years*, which is so powerful, may be seen as a triumph of craft or a failure of nerve or a little of both'. She herself laments the fact that Woolf 'abandoned the self in the thirties, responding to the demand for public commitment not with a frank assertion of the value of private

experience, but by embracing impersonality and anonymity' (Rose, *Woman of Letters*, pp. 216, 218).

3. Showalter, *A Literature of their Own*, pp. 282–3, 285.
4. Ibid., pp. 289, 264. Phyllis Rose, similarly, suggests that *The Years* betrays 'a perilous reticence in the author' (Rose, *Woman of Letters*, p. 215).
5. Echoing Q. D. Leavis's *Scrutiny* review of 1938, Showalter criticises *Three Guineas* for its 'class assumptions', and 'political naïvete', 'its empty sloganeering and cliché' and its 'stylistic tricks of repetition, exaggeration, and rhetorical question' which are, she says, 'irritating and hysterical' (Showalter, *A Literature of their Own*, pp. 294–5). Jane Marcus rightly points out that the view – which Marcus considers to have been propagated primarily by Quentin Bell and, to a lesser extent, Leonard Woolf – that Woolf was an upper-middle-class aesthete who dabbled in politics, without being capable of a rational understanding of early twentieth-century political events, is widely off-mark. Marcus suggests that Bell is amongst those readers who dismiss *Three Guineas* as confused and unimportant because they feel threatened by the devastating rationality of Woolf's argument (Marcus, ' "No more horses" ', pp. 265–90). There is nothing simple-minded or muddled about the superb mastery with which Woolf follows through her argument in this essay, linking fascism with more general instances of patriarchal power, and warning women that as they become 'liberated' they must avoid the many temptations inherent in the freedom which they have won.
6. Stubbs, *Women and Fiction*, pp. 230–1.
7. One cannot, then, accept Phyllis Rose's objection to the novel's 'scrupulous impartiality, Woolf's refusal to define a central character or to shape a narrative, while heaping upon us the kind of detail that demands such a shape' (Rose, *Woman of Letters*, p. 213).
8. Stubbs, *Women and Fiction*, p. 232.

Bibliography

WORKS OF VIRGINIA WOOLF

Woolf, Virginia, *Between the Acts* (London: The Hogarth Press, 1941).
——, *Collected Essays*, ed. Leonard Woolf, 4 vols (London: The Hogarth Press, 1966).
——, *The Complete Shorter Fiction of Virginia Woolf*, ed. Susan Dick (London: The Hogarth Press, 1985).
——, *Contemporary Writers*, ed. Jean Guiget (London: The Hogarth Press, 1965).
——, *The Diary of Virginia Woolf*, ed. Anne Olivier Bell and Andrew McNeillie, 5 vols (London: The Hogarth Press, 1977–84).
——, *Jacob's Room*, 2nd edn (London: The Hogarth Press, 1945; 1st edn 1922).
——, *Letter to a Young Poet* (London: The Hogarth Press, 1932).
——, *The Letters of Virginia Woolf*, ed. Nigel Nicolson, 6 vols (London: The Hogarth Press, 1975–80).
——, *Mrs Dalloway*, 3rd edn (London: The Hogarth Press, 1947; 1st edn 1925).
——, *Night and Day* (London: The Hogarth Press, 1919).
——, *The Pargiters: The Novel-Essay Portion of 'The Years'*, ed. Mitchell Leaska (London: The Hogarth Press, 1978).
——, *A Room of One's Own* (London: The Hogarth Press, 1929).
——, *Three Guineas* (London: The Hogarth Press, 1938).
——, *To the Lighthouse* (London: The Hogarth Press, 1927).
——, 'The Tunnel', *The Times Literary Supplement*, 13 February 1919, p. 81.
——, *Virginia Woolf Manuscripts (Monks House Papers)* (Brighton: Harvester, 1985).
——, *The Voyage Out* (London: The Hogarth Press, 1915).
——, *The Waves*, 2nd edn (London: The Hogarth Press, 1943; 1st edn 1931).
——, *The Years* (London: The Hogarth Press, 1937).

WORKS BY OTHER AUTHORS

Abel, Elizabeth (ed.), *Writing and Sexual Difference* (Brighton: Harvester, 1982).

Annan, Noel, *Leslie Stephen: The Godless Victorian* (London: Weidenfeld & Nicolson, 1984).

Austen, Jane, *Emma* (London: Murray, 1816).

——, *Mansfield Park* (London: Egerton, 1814).

——, *'Northanger Abbey' and 'Persuasion'* (London: Murray, 1818) vol. I.

Barrett, Michèle (ed.), *Women and Writing* (London: The Women's Press, 1979).

Bayley, John, 'Diminishment of Consciousness: a Paradox in the Art of Virginia Woolf', in *Virginia Woolf: A Centenary Perspective*, ed. Eric Warner (London: Macmillan, 1984) pp. 69–82.

——, *The Uses of Division: Unity and Disharmony in Literature* (London: Chatto & Windus, 1976).

Beauvoir, Simone de, *The Second Sex*, trans. H. M. Parshley (Harmondsworth: Penguin Books, 1983; 1st edn 1949).

Beckett, Samuel, *Proust* (London: Chatto & Windus, 1931).

Bell, Alan (ed.), *Sir Leslie Stephen's Mausoleum Book* (Oxford: Oxford University Press, 1977).

Bell, Barbara Currier, and Carol Ohmann, 'Virginia Woolf's Criticism: A Polemical Preface', in *Feminist Literary Criticism*, ed. Josephine Donovan (Lexington, Ky: University of Kentucky Press, 1975) pp. 48–60.

Bell, Quentin, *Virginia Woolf: A Biography*, 2 vols (London: The Hogarth Press, 1972).

Belsey, Catherine, *Critical Practice* (London: Methuen, 1980).

Bennett, Arnold, *The Old Wives' Tale* (London: Chapman & Hall, 1908).

Bennett, Joan, *Virginia Woolf: Her Art as a Novelist*, 2nd edn (Cambridge: Cambridge University Press, 1964; 1st edn 1945).

Blackstone, Bernard, *Virginia Woolf: A Commentary* (London: The Hogarth Press, 1949).

Brontë, Charlotte, *Jane Eyre* (London: Smith, Elder, 1847).

——, *Shirley* (London: Smith, Elder, 1849) vol. II.

——, *Villette* (London: Smith, Elder, 1853).

Butler, Marilyn, *Jane Austen and the War of Ideas* (Oxford: Oxford University Press, 1975).

Conrad, Joseph, 'Heart of Darkness', in *Youth, a Narrative: and Two Other Stories* (Edinburgh: Blackwood, 1902) pp. 49–182.

——, *Lord Jim* (London: Dent, 1900).

——, *Nostromo* (London: Dent, 1904).

Culler, Jonathan, *Saussure* (Brighton: Harvester, 1976).

Daiches, David, *Virginia Woolf*, 2nd edn (Norfolk, Conn.: New Directions, 1963; 1st edn 1942).

Davies, Margaret Llewelyn, *Life As We Have Known It: By Co-operative Working Women* (London: The Hogarth Press, 1931).

Delattre, Floris, 'La Durée Bergsonienne dans le roman de Virginia Woolf', *Revue Anglo-Américaine*, vol. IX (Paris, December 1931) pp. 97–108.

——, *Le Roman psychologique de Virginia Woolf* (Paris: Librairie Philosophique, 1932).

DeSalvo, Louise, *Virginia Woolf's First Voyage: A Novel in the Making* (London: Macmillan, 1980).

Dick, Susan (ed.), *The Complete Shorter Fiction of Virginia Woolf* (London: The Hogarth Press, 1985).

Donovan, Josephine (ed.), *Feminist Literary Criticism* (Lexington, Ky: University of Kentucky Press, 1975).

Douglas, Ann, Introduction to Harriet Beecher Stowe, *Uncle Tom's Cabin* (Harmondsworth: Penguin Books, 1981) pp. 7–34.

Eagleton, Terry, *Marxism and Literary Criticism* (London: Methuen, 1976).

Edel, Leon, and Gordon Ray, *Henry James and H. G. Wells: A Record of their Friendship, their Debate on the Art of Fiction, and their Quarrel* (London: Hart-Davis, 1958).

Eliot, George, *Middlemarch* (Edinburgh: Blackwood, 1871– 2).

——, *The Mill on the Floss* (Edinburgh: Blackwood, 1860).

Eliot, T. S., *The Sacred Wood* (London: Methuen, 1920).

Ellmann, Mary, *Thinking about Women* (New York: Harcourt, Brace, 1968).

Erlich, Victor, *Russian Formalism: History-Doctrine*, 4th edn (New Haven, Conn.: Yale University Press, 1981; 1st edn 1955).

Faulkner, William, *The Sound and the Fury* (London: Chatto & Windus, 1954).

Forster, E. M., *Howards End* (London: Edward Arnold, 1910).

——, *A Room with a View* (London: Edward Arnold, 1908).

——, *Virginia Woolf* (Cambridge: Cambridge University Press, 1942).

Fry, Roger, 'An Essay in Aesthetics', in *New Quarterly*, vol. II (1909); reprinted in *Vision and Design* (London: Chatto & Windus, 1920) pp. 11–25.

Furst, Lilian, and Peter Skrine, *Naturalism* (London: Methuen, 1971).

Galsworthy, John, *The Forsyte Saga* (London: Heinemann, 1922).

Gaskell, Elizabeth, *The Life of Charlotte Brontë* (London: Smith, Elder, 1857).

Gilbert Sandra, 'Costumes of the Mind: Transvestism as Metaphor in Modern Literature', in *Writing and Sexual Difference*, ed. Elizabeth Abel (Brighton: Harvester, 1982) pp. 193–219.

——, and Susan Gubar, *The Madwoman in the Attic: The Woman Writer and the Nineteenth-Century Literary Imagination* (London: Yale University Press, 1979).

Gissing, George, *The Odd Women* (London: Lawrence & Bullen, 1893).

Gordon, Lyndall, *Virginia Woolf: A Writer's Life* (Oxford: Oxford University Press, 1984).

Guiget, Jean, *Virginia Woolf and her Works*, trans. Jean Stewart (London: The Hogarth Press, 1965).

Heilbrun, Carolyn, *Reinventing Womanhood* (London: Victor Gollancz, 1979).

——, *Towards Androgyny: Aspects of Male and Female in Literature* (London: Victor Gollancz, 1973).

Hillis Miller, J., *Fiction and Repetition: Seven English Novels* (Oxford: Blackwell, 1982).

Huxley, Aldous, *Brave New World* (London: Chatto & Windus, 1932).

——, *Point Counter Point* (London: Chatto & Windus, 1928).

Ibsen, Henrik, *A Doll's House*, trans. W. Archer (London: Fisher Unwin, 1889; 1st edn 1879).

Iser, Wolfgang, *The Act of Reading: A Theory of Aesthetic Response* (London: Johns Hopkins University Press, 1978).

James, Henry, *The Art of the Novel*, ed. Richard P. Blackmur (New York: Charles Scribner's Sons, 1934).

——, *The Awkward Age* (London: Heinemann, 1899).

——, *The Bostonians* (London: Macmillan, 1886).

——, *French Poets and Novelists* London: Macmillan, 1878).

——, *The Golden Bowl* (New York: Charles Scribner's Sons, 1904).

——, *The Notebooks of Henry James*, ed. F. O. Matthiessen and Kenneth B. Murdock (Oxford: Oxford University Press, 1947).

——, *Notes and Reviews*, ed. Pierre de Chaignon la Rose (Cambridge, Mass.: Dunster House Press, 1921).

——, *Notes on Novelists: With Some Other Notes* (London: Dent, 1914).

——, *Partial Portraits* (London: Macmillan, 1888).

——, *The Portrait of a Lady* (London: Macmillan, 1881).

Jones, Vivien, *James the Critic* (London: Macmillan, 1984).

Joyce, James, *Ulysses* (Paris: Shakespeare, 1922).

Kelley, Alice van Buren, *The Novels of Virginia Woolf: Fact and Vision* (London: University of Chicago Press, 1973).

Kirkham, Margaret, *Jane Austen, Feminism and Fiction* (Brighton: Harvester, 1983).

Lawrence, D. H., *The Rainbow* (London: Methuen, 1915).

——, *Sons and Lovers* (London: Duckworth, 1913).

Leaska, Mitchell, *The Novels of Virginia Woolf: From Beginning to End* (London: Weidenfeld and Nicolson, 1977).

—— (ed.), *The Pargiters* (London: The Hogarth Press, 1978).

Leavis, Q. D., 'Caterpillars of the Commonwealth Unite', *Scrutiny*, vol. VII, no. 2 (September 1938) pp. 203–14.

Lee, Hermione, *The Novels of Virginia Woolf* (London: Methuen, 1977).

Lehmann, Rosamond, *The Weather in the Streets* (London: Collins, 1936).

Lemon, Lee, and Marion Reis (eds), *Russian Formalist Criticism: Four Essays* (Lincoln, Nebr.: University of Nebraska Press, 1965).

Lessing, Doris, *The Golden Notebook* (London: Michael Joseph, 1962).

Lodge, David, *Language of Fiction: Essays in Criticism and Verbal Analysis of the English Novel*, 2nd edn (London: Routledge & Kegan Paul, 1984; 1st edn 1966).

——, *The Modes of Modern Writing: Metaphor, Metonymy and the Typology of Modern Literature* (London: Edward Arnold, 1977).

Lubbock, Percy, *The Craft of Fiction* (London: Jonathan Cape, 1921).

MacCarthy, Desmond, 'An Olive-Branch', *The Sunday Times*, 26 January 1930, p. 8.

Marcus, Jane, ' "No more horses": Virginia Woolf on Art and Propaganda', *Women's Studies*, vol. IV, nos 2/3 (1977) pp. 265–89.

Marder, Herbert, *Feminism and Art* (London: University of Chicago Press, 1968).

Megay, Joyce, *Bergson et Proust* (Paris: Librairie Philosophique, 1976).

Meredith, George, *Diana of the Crossways* (London: Chapman & Hall, 1885).

——, *The Egoist* (London: Kegan Paul, 1879).

Middleton, Victoria, 'The Years: "A Deliberate Failure" ', Bulletin of the New York Public Library, vol. LXXX (1976–7) pp. 158–71.

Mill, J. S., The Subjection of Women (London: Longmans, Green, Reader & Dyer, 1869).

Millett, Kate, Sexual Politics (London: Hart-Davis, 1971).

Moi, Toril, Sexual/Textual Politics: Feminist Literary Theory (London: Methuen, 1985).

Neale, Steve, 'Propaganda', Screen, vol. XVIII, no. 3 (Autumn 1977) pp. 9–40.

Nightingale, Florence, 'Cassandra', in Ray Strachey, The Cause (London: Bell, 1928), pp. 395–418.

Poovey, Mary, The Proper Lady and the Woman Writer: Ideology as Style in the Works of Mary Wollstonecraft, Mary Shelley and Jane Austen (London: University of Chicago Press, 1984).

Poulet, Georges, Proustian Space, trans. E. Coleman (London: Johns Hopkins University Press, 1977).

Proust, Marcel, Remembrance of Things Past, trans. C. K. Scott Moncrieff and Terence Kilmartin (London: Chatto & Windus, 1981).

Radin, Grace, ' "Two Enormous Chunks": Episodes Excluded During the Final Revisions of The Years', Bulletin of the New York Public Library, vol. LXXX (1976–7) pp. 221–51.

Richardson, Dorothy, 'Data for Spanish Publisher', in Joseph Prescott (ed.), London Magazine, vol. VI, no. 6 (June 1959) pp. 14–19.

——, Pilgrimage, 4 vols (London: Dent, 1938).

Rogers, Katharine, The Troublesome Helpmate: A History of Misogyny in Literature (London: University of Washington Press, 1966).

Rose, Phyllis, Woman of Letters: A Life of Virginia Woolf (London: Routledge & Kegan Paul, 1978).

Schreiner, Olive, From Man to Man (London: Fisher Unwin, 1926).

——, The Story of an African Farm (London: Chapman & Hall, 1883).

——, Woman and Labour (London: Fisher Unwin, 1911).

Shaw, George Bernard, 'Mrs Warren's Profession', in Plays Pleasant and Unpleasant, vol. I (London: Grant Richards, 1898).

——, The Quintessence of Ibsenism (London: Scott, 1891).

——, An Unsocial Socialist (London: Swan, Sonnenschein, Lowrey, 1887).

Shklovsky, Victor, 'Art as Technique', in Russian Formalist Criticism: Four Essays, ed. Lee Lemon and Marion Reis (Lincoln, Nebr.: University of Nebraska Press, 1965) pp. 3–57.

Showalter, Elaine, 'Feminist Criticism in the Wilderness', in Writing and Sexual Difference, ed. Elizabeth Abel (Brighton: Harvester, 1982).

——, A Literature of their Own: British Women Novelists from Brontë to Lessing (London: Princeton University Press, 1978).

Sinclair, May, The Three Sisters (London: Macmillan, 1914).

Spender, Dale, Man Made Language (London: Routledge & Kegan Paul, 1980).

Spender, Stephen, The Struggle of the Modern (London: Hamish Hamilton, 1963).

——, World Within World (London: Hamish Hamilton, 1951).

Starkie, Enid, *From Gautier to Eliot: The Influence of France on English Literature, 1851–1959* (London: Hutchinson, 1960).

Stephen, Karin, *The Misuse of Mind: A Study of Bergson's Attack on Intellectualism* (London: Kegan Paul, Trench, Trubner, 1922).

Stephen, Sir Leslie, *Sir Leslie Stephen's Mausoleum Book*, ed. Alan Bell (Oxford: Oxford University Press, 1977).

Sterne, Laurence, *Tristram Shandy* (Oxford: Blackwell, 1926; 1st edn 1759–67).

Stowe, Harriet Beecher, *Uncle Tom's Cabin* (Harmondsworth: Penguin Books, 1981; 1st edn 1852).

Strachey, Ray, *The Cause* (London: Bell, 1928).

Stubbs, Patricia, *Women and Fiction: Feminism and the Novel, 1880–1920* (Brighton: Harvester, 1979).

Sturrock, John, 'Jamboree', *London Review of Books*, vol. viii, no. 3 (20 February 1986) pp. 13–14.

Taylor, Barbara, *Eve and the New Jerusalem: Socialism and Feminism in the Nineteenth Century* (London: Virago, 1983).

Tennyson, Alfred Lord, *The Princess* (London: Moxon, 1847).

Turgenev, Ivan, *On the Eve*, trs. C. E. Turner (London, Hodder & Stoughton, 1871; 1st edn 1860).

Turner, Paul, *Tennyson* (London: Routledge & Kegan Paul, 1976).

Waldron, R. A., *Sense and Sense Development* (London: André Deutsch, 1967).

Warner, Eric, 'Some Aspects of Romanticism in the Work of Virginia Woolf' (D. Phil. thesis, Oxford University, 1980).

—— (ed.), *Virginia Woolf: A Centenary Perspective* (London: Macmillan, 1984).

Warner, Sylvia Townsend, *Lolly Willowes: or The Loving Huntsman* (London: Chatto & Windus, 1926).

West, Rebecca, *The Judge* (London: Hutchinson, 1922).

Willett, John (ed.), *Brecht on Theatre* (London: Methuen, 1964).

Wollestonecraft, Mary, *A Vindication of the Rights of Woman: With Strictures on Political and Moral Subjects* (London: Johnson, 1792).

Index

238 *Index*